5/06

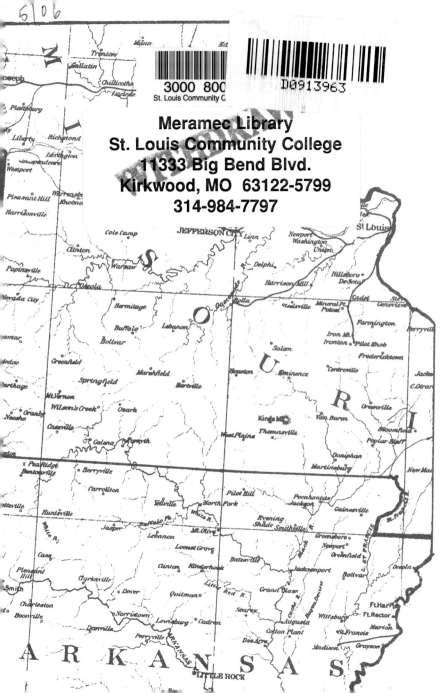

ROBERT E. MILLER HISTORY COLLECTION

MEMOIRS

OF THE

REBELLION

ON

THE BORDER, 1863,

BY

WILEY BRITTON,

Late Sixth Kansas Cavalry.

———

CHICAGO:
CUSHING, THOMAS & CO., PUBLISHERS.
1882.

New Material Copyright ©1986 By Inland Printer Limited

Library of Congress Catalog Card Number 86-082410

International Standard Book Number
0-940435-01-2
Facsmile Edition
Original Printing By
Cushing, Thomas and Co., Chicago
1882

Printed and Bound in the United States of America

Inland Printer Limited
Florissant, MO 1986

THIS BOOK IS DEDICATED BY THE AUTHOR TO THE MEMORY
OF THE DECEASED OFFICERS AND SOLDIERS, AND TO
THE SURVIVING OFFICERS AND SOLDIERS,
WHO SERVED IN THE FEDERAL ARMY
ON THE BORDER DURING THE
LATE WAR OF THE
REBELLION.

Forward

In order to garner the most information from a historical text, the reader must understand not only the times but the author's relationship to those times. Wiley Britton's observations of the Civil War on the western border are of special value because they are firsthand. As a member of the Kansas 6th Cavalry, Britton was a participant in the events recorded in *Memoirs of the Rebellion on the Border, 1863*. He knew the times as well, if not better, than most who have written of them.

During the time Wiley Britton was recording his experiences, the nation had been at war for nearly two years. East of the Mississippi, the Confederacy still held the military advantage it had earned in the first months of fighting. The same could not be said of the Trans-Mississippi Department. If the Confederacy had ever held an advantage west of the Mississippi, it no longer did so. The Union Army had pushed the Confederates out of Missouri and into the wilds of northwest Arkansas and the Indian Nations. In 1862 defeats at Pea Ridge, Island Number 10, New Madrid, and Maysville had seriously depleted the supplies and the spirits of the Confederate troops in the west. Even the late victory at Prairie Grove, Arkansas accomplished little more than a rekindling of Southern esprit de corps.

For Northern troops, service in the Trans-Mississippi was both dull and dangerous. Dull because duty there involved days of routine patrolling of occupied territory. The danger came from ardent southern sympathizers dwelling in the region and from bands of marauders, from both North and South, that had raided the borderlands between Missouri and

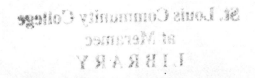

Kansas since the 1850's. The martial law established by the Union Army was tenuous at best and life for the Union soldier precarious. It was during this time that Wiley Britton served.

Born October 8, 1842, in Newton County, Missouri, Wiley Britton enlisted with the Kansas 6th Cavalry at the outbreak of the war. His Civil War experiences were published first as *Memoirs of the Rebellion on the Border, 1863* and were later expanded into a two-volume edition entitled *Civil War on the Border* (1890). In both editions, Britton displays a sense of fairness, and even compassion, toward the southern soldier. With the end of the war Britton began working for Senator John J. Ingalls of Kansas. Through the senator's recommendation Britton gained a post with the United States War Claims Department. He served in the states of Missouri, Arkansas, and Tennesse and remained with the War Claims Dept. for thirty years. He also worked for the Interior Department in Washington, D. C.

Out of his experiences during the war and reconstruction, Britton penned several books of note. These include *The Union Indian Brigade in the Civil War* (1922), *The Aftermath of the Civil War* (1924), and *A Traveling Court . . .**(1926). The latter relates stories of departmental procedures and incidents involving the War Claims Department during reconstruction.

Nor did Britton's writing remain solely in the field of military history. He wrote articles for scientific publications of the day and produced a study of unionization in industry entitled "Trades Union System". In 1929 he published *Pioneer Life in Southwest Missouri*. This book recounted his experiences as a youth growing up in that region. He also wrote several articles for the Missouri State Historical Society journal.

Wiley Britton died at the Soldiers Home in Levenworth Kansas on September 14, 1930.

*complete title: *A Traveling Court Based on Investigation Of War Claims*

Dennis Babbitt
Florissant, MO 1986

PREFACE.

---⊁---

Durıng the year 1863, I chronicled the various events
mentioned in the following pages, just as they impressed me by actual observation, or by authorities
deemed reliable. Though my manuscript contained
all the facts here presented, except a few notes made
from official data, I have never considered it in suitable shape for publication. In rewriting it, I have
stricken out certain criticisms and passages hastily set
down in camp or on the march, and I hope that I have
improved the expression in various ways. I have endeavored to make the work a *panoramic* view of
military operations and events on the borders of Missouri, Kansas, Arkansas and the Indian Territory during the year 1863. Eighteen years have now elapsed
since I collected the material from which my *Memoirs*
are written, and I have not as yet met with a single
book pretending to give any kind of an account of

the military operations of our army for any one year during the rebellion, in that portion of the Trans-Mississippi region mentioned in the following chapters. Though one might, by rummaging the archives of the War Department, get material enough out of general orders and official reports of battles, skirmishes, etc., in that region, to enable him to write a small volume, he would get very little of the kind of material that I collected. I noted not only the movements of the army with which I was connected, and the battles and minor engagements which it fought, but I also turned aside now and then to note a good many other things ; as, for instance, the thoughts and feelings of the soldiers on various subjects, as reflected in their conversations around their camp fires and on the march. I have also given short descriptions of the country we marched over and around our camps; the *pro* and *con* opinions of officers and soldiers in regard to the policy of the Government, in emancipating the slaves and of enlisting the freedmen into the army. And on several occasions I give a moment's thought to natural phenomena, which were subjects of conversation in the camp.

The critical reader may, perhaps, think that I have in one instance purposely arranged my composition to show that "coming events cast their shadows before." But I have not. The facts, however, show that they sometimes do. Gen. Shelby's raid through Missouri in October, 1863, affords an example. The approaching storm was indicated nearly a week before the invasion by the main force took place, and we are almost made to hear the distant rumbling of artillery carriages and caissons, and the faint tramping of marching squadrons.

Should it be asked why I have allowed eighteen years to elapse before printing my *chronicles*, I reply because I felt that they should have a more careful and critical revision than I have been able to give them until lately, before going to the public. A literary composition even of this kind, like other art compositions, as in painting and sculpture, for instance, is always susceptible of improvement in the manner of presentation, without affecting its truthfulness in regard to the matter treated of. I have no doubt but that much more trimming and pruning might have been done to good advantage.

I felt such an interest in the anti-slavery cause before the war, that Kansas, to me, always meant a principle, and I left home at an early age to join the Free State party. It was, therefore, a real pleasure to me to chronicle everything that I thought would be of interest in the future pertaining to Kansas soldiers in the war. At the same time I endeavored to do full justice to the soldiers of other States serving with us in that section.

Though, no doubt, I always clearly show where my sympathies lie in the discussion of any given question, yet I do not believe that I have, in any instance, displayed strong partisan bias. Nor have I been tempted to write anything for the purpose of producing a sensation.

Future generations of that portion of the Trans-Mississippi country covered by my *Memoirs* will doubtless wish to know what part, if any, the people took in the Great War of the Rebellion. But there has been, as yet, very little published in permanent and accessible form, from which they will be able to obtain the desired information, although nearly all the able-bodied men were in the Federal and Confederate armies, and the storms of war raged furiously over that section. A few sketches of one or two campaigns have been written, but mere sketches are evanescent and pass away in a generation. I hope that I have done something towards filling up the hiatus which exists during the period of the most exciting events in our history.

If the reader will endeavor to put himself in my place during the period covered by my *memoirs*, he will then see the marches, battles, skirmishes, reconnoissances, reviews, etc., as I saw them. As he passes about the camp alone from time to time, he will see refugees, men, women and children, of almost every conceivable color and condition, except that none of them appear to be provided with much of this world's goods and means of happiness. Passing to the hospitals, he will see the sick and wounded, men bleeding and mangled and torn by shot and shell, by small arms, and by the cuts and thrusts of swords and bayonets; he will see them bearing wounds, from the slightest contusions to limbs torn from their bodies; he will hear men groaning and pleading to die, that they may be relieved from their intense suffering; he will hear others, with piteous expressions upon their quivering lips, praying to be taken to their homes to die surrounded by their families and friends; he will see comrades who, but a few days before, were beaming with health and buoyant with life and hope, with the dark shadows of death seizing upon their countenances; and the grief-stricken forms of the dear ones these noble men left behind, when they staked their lives in defense of their country and their homes, will rise up before him.

But passing from these scenes of death and woe, his mind is permitted to dwell upon other subjects less gloomy, and which tend to make the heart glad instead of making it ache. On the march and under clear blue skies, he will cross silver-eddying streams or mountain-brooks leaping and splashing and foaming along. And by the wayside he will drink from crystal springs bubbling out of the earth, as beautiful as spark-ling fountains. The scenes are constantly changing, and always interesting to anyone of healthy mind and body; and he will see landscapes of every conceivable variety, from the forest-covered mountains and hills of Arkansas to the grass-covered prairies and plains of Kansas, and from the deep green of spring to the rich and variegated tints of autumn, and the snow-covered ground of winter.

It is proper that I should express my indebtedness to Captain William Gallaher, Colonel Phillips' Assistant Adjutant-General, for many kindnesses and courtesies in connection with the writing of my *Memoirs* while we were attached to the Indian division. And during the latter part of the year I received from General C. W. Blair, the commanding officer of the post of Fort Scott and the District of Southern Kansas, many acts·of kindness and words of encouragement, for which I feel under deep obligations to him. As he was one of the most accomplished orators in the State, and a man of rare culture and refinement, I have always considered myself fortunate that I made his acquaintance, and was permitted to regard him as my friend. I have never met any one who came nearer my ideal of the perfectly accomplished gentleman than General Blair.

It will perhaps be thought by some that I have given undue prominence to the operations of Colonel Phillips' division. But I think that any one who will follow the operations of this division, will agree with me that I have not magnified its achievements or overestimated the merits of its commander. Considering the number and kind of troops with which he had to operate, and the long line of communication he had to keep open from his advanced position, there was not perhaps another officer in our army who accomplished so much with a single division of troops.

I hope that I have made the work worthy of being welcomed by the young men and women who have grown up since the war, and who desire to become ac-

quainted with the great events in which their fathers
participated. To thus commemorate the grand achievements of the men with whom I served, has afforded
me real pleasure, for I felt that never before have the
soldiers engaged in a great struggle deserved such a
measure of gratitude of future generations as those
whose heroic actions I have recorded.

WILEY BRITTON.

Washington, D. C., May, 1882.

CONTENTS

CHAPTER I.

Resume of the operations of the Army under Gen. Blunt during the last three months of 1862—The battles of Newtonia and Maysville mentioned—The charge led by Capt. S. J. Crawford, Second Kansas Cavalry, and capture of Gen. Cooper's Artillery—The battle of Cane Hill—Brave charge of Col. Lewis R. Jewell, Sixth Kansas Cavalry—His mortal wound and death—Remarks on his character—After the battle of Cane Hill, Gen· Blunt orders his trains to Rhea's Mills—Couriers sent to Gen. Herron to bring forward his Division on a forced march—Strength of the two divisions—Strength of Gen. Hindman's Army—Battle of Prairie Grove described—It lasts until after dark—Furious charging of the Infantry—Terrific artillery fire—Gen. Hindman defeated, and retreats to Van Buren—Gen. Blunt's trains ordered to Fayetteville—Burying the dead and caring for the wounded—Concluding Remarks_____ 33

CHAPTER II.

General Blunt's trains return to Rhea's Mills from Fayetteville—
Resources of the country around Rhea's Mills—Furnishes
forage for the cavalry and transportation animals—Native animals stand the service better in that section than animals
brought from the north—Preparations for the expedition to
Van Buren—Incidental reflections—The expedition on the
march—Crossing and recrossing the raging, foaming and
splashing mountain stream thirty-nine times—An unpleasant
march for the infantry—The troops bivouac by this stream—
The march resumed—An outpost of the enemy struck by the
Federal Cavalry advance—The chase—Battle Dripping Springs
—Federal charge on the enemy's camp—Flight of the enemy to
Van Buren—Federal pursuit—Capture of Van Buren—Burn-
ing of steamboats and supplies—Artillery duel across the Arkansas River—The enemy shell their own city—Return to
Rhea's Mills....   52

CHAPTER III.

The First Division Army of the Frontier moves from Rhea's Mills
to Elm Springs—All the Federal wounded in the Field Hospitals at Prairie Grove removed to Fayetteville—General
Blunt Relieved and starts North—General Schofield takes
command of the Army of the Frontier—Future Operations to
be conducted according to West Point tactics—The Army to
retreat to the Missouri line—Reorganization of the Army—
Colonel W. A. Phillips to command the Indian Division—A
Battalion of the Sixth Kansas cavalry and Captain Hopkin's
Battery to go with it—Grand Review of the Army of the

Frontier by General Schofield—The author's last visit to his
brother in the General Hospital at Fayetteville—The Reduc-
tion of Transportation—Order from War Department for
Recruiting several loyal Arkansas Regiments—General
Marmaduke marching on Springfield—The Army of the
Frontier on the march, except the Indian Division...... 74

CHAPTER IV.

Colonel W. A. Phillips assumes command of the Indian division—
The author to go with it—The division marches to Maysville
on the western line of Arkansas—A skirmish with guerrillas—
A snow storm and difficulty in getting forage—Colonel Phillips,
not only a military commander but also a governor of several
Indian tribes—His position requires great executive ability
—Skirmishes with guerrillas becoming frequent—Bushwhackers living in a cave—Remarks on how caves are formed
—How Stalactites are formed—How stalacmitic matter may
preserve to distant ages in the future some account of the
war—In a few years all external evidences of the war will
have disappeared—Description of the country and of its
resources—Colored refugees increasing—Their destitute condition—Col. Phillips' orders—Repairing of the mills—The
battle at Springfield—Gen. Marmaduke defeated........ 88

CHAPTER V.

The author at Neosho, Missouri, for a few days—*Ante-bellum* times
and reminiscences—Description of the town——The Grand
Falls and water-power mills in the country—Fertility of the

soil on the river bottoms—Fencing which enclosed most of the farms destroyed—About half the people loyal—Indiscriminate destruction of property condemned—A double sacrifice put upon Missouri loyalists—A picture of desolated homes—Guerrilla warfare and Federal losses in the State—The Militia occupying Newtonia and fortifying it—Their efficiency—Mostly State troops that opposed General Marmaduke at the battle of Springfield on the 9th—Flag raising at Neosho—The National Flag scornfully regarded by rebels—Geurrillas at Granby—The rich lead mines there, but no longer worked —Author informed of the death of his brother at Fayetteville —A mother's picture of a united family_____ 107

CHAPTER VI.

The Author's return to his division at Scott's Mills—Colonel Phillips' popularity with his troops—Rebels returning and taking the oath of allegiance—Indians make good troops to fight bushwhackers—Increase of wild game since the war—A detachment of Federal troops worsted in a skirmish with guerrillas—Captain Conkey loses eleven men by capture—Guerrilla chieftains commissioned by the Rebel authorities—Comments on plans proposed by some to break up the guerrilla warfare—Sickness and heavy mortality among the Indian Refugees at Neosho—Sick and wounded being removed from Fayetteville to Fort Scott—The classes of the enemy the Federals have to deal with—Bushwhackers—Guerrillas—Detachments returning to and leaving the State—The regular forces in our front—Illustrations—Incidents from the Expedition to Lone Jack—The battle of Coon Creek—Concluding remarks on the Indians_____ 125

CHAPTER VII.

The Indian Division moves to Pineville, Mo--Remarks on the physical aspect of the country and its resources—Few depredations committed considering the general character and condition of the refugee camp-followers—The President's Emancipation Proclamation—A good many officers and soldiers opposed to it—It is a military necessity—It is just and is warmly commended—The Government will soon have colored troops in the field—Colonel Phillips' brother wounded —Colonel Judson's brigade at Mount Vernon—The Indian division marches to Bentonville, Arkansas—Description of the country—Rebel prisoners sent to Springfield—They were brought in by loyal Arkansas troops—A meteor of great brightnsss observed—Reflections on sidereal worlds and meteoric displays—The Indian Delegation go to Washington_____ 145

CHAPTER VIII.

Colonel Phillips invited to address a Mass Meeting of the Union Citizens of Northwestern Arkansas, at Fayetteville—The great difficulty in getting Forage—A Scouting Party returns from Van Buren—The Indian Division encamped on the edge of the Battle Field of Pea Ridge—An account of the Battle from data collected on the Field and from Eye Witnesses—Rebel raid on Neosho and Capture of Negroes—A Deserter from the Enemy gives Position and strength of their forces—The Enemy's wounded from Prairie Grove at Cane Hill still—Great Mortality among them— Skirmish with Bushwhackers—Arrival of Forage Trains from White River—Horses eat each others Manes and Tails off—The Small-pox among the Indians—Very few of them Vaccinated—Only a few cases among the White Soldiers—Remarks on the Disease—The Government should stock a farm with Animals to furnish Vaccine Virus for the Army---------------------------------- 161

CHAPTER XI.

The march to Camp Moonlight—Captain Mefford, Sixth Kansas Cavalry, defeats Livingston's band—Grass sufficient for grazing purposes about Fort Gibson—Supply train reinforced—A bushwhacker killed near camp—The people should be better informed by proclamation of the Federal purposes—Officers for the Fourth and Fifth Indian regiments report to Colonel Phillips—No such regiments exist—Criticisms concerning the matter—Near Rhea's Mills again—Two loyal Arkansas regiments organized—After a battle the people show on which side their sympathies are by their expressions—The people of a less haughty spirit than in Missouri—Reconnoissance returned from Dutch Mills—Women and children raise their own foodstuffs—The soldiers exchange their surplus rations for butter, eggs, &c—The Army ration—A party of Union men arrive from Texas—They were hunted by the enemy with blood hounds--------------------------- 179

CHAPTER X.

April Fool's day—Seven Pin Indians killed at Park Hill, C. N., by the enemy in federal uniform—The march to Cincinnati on the State line—War paint and yelping of the Indians when

they start out—Commendable conduct of the Indian soldiers
while in Missouri and Arkansas—The division crosses the
line into the Indian country—On the march to Park Hill—
The country becomes more inviting and the vegetation more
advanced—Rebel scouting party near Fayetteville—Arrival at
Park Hill and meeting of the Indian refugee families from
Neosho—Great manifestations of joy and affecting scenes—
Standwaitie commanding the rebel Indians—Colonel Phillips
sends out a strong reconnoissance—Webber's Falls—He
drives the enemy into the Arkansas River and takes Fort
Gibson—Description of the place—Its importance—The
beautiful Grand and Verdigris Rivers................... 197

CHAPTER XI.

Fort Gibson the Key to the Indian country—The enemy showing signs of activity—The troops at Gibson commence to
build bake ovens—Anxiety for the supply train—Creek
Indians coming in—The enemy concentrating at Webber's
Falls—Celebrating the event of hoisting the United States
Flag at Fort Gibson—A sad accident—Arrival of supply train
from Fort Scott—Part of Neosho burned—The enemy attack
Fayetteville and are defeated—A young man as a spy caught
dressed in a woman's suit—The troops commence to throw up
fortifications at Fort Gibson—Strength of the Federal position—Engagement at Webber's Falls—Capture of the enemy's
camp—Assassination of Dr. Gillpatrick—Arrival of rebel
officers under a flag of truce—They are on business in connection with exchanging of prisoners—Reconnoissance of Colonel
Schaurte to the Arkansas line—Colonel Harrison abandons
Fayetteville—Colonel Phillips reviews his division...... 213

CHAPTER XII.

The author sent with dispatches to Colonel Harrison at Cassville, Missouri—The first night's march in a storm of thunder and lightning—The next morning on the battle-ground of Locust Grove—Account of the battle and of the capture of Colonel Clarkson's command—Passing over the ground of an exciting chase of last year—Camp in the forest—On the look-out for the enemy—In Missouri—Arrival at Cassville—Detention at Cassville—The troops there daily expecting to be attacked—Large number of troops, including the State militia, in Southwest Missouri—Activity of the militia—The First Kansas colored infantry organized, and at Baxter Springs—Remarks on arming the freedmen—Many small tracts being cultivated in Missouri—By whom—On the march to Fort Gibson—A fight with Guerillas—Stopping in a lonely retreat—Return to Fort Gibson............................ 231

CHAPTER XIII.

The enemy occupying the heights south of the Arkansas River in sight of Fort Gibson—Picket firing across the river all day long—Strength of General Cooper's force—He is preparing to capture Colonel Phillips' supply train—Name of post of Fort Gibson changed to Fort Blunt—Colonel Phillips contending single-handed with two Generals of the enemy—Hard service for the cavalry—Capture of horses and mules from the enemy—Activity in the enemy's camp—The enemy kill the Federal pickets, and capture a good many animals—The battle—Enemy driven from the field and pursued—Recapture of some animals—Large force of the enemy cross the Arkansas

River, and march to meet the Federal supply train—Convalescent soldiers coming in from Tahlequah—The troops move
inside the fortifications at Fort Gibson—The engagement at
Rapid Ford, Sunday afternoon—Colonel Phillips intended the
movement only as a demonstration...................... 251

CHAPTER XIV.

The enemy makes a night attack on the Federal supply train—
Gallant charge led by Colonel Phillips, and total route of the
enemy—Only a sutler's wagon partially plundered—The
enemy had another force which failed to co-operate—The paymaster paying off the troops—The Government should adopt
a system to enable officers and soldiers to send their money
home—Activity noticed in the enemy's camp again—The
Arkansas River rising—Friendly conversations between Federal and Rebel Pickets—The Federal supply train returns to
Fort Scott with a heavy escort—Engagement between Livingston and the colored troops at Baxter Springs—The enemy
anxious to know if the colored regiment is coming down—A
woman takes one of the enemy's horses and comes into the
Fort—Colonel Phillips to be reinforced—Skirmish near Park
Hill—Standwaitie's Indians in the northern part of the
Nation.. 266

CHAPTER XV.

An agreement in regard to the cessation of picket firing—Mostly
young men in the army—They have no Alcestis to die for
them—General Cooper's army moves back twenty miles,
perhaps to find better grazing—A rebel reconnoitering force

west of the Fort—General Cabell's force near Cincinnati—
The Indians harvesting—The wheat crop good, what there is
of it—Major Foreman after Standwaitie—Engagement on
Green Leaf prairie—The enemy finally driven from the field
—Federal and Rebel pickets in swimming together—The
Federals exchange coffee for tobacco—Desertion of rebel
soldiers—Rebel discipline believed to be more severe in some
respects than the Federal—Remarks on flogging and severe
discipline—Major Foreman with six hundred men sent to
meet Federal supply train—The enemy preparing to attack it
again—An Indian prophet and the superstitions of the
Indians... 234

CHAPTER XVI.

The rebel pickets shout across the river that the Federal supply
train is coming—Another rebel force gone to meet the Federal
supply train—Movements of the Confederate armies in
the East as reported by rebel pickets—Vicksburg closely invested by General Grant—Federal troops in southwest Missouri—Federal supply train detained by high water at Neosho River—Federal supplies running short at Fort Gibson—
High water in Grand River—Indian women report heavy firing in the vicinity of Cabin Creek—General Cabell on the east
side of Grand River, near Cabin Creek, with artillery—The
suspense—A National Salute fired in honor of Independence
Day—Beef and Beans for barbecue—The pinch of hunger—
Horses and dead rebels floating in the river—Two days' fighting at Cabin Creek—Gallant charge of the Colored regiment—
Total rout of the enemy—How the Federal troops crossed

Cabin Creek under fire—General Cabell unable to join General
Cooper's division on account of high water—Arrival of supply train at Fort Gibson................................ 302

CHAPTER XVII.

The Federal supply train returns to Fort Scott—The Battalion of
the Sixth Kansas Cavalry and the author accompany it—Colonel Phillips commended for his successful military operations
—Federal troops with which author has acted for two years
have been uniformly successful—The colored soldiers anxious
to meet the enemy—Their physical endurance—Well adapted
to campaigning in warm climate—Colonel Phillips will be
able to cross the Arkansas river and attack General Cooper—
Large quantities of hay should be put up at Fort Gibson—
Salt works at Grand Saline—Families of English blood cling
to their homesteads—On the march up the beautiful Grand
River country—Looking out for General Cabell's force—The
escort meets General Blunt at Cabin Creek—Examination of
the battle-field—Active operations to be commenced against
General Cooper immediately—The train and escort pass
the section of Livingston's operations—Arrival at Fort
Scott... 330

CHAPTER XVIII.

The battalion of the Sixth Kansas Cavalry to remain at Fort Scott
a few weeks—News of the battle of Gettysburg and surrender
of Vicksburg and Port Hudson — Remarks on the progress of the Federal arms—Backbone of the Confederacy

broken—Frequent contests between the State Militia and
guerrilas in Southwest Missouri—Guerrilla warfare leads to
retaliation and personal grudges—Major Livingston, the
guerrilla leader, killed by the Missouri Militia—Remarks on
the nature of his operations—Colonel Crittenden, commanding the Militia in Southwest Missouri, after the enemy—Colonel Cloud on the march to Fayetteville—General Blunt attacks
General Cooper's army at Honey Springs—Preparations for
the battle—Furious charge of the Federal troops—Complete
rout of the enemy and capture of one piece of artillery, colors and prisoners—General Cabell came up after the battle
was over_____ 346

CHAPTER XIX.

The enemy burn the Court House and Academy at Carthage—
County records carried away in Missouri—Rebel guerillas
near Fort Scott—Rebel women carry information to the
enemy—Cholera and Small-pox at Fort Gibson—Probable
cause of Cholera breaking out—A soldier killed by Captain
Tough—A little too much drunkenness—Major Blair closes
the whisky shops—Resisting the draft—Great riot in New
York City—Remarks on neutrality—Arrival of Colonel Phillips from the front—The supply train starts to Fort Gibson—
Recruiting of the Fourteenth Kansas Cavalry—Large bounties
paid by the government for recruits—State bounties in some
of the States—Skirmish between several squadrons of Federal
troops through mistake—Skirmish with guerillas near Balltown—Appeal of the rebel government for more troops—Description of the country around Fort Scott—Recruiting colored troops_____ 363

CHAPTER XX.

A Post established at Baxter Springs, with a Detachment of Cavalry—Bombardment of Charleston and probable fall of Forts Sumter and Wagner—Guerrillas along the Border displaying unusual Activity—Large quantities of Hay being put up for the Government at Fort Scott—Burning and Sacking of Lawrence by Quantrell—Murder of one hundred and fifty of her Citizens—Escape of the Desperadoes into Missouri—Federal troops in pursuit—The Guerillas break up into small Detachments—Kansas needs a State Militia—Looking around for some one to blame—Generals Ewing and Schofield Denounced—Some favor the wild notion of a Grand Army of Invasion, to destroy everything in Missouri for a distance of forty miles from Kansas—Folly of the Scheme—Generals Cooper and Cabell threatening General Blunt—Paola Mass Meeting—Plan of removal of Rebel Families considered... 381

CHAPTER XXI.

General Schofield coldly received by the people of Leavenworth City—Colonels Jennison and Hoyt speak in Fort Scott—The crowd sing "John Brown's body lies mouldering in the grave," &c.—More of General Lane's Grand Army of Invasion —Few trophies to bring back—General Schofield issues an order against invasion—The Missouri State troops would resist it—Battle of Perryville and defeat of General Cooper— General Blunt captures Fort Smith—Generals Steele and Davidson capture Little Rock—Colonel Blair sends out a reconnoissance—A new department wanted—General Gillmore

captures Forts Wagner and Gregg in Charlestown Harbor—
Sympathizers of the rebellion receive anonymous notices to
leave the city—Supposed to be the action of the Union League
—Arrival of General Blunt and Staff and Colonel Judson—
The Bourbon County Fair—Activity of the enemy along the
border again... 397

CHAPTER XXII.

General Blunt, Staff and Escort start to Fort Smith—Two Soldiers killed near Fort Scott by the enemy—Signs of an approaching storm—The enemy endeavor to capture or kill the
Federal pickets, and to make a dash on Fort Scott—General
Blunt's escort attacked by Quantrell near Baxter Springs, and
nearly all killed—Colonel Blair with a cavalry force to the
rescue—Members of the Band burned in the Band wagon—
The enemy defeated by Lieutenant Pond at Baxter Springs—
The invasion of Missouri by General Shelby, with two thousand cavalry and three pieces of artillery—The Missouri
State militia in pursuit of him—The Militia capture his artil-
lery and disperse his force—General Ewing's force joins in
the pursuit of the enemy—The enemy driven from the State—
General John McNeil to take command of the Federal troops
at Fort Smith—General Lane speaks in Fort Scott—General
Blunt starts to Fort Smith again...................... 413

CHAPTER XXIII.

All quiet along the Border—Lovely Indian Summer—Theory
accounting for the Smoky condition of the Atmosphere—

Reprehensible conduct of a Detachment on scouting service —Discussion over the question, "Who shall be the Commanding General of the District?"—Rebel guerrillas in the vicinity of Humboldt—Colonel Moonlight takes command of the Fourteenth Kansas Cavalry—Lieutenant Josling on a scout to Osage Mission—A Cold Wave—Distressing condition of Refugees—General Blunt authorized to raise another Colored Regiment—Citizens of Fort Scott opposed to Colonel Jennison taking command of the post—The supply train starts South—A Military Telegraph to be constructed to Fort Scott—Twelfth Kansas Infantry *en route* to Fort Smith—Federal expedition towards Texas—"Mountain Federals" in Arkansas—They annoy the enemy....................... 429

CHAPTER XXIV.

General Grant defeats the enemy under General Bragg near Chattanooga—Arrival of a large quantity of Cotton from Fort Smith—Supposed crookedness in regard to it—Guerilla bands in Southwestern Missouri—How the people manage to keep good Animals in some instances—Temporary suspension in the Exchange of Prisoners—General Marmaduke, with two thousand men, near the Southern line of Missouri—Perhaps the last supply train to Fort Smith—General Ewing orders the seizure of the Cotton from Fort Smith—Snow Storm— Removal of General Schofield probable—Quantrell's forces cross the Arkansas River near Fort Gibson, on the way North—Were defeated by Colonel Phillips' troops—General Price threatens Fort Smith—Attempt of the enemy to spike the seige guns at Fort Scott—The Missouri militia defeat Quantrell—A large Rebel force in Southwest Missouri—It is driven South—Concluding Remarks.................. 442

CHAPTER I.

Resume of the operations of the Army under Gen. Blunt during the last three months of 1862—The battles of Newtonia and Maysville mentioned—The charge led by Capt. S. J. Crawford, Second Kansas Cavalry, and capture of Gen. Cooper's Artillery—The battle of Cane Hill—Brave charge of Col. Lewis R. Jewell, Sixth Kansas Cavalry—His mortal wound and death—Remarks on his character—After the battle of Cane Hill, Gen. Blunt orders his trains to Rhea's Mills—Couriers sent to Gen. Herron to bring forward his Division on a forced march—Strength of the two divisions—Strength of Gen. Hindman's Army—Battle of Prairie Grove described— It lasts until after dark—Furious charging of the Infantry— Terrific artillery fire—Gen. Hindman defeated, and retreats to Van Buren—Gen. Blunt's trains ordered to Fayetteville— Burying the dead and caring for the wounded—Concluding Remarks.

WHEN I commenced my *Memoirs* I felt sure that shortly after peace should be established between all sections of the country, the military operations with which I was connected as an humble participant would be regarded by many with deep interest. I therefore thought it worth while to undertake to chronicle the important events that came under my notice during the year 1863, as I had done during the year 1862.*

* Two volumes of my Ms., for 1862, and 1864, were left in the Adjutant General's Office at Fort Smith, Arkansas, the latter part of 1864, and are supposed to have been destroyed by fire the following year.

3

I commenced to write the following memoirs at
Rhea's Mills, Washington 'County, Arkansas, on the
25th day of December, 1862. In my chronicles I said
that as our offensive operations are temporarily sus-
pended; and as we are expecting orders shortly to
move northward towards the Missouri line; a *resume*
of our operations since we came into this section last
fall will be useful.- After the battles of Newtonia on
the 30th of September and 4th of October last, we
moved steadily forward, and defeated the enemy in
every engagement. At the battle of Maysville or *Old
Fort Wayne*, Cherokee Nation, on the 20th of October,
we gained a substantial victory by capturing from
General Cooper four pieces of light artillery, brass
twelve pounders. The Second and Sixth regiments
Kansas cavalry led in the charge which resulted in the
capture of these guns. It is generally conceded however, that the meed of honor should go to Captain
Samuel J. Crawford, Second Kansas cavalry, for
conspicuous bravery displayed on the field that bright
sunny morning. It was one of the most exciting
contests that I had up to that time witnessed. The
enemy were completely routed in less than half an
hour after the engagement commenced, and besides his
artillery, a considerable number of small arms, which
were thrown down by General Cooper's troops in their
flight, fell into our hands.

Passing over minor engagements and skirmishes,
we come next to the battles of Cane Hill and Prairie
Grove. The battle of Cane Hill took place November

29th. Though we drove the enemy through the
mountains from position to position all day, we gained
nothing of consequence, since we lost one of the
bravest and best officers of our command, Lieutenant
Colonel Lewis R. Jewell, Sixth Kansas Cavalry. We
also had two other officers of the same regiment
seriously wounded, Lieutenants John G. Harris and
John A. Johnson, besides some twenty enlisted men.
Colonel Jewell fell mortally wounded while leading a
sabre charge through a narrow pass in the mountains
near the head of Cove Creek just as darkness was
coming on.* The gorges in the mountains through
which we were pressing the enemy made our pursuit
of him exceedingly difficult and hazardous, for we
could rarely display a front of more than fifty men.

I feel that it is eminently right and proper that I
should give Colonel Jewell more than a passing notice
in this *resume*. He permitted me to accompany him
on all scouts and reconnoissances whenever I could be
spared from my regular duties. And when I could
not go with him, he generally made it a point on his
return to report to me such facts as he thought would
be worth noting down. As I endeavored to notice the
chief points of interest covering the area of our
operations, he frequently furnished me with information from higher authorities, which I could not have
otherwise got. When I carried orders on the field at

*Captain J. K. Hudson, Assistant Adjutant General of Colonel
Weir's brigade, who had been on several bold adventures with
Colonel Jewell during the day, was only a few yards from him
when he fell.

Newtonia last September, it was Colonel Jewell that
I saw lead two battalions of the Sixth Kansas Cavalry
on our right against two battalions of the enemy's
cavalry. This force of the enemy, though somewhat
superior to ours, had no sooner drawn several volleys
from our carbines than Colonel Jewell ordered his
bugler to sound the charge, and in an instant, with
drawn sabres and at the head of his regiment, he
swept forward over the prairie like a storm, leaving a
cloud of dust in his rear. The enemy stood for a
moment, but when they saw our cavalry coming
towards them with such impetuosity, they turned and
fled, and sought the covering of their guns. Colonel
Jewell pursued them for about three-quarters of a
mile right at their heels, sabreing some of the rear-
most, until he came near the stone wall or fence,
behind which were posted a large body of rebel
infantry. It was the grandest sight I ever saw—our
bright sabres gleaming in the sunlight of that lovely
afternoon. This short action took place on the open
prarie, and as I was near Colonel Weir and our batteries,
a few hundred yards to the left of Col. Jewell's position,
I could see every movement as distinctly as if I were
watching two of our cavalry regiments going into a
sham battle. In the presence of the enemy he never
sought an excuse to be absent from his regiment or
post of duty. And his men loved him, for he respected their manhood, and shared equally with them
all dangers and hardships. In another way he endeared himself to us more than any other field-officer

of our regiment. He always seemed to me to be more in earnest and devoted to the cause for which we are fighting, and in which I believe we shall be successful, than any of the other field-officers. We had some rather lively discussions around headquarters sometimes in regard to the policy of the Government towards the rebellious States, and I know that he was an ardent supporter of Mr. Lincoln's administration, and believed that the war should be prosecuted without dallying with the enemy.

It is a matter of simple justice to state that no truer and braver soldier has thus far in the war been sacrificed on the altar of liberty, nor has a purer patriot drawn his sword in defence of his country. Though his family and friends and all who knew him will mourn that he has been thus cut down in the prime of his manhood and usefulness, yet there is a sad pleasure in knowing that he fell in the full discharge of a noble duty, the noblest it is given man to perform.

If Kansas shall in the future erect monuments to her heroic dead, I know that none will be more deserving of a monument than Colonel Jewell.

After the battle of Cane Hill, General Blunt ordered forward all his trains from Camp Moonlight to Rhea's Mills, eight miles north of Cane Hill. All the troops of his division, except some detachments which were posted to guard the principal passes in the mountains to the south of us, were collected at Rhea's Mills, for he knew from the information that our scouts brought in each day, that a great struggle was near at hand—a struggle that would require the co-operation of all the Federal troops in southwest Missouri and northwest Arkansas to save us from defeat and utter destruction. General Herron's division of Iowa, Illinois, Wisconsin and Missouri troops, which had been with us during the latter part of October, while we were encamped at Pea Ridge, moved back early in November in the direction of Wilson Creek and Springfield, Missouri. Having received reliable information that a large army of the enemy, consisting of all the available troops from Texas, Arkansas and Missouri, had concentrated at Fort Smith and Van Buren under the supreme command of General Hindman, who had positively fixed the 3d or 4th of December as the day when he would set out with his army to attack and destroy this division and invade Missouri, General Blunt sent couriers to General Herron to bring forward his division on a forced march. General Herron responded with great promptness, marching day and night, and on Sunday morning, December 7th, his advance guard, composed of a battalion of the Seventh Missouri Cavalry, was attacked by General Hindman's advance cavalry division about twelve miles south of Fayetteville, near Illinois river, and some five miles southeast of our camp. The officer in command of General Herron's advanced guard, supposing that he was in the neighborhood of our division, allowed himself to be surprised by the enemy, and in this preliminary engagement lost upwards of one hundred of his men by capture, and some ten or twelve killed and wounded. But I think he cannot be justly censured for this misfortune, since he had a right to suppose that we had not permitted the enemy to pass us. This engagement in the morning, however, stopped the progress of the enemy and enabled General Herron to bring up his infantry and artillery. And in the meantime our division was also coming into position on the enemy's left flank.

With the exception of the above affair, and a reconnoisance by our division, which will presently be mentioned, the early part of the day was consumed by the commanding generals on both sides in bringing up troops and artillery and getting them into position, so that a calm prevailed before the storm which was to break over Prairie Grove in the afternoon.

While the two opposing armies were thus getting ready for the impending conflict, a movement with which I was connected seems worth mentioning. About two o'clock on Sunday morning the 7th, Colonel W. R. Judson, with most of the available men of his regiment and two mountain howitzers, was detailed by Gen. Blunt to occupy a pass in the mountains about twelve miles southeast of Rhea's Mill, as a report came in that the enemy were making a demonstration against an outpost which we had there. When we reached the point designated, we found that all Gen. Hindman's army with the exception of some detachments, which had been thrown out as flankers and as rear guard, had passed. After we struck the Fort Smith and Fayette-

ville road and marched north a short distance, we came
in sight of the enemy's rear column. Col. Judson ordered the howitzer battery to fire a few rounds into it,and
Gen. Hindman supposing that his army was attacked
in the rear by Gen. Blunt's division from Rhea's Mills,
ordered his troops to form in line of battle, facing to the
rear. We saw them forming on the sides of the mountain and in the openings in the woods in large masses·
After discharging a few volleys from our carbines into
their line, we retreated around a section of the mountain and joined our division on the extreme right
about the middle of the afternoon. This movement it
is generally conceded had the effect of delaying Gen.
Hindman in massing his troops in front against Gen.
Herron, as he could not feel sure that the main attack
was not to be made in his rear, until he sent out a
reconnoisance and discovered the true situation. Several rebel wounded with whom I talked on the subject
of the battle, stated that Gen. Hindman had actually
commenced to change his main line of battle to face
south. When we came on to the field the divisions of
Gens. Blunt and Herron had just formed a junction,
and their line of battle must have been fully two and
a half miles long. Gen. Herron's division had already
had several sharp contests with the enemy, and the
engagement was becoming general all along the line.
On both sides the skirmish lines were being pushed back
on the infantry and artillery. The enemy had apparently the best position, as he occupied a side of the
mountain and a plateau or intermediate elevation,

thickly covered with timber, mostly of young growth; while our forces occupied the lower ground north and west of Prairie Grove meeting house. Shortly after we had taken our position, there was a lull in the skirmish firing, which was soon followed by a heavy roll of musketry on our extreme left. Gen. Hindman had thrown forward a division of infantry which attacked Gen. Herron's division furiously. He then dispatched another division against Gen. Blunt. The heavy volleys of musketry now extended all along the lines of both armies. In the meantime the artillery of both sides had not been idle. It furnished the base notes of that awfully grand performance. Our batteries were skillfully handled, and sometimes when they came into new positions with the enemy plainly in view, their terrific thundering seemed to shake the very foundation of the mountains. The storm surged back and forth along the lines of both armies with no perceptible intermission until dark with small arms, and until long after dark with the artillery; for I could distinctly see from our position the enemy's guns on the side of the mountain belching forth long volumes of fire from their horrid throats. My experience at Newtonia and Prairie Grove convinces me that shells from an enemy's guns bursting over one's head at night make quite a different impression upon the mind than when bursting over one's head in broad daylight. The bursting and singing of shells flying through the air, and the crackling and falling of limbs of trees produce an indescribable feeling, such perhaps as is not easy to imagine by anv one who has not had the experience.

As the twilight grew into darkness the volleys of musketry died away gradually, and only the batteries kept up the firing of shot and shell. But when night came and drew a mantle of darkness over the earth, and shortly separated the combatants, neither we nor our foes knew the amount of death and suffering the last few hours had wrought. Nor is it likely that the commanding Generals of either army, until long after silence reigned over the bloody field, felt sure as to the result of the day's contest. At the close of the day both armies occupied very nearly the same positions they had taken up on going into action. Some of the bloodiest parts of the field were neutral ground during the night. Our troops slept on their arms, and all night long active preparations were being made to bring every available man on the field the next day, and to renew the battle at early dawn. The supply and baggage trains of our division at Rhea's Mills, had been in an unsafe position during the day, and were removed during the night to Fayetteville, so that they would be covered by our army in the event of its being compelled to retreat the next day. During the progress of the battle, Gen. Solomons, with the Ninth Wisconsin infantry and some detachments from different regiments, was left to guard our trains. But the next morning was clear and frosty, and the sun, with its disc half obscured, peeped over the distant outlines of the mountain and seemed to smile on

all below. The distant mountain peaks, too, bathed in
a soft haze, seemed to speak words of hope and confidence. We found ourselves in complete possession of
the field instead of another bloody day before us.
Gen. Hindman not being willing to renew the contest,
had during the night ordered the wheels of his artillery carriages and caissons muffled, and drawn off the
field and retreated towards Van Buren. He remained
however with a division of cavalry in the vicinity of
the battle field a short time the next day, and sent a
flag of truce to Gens. Blunt and Herron concerning
the picking up of arms on the field, the burying of the
dead and caring for the wounded. Our victory was
complete. The defeat of the enemy was a severe blow
to the Confederate cause west of the Mississippi.
Gen. Hindman is reported to have boasted that his
horse should drink out of the Missouri river or from
the rivers of Pluto's regions before Christmas. The
morning before leaving Van Buren, he issued a flaming address to his troops to inspire them with courage
and hope, and in it, in speaking of the Federal troops,
he went on to say, "they have desolated your homes,
defiled the graves of your kindred," etc. A copy of
this address I picked up on the field beside a dead
Confederate soldier, and presume it was printed and
distributed among the rebel troops. This bombastic
display of oratory may have had some effect towards
firing the flagging zeal of his troops, for some of his
soldiers that we captured had very exaggerated notions
about alleged outrages committed by our troops, particularly the Kansas division.

This battle is one of the three big battles that have as yet been fought west of the Mississippi river, and as it has resulted so favorable to our arms, it will no doubt do much to strengthen our cause in the west. There are always men who are looking out for the winning side.

It requires time and an immense expenditure of energy and money to organize and equip such an army as Gen. Hindman brought against us. His army has been estimated at sixteen to twenty thousand men. Our two divisions did not bring on the field exceeding ten thousand men. From what I saw and could find out, I estimated that our loss must have been very nearly two hundred men killed, and upwards of eight hundred wounded.* The enemy, I estimated

* The First Division, commanded by Brig.-General James G. Blunt, consisted of the following troops; Kansas: Second, Sixth and Ninth regiments of cavalry, with four twelve pound mountain howitzers; Tenth, Eleventh and Thirteenth regiments infantry, and First, Second and Third batteries light artillery. Indiana: Second battery light artillery commanded by Captain Rabb. Wisconsin: Third regiment cavalry, two battalions, and Ninth regiment infantry. And Colonel Phillips Indiana brigade, consisting of the First, Second and Third regiments.

The Second and Third Divisions commanded by Brig.-General Frank J. Herron were composed of the following organizations: Iowa: Nineteenth and Twentieth regiments of infantry, and First regiment cavalry. Illinois: Tenth regiment cavalry and Thirty-seventh and Ninety-fourth regiments infantry and Peoria battery light artillery. Indiana: Twenty-sixth regiment infantry. Missouri: First, Seventh and Eight regiments cavalry, and batteries "E," "F" and "L" First light artillery. Wisconsin: One battalion Second regiment cavalry, and Twentieth regiment infantry, and First regiment Arkansas cavalry.

from counting different groups of their slain on the field, lost about three hundred men killed, and probably upwards of a thousand wounded.

There was some gallant charging by the infantry on

According to official reports the casualties were as follows in Second and Third Divisions: Indiana: Twenty-sixth infantry, enlisted men killed, 41. Illinois: Thirty-seventh regiment infantry, enlisted men killed,   : wounded,   . Ninety-fourth regiment, enlisted men killed, 2; wounded, 10. Tenth regiment cavalry, enlisted men wounded, 9. Iowa: First cavalry, wounded enlisted men, 1; missing enlisted men, 2. Nineteenth infantry, killed, officers, 3; enlisted men, 42; wounded, officers, 5; enlisted men, 139; missing, officers, 1; enlisted men, 2. Twentieth infantry, killed, officers, 1; enlisted men, 7; wounded, officers, 5; enlisted men, 34. Missouri: Seventh cavalry, killed, officers, 2; enlisted men, 4; wounded, enlisted men, 6; missing, officers, 1; enlisted men, 105. Eighth cavalry, missing, enlisted men, 4. Batteries E, F and L, First Light artillery, killed, enlisted men, 1; wounded, 2. Wisconsin: Twentieth infantry, killed, officers, 2; enlisted men, 51; wounded officers, 8; enlisted men, 154; missing, enlisted men, 10. Battalion Second cavalry, wounded, enlisted men, 1.

First Division: Kansas: Second cavalry, killed, enlisted men, 3; wounded, officers, 1; enlisted men, 11. Sixth cavalry, missing, enlisted men, 3. Tenth infantry, killed, enlisted men, 7; wounded, officers, 2; enlisted men, 58. Eleventh infantry, killed, enlisted men, 2; wounded, officers, 2; enlisted men, 19. Thirteenth infantry, killed, enlisted men, 7; wounded, officers, 2; enlisted men, 33; missing, enlisted men, 6. First Battery, killed, enlisted men, 1; wounded, enlisted men, 8. Indiana brigade: First regiment, killed, enlisted men, 1; wounded, enlisted men, 1. Third regiment, missing, enlisted men, 3.

There were according to the official reports of Gens. Blunt and Herron, killed, 167, wounded, 798; missing, 183, making a total of casualties of 1,148. I make 175 killed, which I think is very nearly correct. This is 28 less than the number of men killed at Pea Ridge during three days' fighting.

both sides to capture batteries and to secure certain desirable positions. In Gen. Herron's division the Twentieth regiment Wisconsin infantry, Twenty-sixth Indiana Infantry, the Nineteenth and Twentieth regiments of Iowa infantry, and Thirty-seventh and Ninety-fourth regiments Illinois infantry were most fiercely assaulted by the enemy, and sustained the heaviest loss in charging the enemy at the point of the bayonet. Never was greater bravery and firmness displayed by troops in action, and no general ever handled his men more skillfully than Gen. Herron.

On that bloody day several of the enemy's batteries, after every horse belonging to the gun carriages had been killed, were captured by our infantry, and while they were being hauled off the field by the hands of the men, the enemy rallied and came down in lines of six deep, and recaptured them just before they were drawn to the foot of the hill. Gen. Herron strengthened his line at this hotly contested spot, and in a few moments a strong force of infantry charged up the hill through the woods and at the point of the bayonet retook one of the batteries and held it. Shortly after this fierce contest Gen. Hindman sent a division of infantry against our right with a view of breaking through Gen. Blunt's line. Again the enemy came down in line of battle six deep. Gen. Blunt ordered his batteries into positions from which they were able to use grape and canister against the enemy with terrible effect. The Tenth, Eleventh and Thirteenth regiments Kansas infantry

suffered the heaviest losses in this fierce engagement.
Our batteries were well handled and did excellent service. They dismounted several of the enemy's guns,
knocked the wheels off some of their gun carriages
and caissons, and by exploding shells killed a good
many of their artillerymen and artillery horses. I
saw near the peach orchard on the hill where this
fierce contest was waged over the taking and retaking
of the batteries above mentioned, nearly all the horses
that belonged to those batteries within a radius of
fifty yards, and I noticed that many of them had been
killed by exploding shells. Indeed in some instances
they were dreadfully mutilated.

I account for the enemy's loss in killed and
wounded being larger than ours in this way. In the
first place I am satisfied that Gen. Hindman's army
was not as well organized and equipped as ours;
though he unquestionably had several divisions of well
organized troops. In the second place, I don't believe
that the great body of his troops were as eager for the
fray as ours. I sincerely believe that a large proportion of our soldiers were actually eager for the contest,
and went into it with confidence of their strength
and in the justice of our cause. They felt too, that
our officers would not blindly lead them into a contest
in which they would be put to disadvantage in every
respect. Our small arms also were perhaps as a
general thing superior to the small arms of the enemy,
though some of their infantry regiments were armed
with fine Enfield muskets with the crown stamped

upon them. When it could be done conveniently it
was probably the intention to pick up these costly
arms whenever a soldier was killed or fell severely
wounded, but in many instances this would have been
impossible, hostile bullets were flying so thick and
fas

Several women whom I saw on the field the second
day after the battle, looking for dead or wounded
relatives and friends, told me that the rebel authorities
had conscripted every able bodied man in the State
they could get, and put him into the army, and that
the conscripts were always sure to be put into the
front ranks, poorly armed and equipped, so as to draw
our first fire, and so that their best trained and
equipped soldiers could be reserved for the fiercest and
most important contests. From inquiries that I have
made, I have no doubt but that a good many men who
were indifferent as to the results of the war, and many
others whose sympathies were more with the Government than with the Confederacy, were killed and
wounded in this battle. But in times like the present,
if not indeed upon all questions of public and private
interests, men should have decided convictions, and
support them by all honorable means in their power.
If a man is not in sympathy with the rebellion
he should at once either join the Federal army or seek
its protection. It is an unsafe time to attempt to sit
a straddle the political fence. Whoever attempts it is
liable to get knocked off by either party, and to receive
very little sympathy from neither.

And thirdly, I don't think that the enemy were able to use their artillery as effectively as ours was used. Gen. Hindman's position on the side of the mountain and on the plateau below, though covered with a dense young forest, was not much advantage to him, if not indeed a positive disadvantage. On account of the few openings in the woods, his batteries could not find a sufficient number of good positions from which to sight our troops and batteries. And being obliged to stick to the same positions all the afternoon, our batteries soon got their range from the smoke which arose from them, and knocked them to pieces fearfully. Our batteries constantly shifted their positions and consequently suffered very little loss. Only at the peach orchard above mentioned, did the enemy attempt to use any of his batteries at short range with grape and canister, and we have seen how that performance ended. The batteries of both our divisions, about forty-two pieces, all the afternoon poured a constant and terrific shower of shot and shell into the dense woods which seemed to afford the enemy shelter. The day after the battle, in passing through this woods with an officer and several comrades, the number of torn and multilated bodies of rebel soldiers, scattered here and there, told us plainly enough that the forest had afforded the enemy very little shelter, that though it had concealed them from our view, it had not concealed them from our exploding shells. On one occasion when General Hindman massed a large force of infantry in front of our right, and directed them to break our line, two of our batteries took positions well selected, and cross-fired them with grape and canister, as soon as they came within range, with terrible effect.

The names of many officers who displayed conspicuous bravery on the bloody field of Prairie Grove could be mentioned, but as there were probably others, whose names I did not get, who displayed equal bravery, it would be unjust to make any discrimination. The officer of highest rank killed on our side, was Lieut.-Colonel Samuel McFarland, Nineteenth Iowa infantry, while gallantly leading his regiment.

The smoke of the battle having cleared away, and it having been ascertained that the enemy had not stopped in his retreat until he reached Van Buren, our next care was to bury our dead and look after our wounded. The enemy also, under a flag of truce, had men and surgeons on the field gathering up their dead and wounded. I visited a number of our Field Hospitals, and it was the most affecting sight I ever saw to see so many of our poor fellows breathing out their noble lives. A young man to my left, as I passed through a ward in which most of the patients were regarded as mortally wounded, knowing that dissolution was near, was dictating a last message to his young wife; and another to my right was directing a comrade by his side to send some loving word to his mother; and near by another, whose countenance showed that life was fast ebbing away, looked intently on a picture of some dear one at home for a moment and then fell to weeping. Others were undergoing great mental as well as physical suffering, because

they were conscious that they were. going to die far
away from homes and friends. But the groans and
agonies of these brave men shall not have been in vain.
Future generations will enjoy the blessings that their
blood has helped to purchase. It would be base in-
gratitude on the part of those for whom they died,
were they to make no effort to commemorate their
glorious actions.

CHAPTER II.

General Blunt's trains return to Rhea's Mills from Fayetteville—
Resources of the country around Rhea's Mills—Furnishes
forage for the cavalry and transportation animals—Native animals stand the service better in that section than animals
brought from the north—Preparations for the expedition to
Van Buren—Incidental reflections—The expedition on the
march—Crossing and recrossing the raging, foaming and
splashing mountain stream thirty-nine times—An unpleasant
march for the infantry—The troops bivouac by this stream—
The march resumed—An outpost of the enemy struck by the
Federal Cavalry advance—The chase—Battle Dripping Springs
—Federal charge on the enemy's camp—Flight of the enemy to
Van Buren—Federal pursuit—Capture of Van Buren—Burn-
ing of steamboats and supplies—Artillery duel acrsss the Arkansas River—The enemy shell their own city—Return to
Rhea's Mills.

BEFORE saluting the new year we must notice some
further operations of considerable importance. A few
days after the battle of Prairie Grove, General Blunt
ordered his supply and baggage trains back from
Fayetteville to Rhea's Mills, and our division went
into camp again. General Herron's division went
into camp on the ground it occupied during the battle.
The battle will probably always be known in history
as the battle of *Prairie Grove*, for the two opposing
armies met near Prairie Grove meeting house, on a
northern slope of the Boston Mountains.

This section is regarded as the wealthiest and most
fertile region in northwestern Arkansas, if not indeed

of the State. The climate and soil seem peculiarly
adapted to raising sweet potatoes, apples, pears, peaches
and many other kinds of fruit. Wheat, corn and
oats are also raised in considerable abundance. But
the farms are not large like the farms in Missouri.
We have found almost sufficient forage to supply our
animals, and we have also replenished the larder of the
commissariat to some extent. The cattle and hogs
taken from disloyal people of this section furnish us
with fresh beef and pork.. The water-power mills on
the never-failing mountain streams, have rarely been
burned, and turn out a good deal of flour, which is
applied to subsisting the army. All commissary and
quartermaster supplies for our division, with the exception of those that this section furnishes, are transported by four-mule teams from Fort Scott, Kansas, a
distance of one hundred and forty miles. Gen.
Herron's division is supplied from Springfield, Missouri. Though our base of supplies is this great
distance from us; and though most of the country our
trains pass over is infested with guerrilla bands that
annoy our escorts by now and then picking off a
trooper with their rifles or muskets, yet we have not,
up to the present time, lost a train or suffered any inconvenience for want of full rations. A considerable
body of our cavalry has, however, been detached from
actual field service to perform escort duty, during the
autumn and winter. But taking into account the
amount of this kind of service, and the fact that scouting parties or reconnaissances are daily sent out in
every direction, our cavalry horses are in remarkably

good condition. That they have stood the campaign
so well, I think is due to the fact that they have been
collected mostly from Missouri and Kansas, a climate
not differing perceptibly from this. Last spring the
Second Ohio cavalry accompanied us on an expedition
known as the "*Indian Expedition*." The men of
that regiment were mounted on fine horses brought
from northern Ohio, which were in splendid condition
when the regiment left Fort Scott. But when we
returned to Southern Kansas in August, after an
absence of less than four months, nearly all the horses
of this finely equipped regiment had either died or
been abandoned in the Indian country. Very few of
the troopers of the Second and Sixth regiments,
Kansas cavalry, were dismounted on our return. I
have therefore felt convinced since that "Expedition"
that our native animals are more suitable for
army service in this section than horses raised four or
five hundred miles north of this latitude. Animals,
like men, in few generations become adapted to the
conditions of particular localities, and in a measure
unadapted to the conditions of other localities.

After an active campaign, camp life becomes monotonous to the soldier, and he begins to crave new excitement. We remained in camp at Rhea's Mills
about three weeks after the battle of Prairie Grove
without undertaking any other important movement.
Reconnaissances have of course been sent out at intervals of a few days, but in each instance return to camp
without discovering any indications of the enemy in
force. But, on the evening of December 26th, I re-

ceived instructions to issue to the number of men reported present for duty in each company of our regiment, five days' rations suitable for carrying in haversacks, and to be ready to march at 3 o'clock on the morning of the 27th. At the time designated all the cavalry, infantry and artillery, except a force deemed sufficient to guard our trains and camp, under Brig.-General Solomons, were in column and in readiness to march. Very few, if any, of the officers knew where we were going, or the exact object of the expedition. It was thought by some that we were going to attack the rebel army in the vicinity of Van Buren and Fort Smith. It did not seem probable that it was the intention of General Blunt to attack the main body of the rebel army, as we had recently received information that it was encamped around Fort Smith, on the south side of the Arkansas river, four miles above Van Buren. Even if our force had been sufficiently strong to make our success reasonably certain, it was difficult to see how we should get our army across the river as rapidly as would be required, as we have had no pontoon trains such as the eastern armies are furnished with. We thought it possible that the commanding general wished to take a more advanced position, to occupy Van Buren, and to clear the country all north of the river of the enemy. There were, however, serious difficulties to be encountered in taking this view of the matter. Our base of supplies would be further removed from us; besides our supply trains would be obliged to pass over the Boston Mountains, a rough and rugged region. But with a line of stations in our rear we thought that the army might move to Van Buren, as we were in complete possession of western Arkansas north of the river.

I need not, however, recount further what our thoughts were in regard to the ultimate object of the expedition. Suffice it to know that General Blunt had information that a brigade of Texas cavalry, under command of Colonel Crump, was encamped at Dripping Springs, eight miles north of Van Buren, and that he wished to capture them or break up their camp. He was also informed that large quanties of quartermaster and commissary supplies were stored at Van Buren, and that four or five steamboats were coming up the river from Little Rock with cargoes of supplies for General Hindman's army encamped in the neighborhood of Fort Smith, and that the steamboats would probably reach Van Buren about the time he calculated we would get there. If we could capture and destroy those supplies and steamboats, and capture or break up Colonel Crump's camp it would of course cripple the rebel army in Arkansas to a very great extent, besides it would add to its demoralization, which was already great since the battle of Prairie Grove. We heard even before that battle that their supplies were scanty in many respects. I don't think that the rebel soldiers had any genuine coffee. We heard that they had not, and I saw in the haversacks on a number of their dead bodies at Prairie Grove, nothing but a kind of meal made of parched corn, a piece of bacon and a piece of black looking bread, which we could not eat unless we felt the pinch of hunger more keenly than we have at any time in the past. When I saw their dead bodies scattered over the field, I could not help feeling that most of them surely had no definite notion of what they were fighting for. Though in death, particularly of a soldier who has died on the battle field in the midst of fire and smoke and dust and excitement, I suppose we cannot judge accurately how he looked when living; yet I think that most of the enemy's dead I saw on the field must have been poor men; who probably never owned a slave, nor never would have owned one even if slavery were permitted to remain an institution of the South. Under such circumstances I sincerely pity those men who are sacrificing their lives to perpetuate and sustain an institution that never has had, and never will have, any sympathy for them in their ignorance and poverty. Should I or my brother fall any day, we know that we shall have fallen in defense of our government, which is, perhaps, the best the world has yet seen; but we also know that we shall have fallen in defense of a principle which has for its object the making of all men free and equal before the law. Had not such thoughts as these been in my mind, I could never have pursuaded him to leave his home and young wife, to enlist into the Federal army. If we come out of the war safe, we feel that we will have an interest in the future, but that if we do not come out safe, that our sacrifice will not have been for nothing. We know that the cause for which we are striving does not tend to establish an aristocracy or privileged class, which shall in various ways be favored by the laws of the land. Though we may not live to enjoy the blessings we hope will come when the storms of war shall have passed away, there is at least a satisfaction in believing that there are those who are dear to us who will enjoy these hoped-for blessings.

But let us not dwell too long upon such thoughts. The expedition is all ready to start. At 3 o'clock it is rather chilly, for the temperature is a little below the freezing point, as the puddles in the road are covered with thin sheets of ice. The three or four inches of snow that fell a few days ago, have not quite disappeared, and as all the little depressions in the road are filled with water or slush, the outlook for the infantry and artillery is not very cheerful. But a few hours marching brought us daylight and into a region where the snow and ice had entirely disappeared, and where the roads were firmer and inclined to be somewhat rocky. By ten o'clock we had struck the head of Cove Creek. It winds through the mountains in a southerly direction, and as it is fed by mountain streams, now regular torrents, it of course increased in size and volume as we descended it, The rapid melting of the snow in the mountains, and the heavy rain-fall the day before we set out, swelled it to overflowing. We had crossed it when we bivouacked at ten o'clock, that night, according to my count, thirty-three times. We were on the march the next morning at three o'clock and crossed it five or six times before daylight. We had heard that we should be obliged to cross it thirty-nine

times; and I think we did. This would be crossing it
somewhat more than once every mile on an average.
The infantry, when they first came to it, could cross it
dry shod, by stepping from stone to stone, as its swift
current ran splashing and foaming along. When they
crossed it the next time they got their feet wet, but
kept their pantaloons dry by turning them up. The
fourth and fifth times they waded it with their shoes
on and their trousers rolled up. After this they fenced
against the waters no further, except to see to it that
their cartridge boxes were kept dry inside, and they
themselves should not be washed down the swiftly
running current, for when we bivouacked that night
at the most favorable crossings that could be found,
the water was well nigh to the armpits of the men. It
was almost ice-cold, for it came mostly from melted
snow that had just run down in the mountain brooks.
The men, however, stood this extraordinary day and
night's march without a murmur, and in fact from conversations with several infantry-men just before we bivouacked, appear to have suffered less discomfort than
I supposed they would. Though their clothing to
their waists was wet all the afternoon and evening,
the physical exercise of marching kept them from getting chilled. Immediately after we halted that night
on the bank of Cove Creek, a thousand blazing fires
were kindled, and the infantry-men dried their clothing; and food and a refreshing sleep prepared them for
the next day's march, which would determine the object and success or failure of the expedition. A few

moments after the bugle sounded the halt, I rode back towards the rear of the column, and listened to the conversations of the men, and talked to some of them myself, so that I might form some idea of the feelings of those whose march had been so disagreeable and fatiguing, for we had marched since we left Rhea's Mills, upwards of thirty miles. I found the infantrymen quite cheerful, and the artillery men thought that their ammunition had not been perceptibly damaged by the water splashing against the caissons. Late in the evening the caissons of our howitzers were detached and put into an ambulance to keep the amunition dry. The ambulances had been obliged to take up also a few men during the day, but the number was much smaller than I supposed it would be. After the men had dried their clothing and taken such food as their appetites demanded, they spread their blankets on the ground, and threw themselves upon them, and soon sweet sleep closed their eyes, and they were wandering through the realms of dream land. If during their waking moments the cares and fatigues of the day had prevented their thoughts from often turning homewards, no doubt but that in their calm sleep many dreamed of pleasant conversations with their families and dear relatives and friends at home, And perhaps pleasant smiles played upon the faces of some who, in dreamland, thought that they were watching the pranks of their rollicking children. Such were the thoughts that came into my mind concerning my comrades, until gentle sleep came to me, bringing that which nature demanded I should accept, rest.

Within a space of less than two miles, in a narrow gorge in the mountains, near the margin of the noisy, foaming and gurgling stream, thus slept three thousand men.

At three o'clock next morning the bugles sounded, and in a few moments our entire force was in readiness to resume the march. About twenty minutes, however, were given us to feed our horses and take such food ourselves as would satisfy the pinch of hunger. A few hours of refreshing sleep is beyond doubt very beneficial to an army, after constant marching all day. The sky had become partly overcast during the night, so that it was pitch dark when we resumed the march. I could not distinguish the color of my gray horse sitting on him. The proximity of the steep sides of the mountains would have made it quite dark even had it been a clear moonlight night, unless the moon had been high in the heavens near the zenith. Several companies of the Second Kansas cavalry, under command of Col. W. F. Cloud, one of the most dashing cavalry officers of our division, was given the advance. Then came the Sixth Kansas cavalry, under command of Col. W. R. Judson, with whom I rode. As already mentioned, we crossed the provoking stream five or six times before daylight and left it, having passed the mountains. In the course of five or six hours Cove Creek had run down considerably; still it was up to the bellies of our horses, and being so cold was anything but inviting to the infantry. They probably wished it was not necessary to take a cold water plunge so soon after awakening from profound sleep.

But when we crossed Lee's Creek we were still about twenty miles from Van Buren. We continued to march along leisurely, occasionally halting a few moments to allow the infantry and artillery to close up, until towards eight o'clock, when a report came along the column that our advance guard had come upon the enemy's pickets who, on discovering us, fled towards their camp in the direction of Van Buren. Our advance pursued them closely, so that they should not reach their camp in time to give the rebel troops many moments warning of our approach. Our movements gradually quickened, and shortly our cavalry was in full gallop, which was kept up for five or six miles and until we came in sight of the enemy's camp at Dripping Springs. In the meantime Gen. Blunt, who had kept up with us, sent back an order for the artillery and infantry to move forward with a quick step. The enemy, under command of Col. Crump, of a Texas cavalry regiment, were encamped along the north side of a hill, and immediately north of their camp were several fields with intermediate spaces covered with undergrowths of woods. But when we came to the fences inclosing the fields, there was scarcely a moment's delay, for they were instantly thrown down and we came into line of battle in a trot, and charged across the field in a full gallop, and when within fifty yards of the enemy's camp, delivered a volley into the ranks of those who had formed in line and thought of making a stand. The Second Kansas cavalry took the left of our line, and the Sixth Kansas cavalry and several companies of the Third Wisconsin cavalry the right. After firing a few rounds from our carbines, Gen. Blunt ordered the bugles to sound the charge, and with gleaming sabres we dashed forward like a whirlwind, throwing up a perfect cloud of dust. The enemy did not wait to feel the edges of our sabres, but fled in the direction of Van Buren, and in their flight left their tents, camp, and supplies of every kind in our possession.

After charging through their camp we could not preserve our line of battle in perfect order, on account of the broken condition of the ground. Nor was it necessary, as the enemy had broken up completely, and thought only of saving themselves. We were cautious, however, as we did not know but that they had formed another line back some distance, with the determination of contesting our advance. The Sixth Kansas cavalry and Third Wisconsin cavalry, therefore, moved right straight forward over the steep hill south of their camp. But when we were passing down the southern slope of the hill, we saw from the clouds of dust hanging over the high road leading to Van Buren, that they had no intention of making a stand short of that place. We also learned from several rebel soldiers and teamsters, whom we had captured, that they were completely surprised, and that their retreat had become a stampede. We now changed from line of battle to columns of fours, and struck the gallop again, preserving such or-

der as was possible, and chased the flying enemy to
Van Buren, and when they passed through the city
we were right at their heels. General Blunt sent out
detachments of cavalry on both sides of the main road
to scour the country and pick up their stragglers. If
the city had any Home Guards or military organization to defend it, the men disappeared on our
approach. We therefore followed the enemy right
through the city, making the dust fly in the streets so
that they had no time to form in line, or to take the
steamboats lying at the wharves to cross the river, but
continued their flight on the road along the north bank
of the Arkansas. A squad of rebels, however, attempted
to escape over the river on a horse-power ferry, but
they had scarcely reached the middle of the stream
when they were discovered. The two mountain howitzers of the Sixth Kansas cavalry, which had kept up
with us during the entire chase, were immediately
brought down to the wharf, and after firing several fuse
shells at the boat, struck the horse at the wheel and
killed him. Another shell exploded, wounding several
men. As the boat had by this time got into shallow
water, the rest of the men jumped overboard and
escaped. Four steamboats with cargoes of supplies
for the rebel army, on the first signal of our approach,
got up steam and made an effort to escape down the
river. Two of them had proceeded a mile or so down
the river, but as the channel now changed to near the
north bank, and as our cavalry and one of our howitzers were waiting for them, a single shot from the

howitzer convinced the officers that it was useless to
make further efforts to escape, and hastened to display
a white flag. The boats were boarded by several of
our officers and two squads of soldiers, and then
directed to steam back up the river to Van Buren. The
other two boats did not get more than a half mile below the city, as they were detained some time in endeavoring to find a landing on the opposite shore for
a party of rebel officers and citizens they had taken
aboard. They got near enough to shore, however, to
allow nearly all the rebels to escape in small boats. It
was the intention to also leave the steamboats at a
landing near the opposite shore, but, as the engineers
and officers had not left them, they were compelled,
when the two lower boats came up with the armed
Federal soldiers on board, to get up steam and take
their boats back to the city.

The pursuit of the flying enemy having been given
up, our cavalry having returned to the city, and the
boats having been made fast to their moorings, we dismounted on vacant lots and squares, and soon found
abundance of forage for our tired and hungry horses.
Nor had we any difficulty in replenishing our haversacks
from the rebel commissary supplies. Such of the non-
combatant population as showed themselves seemed
perfectly amazed. A few hours before their city was
as peaceful as the mist we had lately seen resting on
the mountain side. No one dreamed that the "Yankee" foe was rapidly approaching; and being a bright
Sunday morning many of the good people had been to

5

church, and were just returning home when the alarm
was given that we were near at hand.

Immediately after the boats had been made fast,
several more of our officers went aboard them to examine their cargoes and to obtain such information as
they could get from those who had remained in charge
of them, in regard to the strength, movements and intentions of the rebel army in the vicinity. As we
seemed to be in quiet possession of the city, a good
many of our officers and soldiers left their horses where
they had dismounted to feed them, a few blocks back
from the river, and also came down to the river front
to look at the captured boats.   Col. Judson and I had
just walked down and were taking a survey of the situation and talking over the exciting transactions of the
morning, when suddenly the sound of artillery re-
sounded in our ears, and then an instant after, with a
crash came a solid shot or shell, striking the ground not
more than two or three yards from us. After an interval
of a few seconds there came another, and still another,
and we looked in the direction from whence they came
and saw a rebel battery near the opposite shore and
the smoke rising from it.   We retired to our horses to
await orders.   Gen. Hindman, having heard by telegraph or special messenger that we were in Van Buren, sent down from Fort Smith a force of artillery and
infantry to let us know that he was there.   But in the
meantime our infantry and artillery were coming up
and soon arrived on the heights overlooking the city,
the river and the country far off to the south.   It was

now perhaps after two o'clock, and the artillery duel over the river immediately commenced and lasted until dark. The distance, however, which separated the combatants was so great that no loss was sustained by our troops, and probably not much by the enemy. The shot and shell from the enemy's guns fell short of our position on the heights of the city. But the percussion shells from our rifled guns I could see flew over the river and struck very near where the enemy's batteries were posted. I could not see whether they inflicted any damage to the enemy, as they were covered by the timber. Whenever one of our percussion shells struck a tree or solid object, I could see by the smoke that arose that it exploded with terriffic violence. It was not necessary for our cavalry to make any material change in position after the cannonade opened, as it was covered by blocks of brick buildings. Some of the officers and soldiers, however, desired to occupy positions where they could get a good view of the rebel batteries. Late in the afternoon the echo of the thundering artillery seemed to roll down the river to a great distance, gradually growing fainter until it had died away.

While we were not much disturbed by their cannonade, the people of Van Buren were greatly agitated; and well they might be, for it was their friends who were firing shot and shell into their city, and endangering their lives. We felt somewhat surprised that Gen. Hindman should have permitted the shelling of the city without any warning to the inhabitants, inasmuch as they were nearly all his own people. Even we, as enemies, would not have committed such an act without giving the women and children and old men an opportunity of leaving the city. I heard that several persons, women and children, were killed and injured by exploding shells from the enemy's guns. I was unable, however, to collect exact information of the casualties in the city, as we were under *strict* orders to observe great vigilance. It was not known but that Gen. Hindman would show fight, as we understood that he had an army of ten or twelve thousand men in the neighborhood of Fort Smith. Night came on, and we could see from the heights of the city to the heights on the south side of the river, that the enemy were displaying great activity from some cause. But whether they were retreating or concentrating their forces at some point in the vicinity, we were unable to decide.

After dark, the enemy withdrew his batteries and the thundering of the artillery ceased. And now the disposition of the contraband property awaited the orders of Gen. Blunt. The steamboats, after taking from them such supplies as he wished to take back with us, he ordered burned. Before setting fire to them a number of officers and men were permitted to take from them something of insignificant value, to serve as a memento of the expedition. I got a blank book from the "*Steamer Rose Douglas*" to keep my Chronicles of our operations. The burning of the boats made a tremendous fire, and lighted up the country for miles around. When the flames, which were soon climbing high in the sky, were first noticed by the people, they thought we were going to burn the city. But their fears were soon dispelled when they were assured that only the destruction of contraband property was intended. Private property was respected. Though the population of the city is perhaps upwards of two thousand, yet I did not hear of a single complaint of trespassing upon private premises; or of any rude conduct of our officers or soldiers towards the ladies of Van Buren. I speak of this with some pride, for I found that the non-combatants were strongly impressed with the notion that our Kansas troops were a kind of Vandals or barbarians, lawless, and utterly disregarded the methods and usages of civilized warfare. As our division is composed of Kansas troops, with the exceptions already noted, I think we may justly feel proud of their conduct upon every field, and of the results of the campaign up to this point. Since we attacked the enemy in the last engagement at Newtonia on the 4th of October, we have driven him, step by step, before us; so that now there is not a rebel organized force north of the Arkansas River, excepting guerrilla bands. But notwithstanding the series of splendid achievements, we hear that Gen. Blunt has made this expedition in the face of orders to fall back from Rhea's Mills to the southern line of Missouri.

If this be true, it is to be deeply regretted, for our toils in this campaign will count for almost nothing;

and we surrender back to the enemy all that we have gained. I do not believe that, if the Department Commander thoroughly understood the situation here, he would permit this army to abandon this section after we have gained it at the cost of so many bloody contests. Though we have reliable information that the enemy are greatly demoralized; yet if we fall back from our present position, it will be almost equivalent to a defeat on the field, and he will doubtless feel encouraged to quickly organize his shattered forces and follow us up.

At eight o'clock we received orders to be in readiness to march the next morning (29), at seven o'clock, on our return to Rhea's Mills. But before we commence our return march, let us take a glance at Dripping Springs. When we passed through the rebel camp there, it was about nine o'clock, and the rebel soldiers had apparently just finished their breakfasts, for their mess pans, camp kettles, etc., indicated that their cooks had not yet "washed their dishes." Their tents were standing just as they had occupied them; and broken gunstocks lay scattered over the camp, showing that they had given a moment to the destruction of such property as they could not take with them. A number of teams were harnessed and ready for some service when we came upon them, for on the road to Van Buren I saw not less than twenty wagons partially upset and in attitudes showing that they had been suddenly abandoned by having the mules or horses cut loose from them to enable the driver and parties in them to escape. Articles of camp and garrison equipage, and even ammunition, lay scattered upon the road all the way to Van Buren. When we reached the city, the enemy's Military Telegraph was in perfect working order, but I did not hear whether Gen. Blunt sent his compliments to Gen. Hindman or not. He could have done it had not more important matters occupied his attention. The circuit, however, was soon broken on the Little Rock as well as on the Fort Smith end of the line.

On the morning of the 29th we set out on our return march to Rhea's Mills. Many of the soldiers had their haversacks crammed with sugar and the best things the enemy's commissariat afforded. The troops and animals had a bountiful supper and breakfast, and a good night's rest, and seemed as fresh as if they had been in camp a month. Guards were posted during the night at every necessary point, so that we would not be subject to surprise by the enemy.

The expedition accomplished all that could be reasonably expected of it. We did not capture many prisoners, but we destroyed a large amount of rebel public property, and property pressed into rebel service by the Confederate authorities; besides bringing away with us considerable quantities of such of the captured supplies as we can use.

While the ladies of Van Buren did not, as far as I know, take pleasure in expressing their hatred of "Yankees" as they call us in that section, or show by their actions that they hated us at all, yet I think that they are nearly all strong adherents of the Southern cause. If there were any Union families in the city at the beginning of the war, they probably managed to move north long before we arrived.

We bid good-bye to Van Buren, but not without thoughts of returning again to stay until this contest shall have been decided. Our return march was conducted leisurely; the weather was pleasant and warm, and Cove Creek, the winding mountain stream, had fallen almost to its ordinary dimensions and volume, so that the infantry were much less inconvenienced in crossing and re-crossing it than when we came out on the 27th. They were nearly three days on the march to Rhea's Mills. Most of the cavalry, however, got in on the evening of the 30th.

Thus ended the expedition to Van Buren, and in fact the campaign of the *Army of the Frontier* in northwestern Arkansas.

An expedition of nearly two thousand men, mostly Indians, and a section of light artillery, were sent out under Col. W. A. Phillips, about the time we left Rhea's Mills, in the direction of Fort Gibson. After a short engagement, Col. Phillips captured and destroyed Fort Davis near Fort Gibson, on which the Confederate Government expended upwards of a million dollars. In point of importance, the success of his expedition deserves to be set down among the splendid achievements of the campaign.

Old Year! I bid you adieu. When some future historian writes of the great events which have turned the eyes of the civilized world to this country, he will surely turn to you as having witnessed the greatest events in the history of our Government. You have brought sadness to the hearts of thousands of our people this night. I know, too, that in the hospitals near me there are hundreds of comrades, and among them my brother, whose hearts ache with the thought that they will never again see the faces and sweet smiles of affection of those dearest to them in this world. The lights of many noble lives are going out with you. OLD YEAR, FAREWELL!

CHAPTER III.

The First Division Army of the Frontier moves from Rhea's Mills
to Elm Springs—All the Federal wounded in the Field Hospitals at Prairie Grove removed to Fayetteville—General
Blunt Relieved and starts North—General Schofield takes
command of the Army of the Frontier—Future Operations to
be conducted according to West Point tactics—The Army to
retreat to the Missouri line—Reorganization of the Army—
Colonel W. A. Phillips to command the Indian Division—A
Battalion of the Sixth Kansas cavalry and Captain Hopkin's
Battery to go with it—Grand Review of the Army of the
Frontier by General Schofield—The author's last visit to his
brother in the General Hospital at Fayetteville—The Reduc-
tion of Transportation—Order from War Department for
Recruiting several loyal Arkansas Regiments—General
Marmaduke marching on Springfield—The Army of the
Frontier on the march, except the Indian Division.

Hail, Happy New Year! I welcome you; though
I know not what you have in store for us. We have
no seer or prophet to unfold to us in doubtful and
mysterious language the most important events which
you will disclose to us in due time. But we have
reason to hope that, with honesty of purpose and per-
sistence in the right, on the part of our leaders and of
each of us, we shall have made substantial progress in
accomplishing the objects for which we are striving,
when you shall have expired.

The New Year was ushered in by a national salute

fired from the batteries of General Herron's Division still encamped on the battle-field of Prairie Grove. But to the soldier in the field, in camp and on the march, it has no more significance than any other day. It is impossible for him to observe the forms of polite society. His feelings of happiness find expression in a sterner manner than that of flying around in full dress suit, kid gloves and swallow tail coat, and in indulging in pretty conceits with charming maidens. He takes more pleasure in relating to his comrades around the camp fire some adventure in which he took a part, or some hair-breadth escape; how, for instance, he grasped the guidon or standard from the hand of a fallen comrade, while the enemy's bullets were flying around his head as thick as hail. With all the hardships and dangers which war entails on the soldier in the field, his disposition is generally not only not gloomy, but on the contrary, cheerful and happy. No doubt sad thoughts flit through his mind in regard to loved ones at home, but as fresh excitements are coming up every day, and as old battle scenes and incidents have to be gone over occasionally, his mind is never allowed to dwell long on those ideal pictures which have a natural tendency to produce gloominess.

The rumor that, on the return of our division from Van Buren, the *Army of the Frontier* would move north-ward, turned out to be true. On the morning of January 2d, 1863, the First Division struck tents, left Rhea's Mills, and took up a line of march for Elm Springs, about twenty-two miles north. The General

Hospitals were established at Fayetteville several days ago, and most of the sick and wounded have been removed there. It is the chief town in northwestern Arkansas, and is capable of affording much better facilities for properly caring for sick and wounded soldiers than could easily be provided at Rhea's Mills or Prairie Grove. When it is possible, I think our surgeons prefer substantial buildings for hospitals to the Field Hospital tent. If we were in railroad communication with the rest of the country, a good many of our wounded could be sent to their homes, where they would have loving wives, mothers, daughters and friends to look after them. Those who are conscious that they will never recover from their wounds or sickness, often give vent to the expression, that they would be perfectly content to die if they could only be permitted to die at home, surrounded by their families and friends. If a young man gets severely wounded, the first thing he thinks of is his mother or his sweetheart; if a married man, his wife and children. But a grateful government will not neglect to provide justly for the widow and orphaned children, or mother of the soldier who dies in defense of his country. All this intense longing for the affectionate regard of those at home we know is not unappreciated. The letters we receive from time to time from our relatives and friends, are teeming with love and affection, and are convincing enough that there are lacerated hearts at home as well as in the field. It is the consciousness that there exists these loves and affections that touches so deeply the heart of the soldier; and I believe it is these strong affections that make the effective soldier, for he feels that he is fighting for the protection and happiness of those he loves, and whose lives are as dear to him as his own life. If he thought that by going to war it would ultimately subject his family to greater peril, and bring upon it greater unhappiness, he would not go. We regard a man as having lost his manhood if he shows no concern for the happiness and well-being of his family. And in social organization the family is the social or political unit, and whatever weakens family ties and interests must in time weaken the social fabric.

On the evening of the 2nd we camped on Wild Cat Creek, having marched a distance of about sixteen miles from Rheas Mills. A heavy rain last night put the roads in bad condition for our trains and artillery. But as there is no necessity for rapid movement, and as our backs are turned towards the enemy's heels, we can afford to march leisurely, so as not to injure or break down our animals. Officers and men who have served in a campaign like that we have just closed, soon learn how important it is to take every possible care of their cavalry, artillery and draught animals. We arrived at Elm Springs on the 3rd, and there seems to be a prospect of our remaining here several days, as we hear that there is going to be shortly a reorganization of the *Army of the Frontier*. Gen. Blunt has been relieved, and bade his troops farewell to-day, and, with his staff and escort, started to Forts Scott and Leaven-

worth. On account of his personal bravery and the
brilliant achievements of his campaign, he has greatly
endeared himself to his troops.   I speak from personal knowledge of his bravery.   He was to the front all
day during the battle of Cane Hill, and was only a few
yards from Col. Jewell when he fell mortally wounded.
At Prairie Grove too, he was on the field all the afternoon in dangerous positions, directing the movements
of his troops.   And at Dripping Springs he was at
the front with us when we charged the enemy's camp,
and rode with the advance squadrons when we dashed
into Van Buren.   How well he would succeed in a
campaign which required of the Commanding General
that every movement of his troops should be made
with a distinct but involved end in view, I, of course,
have no means of knowing.   He is probably able to
meet any movement his opponents are able to make
on the military chess board.   My own impression,
however, is, that if a campaign in this section were conducted according to the military science taught at West
Point, and embodied in General Schofield, the enemy could soon put us on the defensive, and we should
never accomplish anything except our destruction.   If
military science is a common sense view of contending
with your foe, of warding off his blows and of striking him most effectively, I believe in it.   But if it be
a mysterious method of directing the movements of
troops, which no one can understand unless he be a
graduate of West Point, then I have little confidence
in it.   A special education for a special purpose is al-

ways desirable, and a military education no doubt
qualifies men for organizing and skillfully handling
large bodies of troops in time of war; but there seems
to be such a tendency among the graduates of West
Point to want to do something incomprehensible to the
common mind, as to make many of them utter failures.
Perhaps only a small percentage of each graduating
class display any special aptitude for military science,
or for any particular arm of the military service. It
amounts to this, a blockhead sent to West Point is as
apt to come out a blockhead as if he had been sent to
any other school. If a boy who has a natural military genius goes to the Military Academy and graduates, and afterwards has an opportunity to develop his
military genius, I think the chances are that he will
make a great military commander. Such special apti-
tudes may be inherited through a line of ancestors, or
they may be due to powerful antenatal influences.
Napoleon's military genius is said to have been due to
the latter cause.

General John M. Schofield assumed command of the
Army of the Frontier on the 4th. I understand that
he has virtually been in command of it since our return from Van Buren. Had he arrived here a few
days sooner, it is probable that the expedition to Van
Buren would never have been made. He is a graduate of the Military Academy, and I suppose that mil-
tary operations will now be conducted according to
the military science taught at West Point. We shall
see. In the first place it seems that we are already

under orders to continue our march further northward, though there is not an officer or soldier in our division who does not feel sure in his own mind that there is not an organized force of the enemy in western Arkansas, north of the river. If this be true, and the Commanding General should know whether it is or not, then why continue to fall back and give up the country we have gained at the cost of so many lives and of so much toil and suffering? Is it because the present Commanding General did not direct the movements of our army in gaining the splendid victories that we have won? The jealousies of military rivals have already in other instances been a curse to our arms.

The reorganization of the *Army of the Frontier*, which I have already mentioned as probable, is to take place immediately. General F. J. Herron is to command the second and third divisions, Colonel William Weir, Tenth Kansas infantry, the first division, and Colonel William A. Phillips, Third Indian regiment, the Indian division, consisting of all the Indian troops, one battalion of the Sixth Kansas cavalry, and Captain Hopkin's battery formerly attached to Colonel Cloud's brigade. With this force I understand that Colonel Phillips will take up a position near Maysville, Benton county, Arkansas, a little town right on the line of the Cherokee Nation. I have been assigned to duty as Commissary Sergeant of this battalion of the Sixth Kansas cavalry, and directed to report to Captain John W. Orahood, the senior officer. Lieutenant John S. Lane, the Regimental Commissary, accompanies the other battalion, together with the other field and staff officers of our regiment.

On the 6th, General Schofield arrived at Elm Springs for the purpose of reviewing the First Division before any important movement shall have been made. The different arms of the service are therefore actively engaged in making preparations for the Grand Review to-morrow. This is a kind of military luxury of which we have had very little experience. During the autumn of 1861, however, when we were in General James H. Lane's command, we had several reviews and sham battles. But since then we have had nothing on as extensive a scale as that which is to take place to-morrow. All the men reported present for duty of the following organizations, are ordered to turn out with their arms and equipments complete, to-wit: Cavalry, Second, Sixth and Ninth Kansas, and Third Wisconsin; infantry—Tenth, Eleventh and Thirteenth Kansas, and Ninth Wisconsin; First, Second and Third Indian regiments; artillery—Capt. Rabbs, Second Indiana battery, First and Second Kansas batteries, and Captain Hopkin's four gun battery, which was captured from the enemy, besides two twelve-pound howitzer batteries, attached to the Sixth and Ninth regiments Kansas cavalry, respectively.

Well, the gala day is over; we have had the Grand Review, and I think that we made a very creditable appearance. We formed in line in an open field, and the ground is rather favorable, considering the general

6

broken condition of the country, for reviewing an army
no larger than ours. After we had gone through a
few evolutions upon the field, we then formed in line,
and in a short time General Schofield and staff, and
several mounted messengers, galloped along our front
and took up a position near our extreme right. Some
of the soldiers within my hearing remarked, looking
at their gay uniforms as they passed along, "Too
much fuss and feathers for a fighting general." The
whole command then formed in columns of companies,
and marched by the place where General Scofield and
staff had posted themselves. The brass bands, marching at the head of brigades and playing soul-stirring
airs, give additional interest to the fine display made
by the troops. Thus ended the Grand Review, after
which we marched to our respective camps. This is
probably the last time the first Division will ever all be
together. It seems to be the intention to break it up
into brigades and detachments, and to scatter these
along the southern border counties of Missouri and
northern Arkansas. If we are not going to make any
effort to hold a more advanced position, or even our
present position, or if we are no longer to assume the
offensive, perhaps to scatter the troops in this manner
is the best policy.

This morning (the 8th) General Schofield, staff and
escort left for Fayetteville, as I understand to review
the second and third divisions under command of
General Herron. It does not appear that General
Schofield has established any headquarters here with

the army. It is therefore thought that his presence
here is only temporary, and that after he shall have
made such disposition of his troops as in his judgment
seems best, that he will return to Springfield or
St. Louis.

As we shall march away from here in two or three
days, I obtained permission to go to Fayetteville to-day
to see my brother who is in the general hospital there.
He was in right good spirits when I came to him,
though he complained that the wound which he received in the shoulder at the battle of Coon Creek last
August, caused him intense suffering at times. He
also informed me that the old wound which he received
through the thigh a little over a year ago, had broken
out again, and gave him much pain when he made certain movements, and his weight came on that leg. He
still clings to the ball that passed straight through his
thigh, touching the femoral artery and lodging on the
opposite side just under the skin. When it was cut
from the wound the conical end of the elongated ball
was found to be considerably flattened, having struck
the femur or thigh bone. But he says that he cannot
bear to have the surgeons probe any more for the ball
which he still carries in his shoulder, as it has either
broken through the encysting and poisoning his blood
or touching some very sensitive part. He expressed
a strong desire to be at home, but thought that he had
not strength enough to be transported in an ambulance
so far, even if he could get permission to go. I encouraged him to be cheerful, and said that I hoped he

would come out of this all right, and be able to report
to his company for duty in a few weeks, or in a few
months at the farthest. I then bid him adieu, but not
without emotion, for I have serious doubts of his re-
covery; the lines of his expression were not natural,
and his life is ebbing away through the wound in his
shoulder. But I will not mourn my brother dead who
is yet living.

The order for the reduction of our transportation
goes into effect to-day. Hereafter each cavalry regiment will be entitled to only sixteen four-mule wagons, and each infantry regiment to twelve four-mule
wagons. This seems a wise measure adopted by the
War Department, for during an active campaign troops
should be encumbered as little as possible with large
trains and useless baggage. Five hundred wagons
and teams in motion, stretch over a distance of several miles, and in an enemy's country always require
a large force of cavalry to protect them. They also offer inducements to the enemy to fit out expeditions
for their capture or destruction. Though officers and
soldiers will have to dispense with certain conveniences
which they have heretofore enjoyed, yet I think that
they will soon see that by doing so, there will be entailed upon them no great hardships. Our object is
to beat the enemy at every point with as little sacrifice of life and public property as possible. If large
trains embarrass our movements, and if we can get
along with smaller ones without decreasing our effec-
tiveness, we should do it without a murmur.

It was reported a few days ago that authority had been obtained from the Secretary of War for raising two regiments of Federal troops in this State, one cavalry and one infantry. This report I find is true, and the recruiting is to commence at once, and the regiments will probably be organized and in the field by spring. For the present, Col. Ferguson is to have charge of the matter, with headquarters at Fayetteville. Once organized and equipped, these regiments will be a valuable acquistion to our army in holding this section. Our troops have shown that they have no hatred or ill will towards the peeple with whom we are contending; that we only want them to lay down their arms and renew their allegiance to the Government. The consequence is, I think, that we have made friends of many of those who had been misinformed and had a rather bad opinion of us before we came into this State. At the beginning of the war there was a strong Union sentiment in nearly all the counties of northwestern Arkansas; and also in other sections of the State. And now that there is an opportunity for those whose sympathies have all along been with the Government, to assist it by organizing for the defense of their lives and homes, we may reasonably expect that these two regiments will soon have their maximum of men. If they see that there is a probability of our permanently holding this part of the State, many of those who are refugees to Missouri and Kansas, will doubtless return and enter the service.

A post has been established at Neosho, Missouri. Major John A. Foreman with a battalion of Indian troops, has already been ordered there. A large number of refugee Indian families are in that vicinity, and they are all to be collected at that point to remain until spring. There is an abundant supply of fine spring water at Neosho, and as it is in a wooded region plenty of fuel can be easily furnished them at a small cost during the winter. Their subsistence supplies can also perhaps be mostly drawn from that section.

Last night, the 8th, the First division, with the exception of the Indian command, having received orders, struck tents and moved out quite suddenly. Some of the troops that left last night, are ordered to Springfield, Missouri, on a forced march, as General Marmaduke with a division of cavalry, and several batteries of light artillery, is reported on the way there, having passed through this State three days ago, about seventy-five miles east of us. General E. B. Brown, with a considerable force of Missouri State troops and some artillery, will doubtles give the enemy a warm reception if they attack him before the reinforcements get there.

That one is obliged to separate from those with whom he has shared the dangers and hardships of the field for more than a year, is cause for profound feelings of sadness. Serving in a common cause, and sharing alike dangers and hardships, tends to unite men by the strongest ties of friendship.

Though many of our troops have been in the service less than sixth months, yet they have moved forward with brave hearts and unfaltering steps, never swerving from the path of duty. Veterans could not have performed more effective service, and service of which the true soldier may well feel proud. Military achievements of less consequence, as far as bettering men's condition is concerned, than the achievements of the *Army of the Frontier*, have been recorded and handed down to us through twenty-five centuries. Many infant children now in the arms of their mothers, when grown to manhood or womanhood, will doubtless refer with pride to the services of their fathers in this campaign.

CHAPTER IV.

Colonel W. A. Phillips assumes command of the Indian division—
The author to go with it—The division marches to Maysville
on the western line of Arkansas—A skirmish with guerrillas—
A snow storm and difficulty in getting forage—Colonel Phillips,
not only a military commander but also a governor of several
Indian tribes—His position requires great executive ability
—Skirmishes with guerrillas becoming frequent—Bushwhackers living in a cave—Remarks on how caves are formed
—How Stalactites are formed—How stalacmitic matter may
preserve to distant ages in the future some account of the
war—In a few years all external evidences of the war will
have disappeared—Description of the country and of its
resources—Colored refugees increasing—Their destitute condition—Col. Phillips' orders—Repairing of the mills—The
battle at Springfield—Gen. Marmaduke defeated.

In some respects perhaps it would have been more
agreeable to me to have remained with that portion of
the Army of the Frontier from which we have been
detached. But with a soldier, preferences should
count for nothing when duty stands in the way. And
looking at the matter in this light, I of course accept
the situation and enter upon the discharge of my duties
in this new field without the slightest dissatisfaction.
How he can be of most service to his country is a
thought that should animate the true soldier, and out-

weigh all other thoughts in his mind. But it may
turn out that our new field of operations will not be
destitute of interest or barren of results worth setting
down. If it should be, however, it will be easy enough
to stop writing, or expunge that which is worthless.
But our new Commander, Colonel W. A. Phillips, I
know is an able and an accomplished officer, and it is not
likely that he will allow us to languish in inglorious
inactivity. No officer of the first division has impressed me more favorably. The first time that I ever
saw him was at the battle of Locust Grove, near Grand
Saline, the 2d of last July, when we captured Colonel
Clarkson and his command of one hundred and ten
men. Even Colonel Jewell, who was also present on that
occasion, did not display more conspicuous bravery than
Colonel Phillips. The night's march, the short and
decisive engagement, just at the dawn of that lovely
summer's morning, will be remembered by those who
participated, while they live. Colonel Phillips received
much praise for the ability with which he handled his
brigade at Indian Creek, Neosho, and Newtonia, last
September. On other occasions, too, he has shown
himself to be a brave officer, and yet one who never
loses his head. It was mainly through his exertions
that authority was obtained from the War Department
to organize and equip the three Indian regiments.
Having been a staff correspondent of the New York
Tribune, and a personal friend of Assistant Secretary
of War, Dana, perhaps no one in Kansas could command more respectful attention from the authorities at
Washington, in such a matter.

I shall not, however, start out with a panegyric, or endeavor to build up hopes of any extraordinary military achievement, for he has taken a command with which I think it will be exceedingly difficult, if not almost impossible, to accomplish anything of great consequence. We must be patient. The future will disclose to us the wisdom or folly of his actions.

We left Elm Springs on the morning of 10th, and arrived at Camp Walker, near Maysville, on the evening of the 11th, having marched a distance of about thirty-five miles. The country that we passed over is generally poor, but has some fine forests, and is supplied with abundance of good spring water. In some of these springs the water is as clear as crystal; it rises out of the earth almost like a fountain, and runs away in a strong swift current. How delightful these springs would be to the thirsty traveller in an arid region. The hills that we passed over are covered with flints of every conceivable shape and size, except that there are few above a hundred pounds weight. They do not, however, seem to have ever been rolled about and worn by the action of water, like pebbles along the sea shore, constantly kept in motion by the tides.

Our camp here is called Camp Curtis, in honor of General Samuel R. Curtis who commanded our forces at the battle of Pea Ridge in this county last March. This locality has been quite noted as a camping ground and rendezvous of the rebel armies of Missouri and Arkansas since the beginning of the war. It is just in the edge of the prairie region, and grounds could scarcely be laid out to better advantage for drilling and maneuvering large bodies of troops. The enemy, however, are not likely to have a camp of instruction here again. We were encamped near here upwards of a week last October, after the battle of Old Fort Wayne, in which we captured General Cooper's artillery.

It looks now as if our chief occupation, for a while at least, is going to be that of fighting and chasing bushwhackers. Captain Anderson, of the 3rd Indian regiment, was sent out on the 12th with a detachment of fifty men, and had a skirmish with a party of guerrillas, in which he lost one man killed and had one wounded. He reports that he killed two of the enemy, the rest having made their escape. The hilly condition of the country to the east of us is favorable for carrying on guerrilla operations. But this is a kind of warfare more suitable to the disposition of our Indian than to our white soldiers. Guerrillas in the vicinity of this command will therefore probably have all they desire of their own kind of warfare.

Col. Phillips sent out on the morning of the 13th, his first train to Fort Scott for supplies, guarded by an escort of two hundred men. At this season, escort duty and teaming are not very desirable kinds of service. We are just beginning to feel the pinch of winter, though we had three or four inches of snow and several rather cold days about a week before we started on the expedition to Van Buren. Men and animals now on the road, especially if they are facing the north-west winds on those bleak prairies which extend for a distance of seventy-five miles south of Fort Scott, will suffer much more from cold than we do in camp. It takes from five to seven days for a train to come down from Fort Scott, the distance being about one hundred and twenty-five miles.

Yesterday morning (15th) a violent snow storm set in and continued all day. We are therefore beginning to experience considerable difficulty in getting sufficient forage for our animals, for when the First division was encamped in this vicinity last fall, we consumed nearly all the forage that could be found for miles around. A large force of the enemy under General Cooper, had also been foraging off this section before our arrival. And as this is not much of an agricultural region, it will be seen that there is just cause for the complaint of scarcity of forage. But Colonel Phillips is watchful of the wants of his troops and public animals, and will no doubt do all that can be done to prevent them from suffering for want of necessary supplies. He sends out daily foraging parties and trains, and they generally go from ten to fifteen miles from camp. This gives us a circuit of about thirty miles, a considerable area of country to forage from. When we shall have exhausted all the forage within fifteen miles of our camp, we will probably establish another camp outside of this radius. If this plan is carried out, as I have no doubt it will be, I think that we can get our animals through the winter in fair condition. Although we have been constantly scouting and marching and skirmishing since we came into this State last fall, we have lost comparatively few animals from having been broken down in the service. Our main losses have of course been cavalry horses. But the safety and comfort of his command, while conducting military operations in this section, are not the sole object of solicitude to Colonel Phillips. Nor is his function that of a military commander alone. He is placed in a position where he must act as governor of several different nations, all in a state of chaos. Since the war commenced, the Indians of the Cherokee, Creek, and Seminole nations, have been almost equally divided on the questions which have arrayed the two sections of the country against each other. But as the rebel authorities sent troops to occupy the country of these Indians immediately after hostilities commenced, and held undisputed possession of it until our expedition of last summer, the loyalists were obliged to leave their homes or contend with unequal odds, with the chances of being continually beaten and finally driven out. Hence when we withdrew from the Indian Territory last August, and brought out the Chief, John Ross, and some of the national archives and treasury, thousands of loyal Indian families, Cherokees, Creeks, and Seminoles, accompanied us as far as Baxter Springs, on the southern line of Kansas. While at Baxter Springs, and indeed since they have been exiles from their homes, the Government has issued them rations, and looked after them to mollify their hardships as much as possible. And though the greater proportion of these Indian families have remained in Southwest Missouri, since the opening of the campaign last September ; and though some have returned to their homes in the nation since we drove the enemy out ; yet there seems to be a fair prospect that the " Refugee Camp " will continue to increase in size during the rest of the winter. The wants and necessities of these people will constantly demand the attention of Colonel Phillips in various ways. How ably and satisfactorily he shall conduct the affairs which devolve upon him, remains to be seen. It will thus also be seen that his position requires of him to be, if he manages matters successfully, not only a judicious military commander, but also to possess, in a fair measure, the knowledge of civil affairs. A man who possesses both of these qualifications in a marked degree, is rarely found. We have reason to believe that we have such a man in the person of Colonel Phillips, for every one has some pride that those with whom he acts in any given venture shall act creditably. That is, no man who possesses a sense of patriotic devotion, likes to have his name associated with inglorious defeat, or any public action upon which rests a stigma or even unfavorable comment.

The skirmishes between our scouting parties and small detachments of guerrillas which infest this section are becoming so frequent, that hereafter I shall not attempt to give the details and result of each day separate, but will endeavor to give some account of the

most important contests. There would be a good deal
of repetition should I detail the movements and skirmishes of every scouting or foraging party sent out.
When any casualties occur they are noted on the muster rolls of the company. That is, if a soldier is killed,
wounded, or taken prisoner, or has his horse killed or
captured, the fact is duly noted. I may add that since
we left Elm Springs, our troops have killed, according
to my daily memoranda, nine bushwhackers, and sustained a loss of three men killed and two wounded.

A woman from the country came into camp yesterday evening (17th) and reported that she knew of
three or four bushwhackers, who were living in a
cave, some eight miles distant from the command.
A detachment of cavalry was sent to the locality of
the cave; but returned without being able to find the
enemy or any indications that they had recently occupied the cave as an abiding place. Our men, however, did not venture into the cave, as it would have required too great a sacrifice of life to dislodge them from
such a fortress, if they were really there and well armed,
unless we should close the mouth of the cave and
compel them to feel the pinch of hunger. What a
novel place for men to take up their abode! But
when we are enjoying freedom and security, and the
rewards of honest toil, it is perhaps difficult for us to
imagine what modes of life we might be inclined to
adopt under the pressure of circumstances. It is well
known that caves do not undergo very radical changes
of temperature during the seasons. I have visited a

cave on my father's estate a good many times, and I remember that it was always almost uncomfortably cool on a warm summer day, and pleasantly warm on a winter day. Considerable attention has recently been given to cavern researches in England and France. And in several instances the bones of men and some domestic implements and rudely-made weapons have been found, which show beyond a reasonable doubt that the human race has existed on this earth for a period much longer than that which we have been taught. While we were encamped at Camp Moonlight, about twenty miles south of here, the early part of last November, I was permitted to accompany a party of officers and soldiers on a visit to a cave much larger than the one near our present camp. We did not go very far into it from the entrance, but we went far enough to see some beautiful stalactites hanging from the roof like icicles which hang from the eaves of a house after the snow has commenced to melt and run down its sloping roof. Were everything favorable, I should like to visit the cave near us, but of course not with the view of making careful investigations, for that would take time and a large expenditure of money. But when peace shall bless our country again, and the spirit of inquiry increases, perhaps interesting researches will be made into the history of these caves, which will throw some light on the various forms of life that once inhabited them. Curious thoughts are apt to come into one's mind after visiting one of these natural wonders. What caused it? How long since it was formed? These are exceedingly interesting questions to those whose minds seek a rational explanation of every natural phenomenon. But when we come to understand something about how a cave has been formed, we are not likely to press the question, " How long since?" It is a notable fact that all the caves in this country are in limestone formations. Now it is well known to every one who has given any attention to chemistry, that a solution of water and carbonic acid will dissolve pieces of limestone, when put into it. Rainwater is known to contain carbonic acid, the proportion, perhaps, depending upon the season. It is easy to imagine, then, that the rain falling on these hills must have always run down through the soil until the water came to the limestone; and that when it penetrated it, it dissolved a portion of it, the extent of dissolution, however, depending upon the amount of carbonic acid the rain water contained. Everyone who has been in a cave can probably call to mind the sound of dropping water from the roof of the cave, which he heard here and there. Well, every drop of water that falls from the roof to the floor, is supposed to hold in solution a very small quantity of the limestone. But when the water comes to separate from the dissolved limestone it leaves a thin film of solid material, different in character from the original limestone. When the water drops from the roof of the cave, it leaves a thin film attached to the roof, which gradually assumes the form and ap-

7

pearance of an icicle.   This is called a stalactite.   The
film that forms on the floor after the water has left it,
is called the stalacmite.

It will thus be seen that the formation of a cave is
a perfectly natural, though an extremely slow process.
It is like removing the sands from the sea shore by
taking a grain at a time.   How long it has taken to
form a stalactite as long as one's arm, we have no
means of knowing as far as the caves in this section
are concerned.   Nor have I ever heard that the thickness of the stalacmite formations of the caves of this
region have ever been measured or any efforts made
to find out the nature of the deposits under them, or
contemporaneous with their growth.

Reflecting on stalacmitic formations and the evidences of ancient life they may contain, this thought has
come into my mind.   Suppose that one of our soldiers
or one of the enemies, on account of the stress of
weather or imminent danger, should take to a cave
and die in it with his arms and accoutrements beside
him.   After a while, perhaps, the drops of water from
the roof of the cave falling on his bones and arms,
would leave thereon a formation of stalacmitic matter.
And should the men of some future age decide to investigate the history of these caves and find the bones
and arms cemented together with stalacmitic matter,
they might be able to determine the age to which they
belonged, and nearly the exact time it had taken to
produce a formation of stalacmitic matter of a given
thickness.   Our pistols and carbines and sabers have

the name of the manufacturer or patentee, and the year they were made, stamped upon them. Though there are many chances that in time these would become obliterated by rust, yet under certain conditions they might not. At any rate the subject is one upon which the mind delights to dwell for a moment. And in this connection there arises the further thought. Is it possible, that in a few years, not a vestige of the storms of war which have recently swept back and forth over this section, will be left to the future inhabitants of these pleasant valleys and prairies ? Is it possible that in a few years and on these grounds a comfortable mansion may arise, whose dwellers will be all unconscious that we were ever here for warlike purposes, and our arms stained with the blood of men who were recently our friends and brothers? Probably in a few years from now there will be many peaceful dwellings by the road-side in this section, whose occupants may never dream that the tramping of marching squadrons, the rattling of artillery carriages, and the clanging of sabers, might have recently been heard upon the public highways. How evanescent are the actions of men! Even the pyramids of Egypt must in time crumble to dust. We do not know but that if the light of the past could be thrown upon these grounds and over these regions, we should see hostile armies of even greater magnitude than ours or that of the enemy, operating against each other. It is now considered by those who ought to be competent authority, that this western country was once occupied by a race of people quite different, in some respects, to our present Indians. At various places in the Mississippi valley mounds are found which are known to have been thrown up by human hands; and in some instances there have also been found human skeletons, pieces of pottery and implements indicative of their domestic life. These mounds are believed to be of high intiquity and not to have been made by any of the existing races of North America. If a numerous people inhabited the Mississippi valley at some distant age of the past, they also probably spread over this region, for its ever-living streams, lovely valleys, and occasional prairies, must always have been very inviting to peoples following a nomadic or pastoral life.

Though our camp is on the edge of a prairie, the country a few miles to the east of us is rugged and hilly, and less adapted to agricultural purposes than the country to the west of us, in the Grand River valley. But as the Grand River country belongs to the Cherokees, no one can say when its agricultural resources will be developed, even should the war close immediately.

The number of negro refugees, who have gained their freedom since we came into this State, are getting to be a good deal of a burden. Their almost destitute condition, causes many of them to commit acts that are not sanctioned by our ideas of strict morality. We find employment for some of them as teamsters and servants, but still there are many more who are unemployed. We send a good many to Kansas every time that our supply trains return to Fort Scott.

Many of them are quite shiftless, and it will probably be some time before they appreciate to a very great extent the value of their freedom. But we should be charitable towards them, and not magnify their short-comings, nor oppress them, so that they will feel obliged to commit unlawful acts. I think that there is a tendency on our part to overlook their many disadvantages, when considering their moral actions. With their past life of slavery and degradation, and with the pinch of hunger and cold affecting them at present, we ought not to expect all their actions to be perfectly free of censure. Those who have tasted of only a small proportion of the fruits of their own toil, are not likely to try before their consciences with much deliberation, the offense of chicken stealing, when they are suffering from hunger. As these people have not been property owners, it will probably be some time before they have very definite ideas of proprietary rights. We should not therefore be surprised to hear of a larger proportion of them during the next generation, guilty of unlawfully appropriating the property of others, than among the white population.

It seems to me that we might be relieved of a good deal of our present embarrassment by organizing a corps of colored troops. The amount of money the Government paid the men for their services would be almost sufficient to take care of their families. There is, however, considerable prejudice yet among our officers and soldiers in regard to organizing them into regiments, but as their freedom throughout the country is sure to come at an early day, I can see no good reason why they should not be taken into the military service at once, indeed just as fast as they see fit to enlist. Having always been accustomed to obey orders, and being naturally of docile dispositions, I am inclined to believe that, if properly organized and officered, they will make excellent soldiers. While I think that intelligent soldiers may be more effective in the field than those of lower intelligence, I do not believe that either are likely to accomplish great deeds under incompetent and inefficient officers.

To relieve as far as possible the demands of hunger among the refugee families on the outskirts of our camp, Colonel Phillips has ordered that all the mills in this vicinity be repaired, so that such grain as can be found may be ground into meal and flour for distribution among those whose necessities are most pressing. He also occasionally makes a tour of personal inspection among the refugees, that he may know from his own observation something of the condition of those whom the fortunes of war have driven to seek our protection.

Yesterday evening (17th) a detachment of cavalry guarding a supply train from Cross Hollows, near Pea Ridge, with rations for this command, brought information that General Marmaduke, whom we fought at Cane Hill last November, attacked Springfield, Missouri, on the 8th instant, with a force of three or four thousand rebel cavalry and artillery. General E. B. Brown who commanded our troops, nearly all of whom were Missouri State Milita, made a gallant defense of the place, and repulsed the enemy after a day of fighting and skirmishing. General Marmaduke captured two unimportant positions in the southern quarter of the city, but after some sharp fighting his men were soon driven from them. Our troops had constructed several temporary forts, which were protected by stockades and trenches, so that a small force could hold the place against a superior force of the enemy. Though the enemy made several gallant charges and captured two positions, he could not hope to capture the stronger positions except by storming them, and he had not made sufficient preparations to undertake this with a reasonable prospect of success. General Marmaduke, finding that General Brown was hourly expecting reinforcements and would soon be able to take the offensive, withdrew from the contest and marched in a southeast direction. Many of the houses of the citizens were badly damaged by shot and shell from the enemy's artillery, and a few were also destroyed by fire. General Brown congratulated his troops for their gallant defense of the city, and regretted that he was unable to vigorously press the enemy in his retreat for want of cavalry.

Our troops that left Elm Springs on the night of the 8th were nearly two days too late to participate in the engagement at Springfield. There was undoubtedly a blunder somewhere, or else our commanding General is not shrewd enough to match General Marmaduke. It was almost stupidity to allow the enemy to march around us without our knowledge of his movements.

We hear now that Colonel Phillips' new command is to be known as the *Eighth* and *Ninth Districts Department* of the *Missouri*. It embraces southwest Missouri, northwestern Arkansas, and the Cherokee Nation. Considering the interests involved and the difficulties of his new position, he is justly entitled to the rank of Brigadier General, particularly if his present assignment is not a temporary arrangement.

In the afternoon of the 21st, Captain Hopkin's battery was taken out on the prairies near camp, for the purpose of spending a few hours in artillery practice. This is the battery that I have already referred to as the one we captured from General Cooper's command at Old Fort Wayne, three miles west of our present camp, the 21st of last October. The guns are in excellent condition, and though most of the artillerymen have had only a few months' drill, yet from the target practice this afternoon, they show that they would do effective work should the occasion shortly arise.

While on this ground I may mention that my father was held as a citizen prisoner near here last April by the rebel Colonel Coffey; and was condemned to be shot, but was exchanged the day before execution was to take place. He was captured by the enemy while guiding Colonel Doubleday's Second Ohio cavalry from Kansas into South-west Missouri, and brought to Camp Walker and held several weeks. The rebel authorities had ordered shot quite a number of Union citizen prisoners, because they charged that our troops had shot a number of disloyal citizens. I doubt whether our troops ever shot any disloyal citizens after they were regularly captured, unless they were among those classed as bushwhackers, and who had committed some outrageous acts.

At eight o'clock on the evening of the 22d, with a detail of fourteen men, I was directed to proceed to Neosho with dispatches for the commanding officer at that post, and for the commanding general at Springfield. As it is the intention of our division to spend the winter in this section ; and as we are not likely to commence any offensive operation until towards spring, I have permission to remain at Neosho two weeks, to see some of my relatives and friends whom I have not seen since the war commenced. I look back upon the past year with a good deal of pride, for I have not been absent from my post of duty a single day. And in the discharge of my duties, I believe that I have given satisfaction to those with whom I have had to deal. Though we have had a Lieutenant and Commissary with us a part of the time, being a subordinate, I have generally had all the work to do, and it is no small task to issue rations to a full regiment of cavalry, as I have had to do when the regiment was all together. If I could issue unbroken packages, of course there would be but little labor. As it is, I am obliged to weigh and measure in all conceivable quantities, sugar, salt, coffee, tea, beans, etc., besides I must cut up the fresh beef and bacon into pieces of just so many pounds weight, and if a scout-

ing party is going out during the night, as generally
happens, it may become necessary to issue to it extra
rations, and to stay up half the night to do it.   I must
be extremely careful in all my calculations, seeing to
it that no company, detachment or the hospital, gets
any more or less than its exact regulation allowance.   This little retrospect of my own duties I hope
is permissible, as I am going to have a respite of a
few days.   The sky was heavily overcast, and there
was no moon, and the night was intensely dark.   But
on this account we thought that we would be less
likely to come in contact with the enemy's guerillas,
and the necessity of being constantly on our guard
would chase sweet sleep from our eyes.

CHAPTER V.

The author at Neosho, Missouri, for a few days—*Ante-bellum* times and reminiscensces—Description of the town——The Grand Falls and water-power mills in the country—Fertility of the soil on the river bottoms—Fencing which enclosed most of the farms destroyed—About half the people loyal—Indiscriminate destruction of property condemned—A double sacrifice put upon Missouri loyalists—A picture of desolated homes—Guerrilla warfare and Federal losses in the State—The Militia occupying Newtonia and fortifying it—Their efficiency—Mostly State troops that opposed General Marmaduke at the battle of Springfield on the 9th—Flag raising at Neosho—The National Flag scornfully regarded by rebels—Geurrillas at Granby—The rich lead mines there, but no longer worked—Author informed of the death of his brother at Fayetteville—A mother's picture of a united family.

We arrived at Neosho on the morning of the 23d, having marched forty-five miles in twelve hours. Our route was through a thickly wooded region all the way. It continued cloudy and was intensely dark, and there was a drizzling rain nearly all night. We had to trust to our horses keeping on the path, as they see better in the darkness than men. It frequently occurred that we could not tell whether we were on the road or not, for we could not distinguish a white handkerchief an arms length in front of us. Immediately

on our arrival at Neosho I delivered the dispatches
and mail to Major John A. Foreman, commanding
officer of the post, who at once sent them by another
detachment on to Springfield.

I breakfasted at home with father and mother and
the family, the first time for nearly two years.   Mother
was nearly wild with delight to see me, so many
exciting events have taken place in this section since
the last time she saw me.   Though we were within
twelve miles of here last September at the battle of
Newtonia, I did not have an opportunity of coming
home.   She heard the booming of artillery all that
day, and knowing that my brother and I were with
our troops, felt great anxiety until she heard that we
were all right.

When we came in sight of the place, I could hardly
bring my mind, I regret to say, into a condition to
greet it with much warmth of feeling.   It is easy to
imagine an instance in which, when one person purposely or carelessly offends another, and afterwards
without having made any apology or explanation, offers his hand, and of the offended party hesitating
whether to take it or not.   Such were my feelings.
I could hardly make up my mind to give the place
the right hand of fellowship, even if the place had
welcomed my return.   Since the Kansas troubles a
large majority of the people of this place have displayed such a spirit of intolerance and want of respect
towards those who differed with them in regard to political issues, that the sight of the town fails to arouse

the slightest thrill of affection and reverence. There were a few abolitionists who resided here before the war, and they were frequently engaged in warm discussions in regard to the slavery question. They could talk with some pro-slavery men with moderation, but others to whom they talked, became passionate and even violent, declaring that no abolitionist should be permitted to live in this section and inculcate his pernicious doctrine. I have always noticed that those who cling tenaciously to principles which they cannot defend, get out of patience if you press them too hard with their illogicalities or inconsistencies. But though the abolitionists were frequently insulted and threatened, they persisted in expressing their convictions to those who desired to know them. Though less than a dozen in the county, they did not deny or make any efforts to conceal the fact that they were abolitionists. There were quite a number of men who were about half in sympathy with them, that is, whose political convictions were gradually undergoing a change, and they were not very decided in their expressions either way. Some people had such peculiar notions about abolitionists that the word was used in a good many families to frighten children. And there were also people quite grown up who regarded an abolitionist as a kind of monster in human form, so one-sided had their education been respecting the views of abolitionists.

I saw to-day several of the men who, in the early part of the war, had so little patience with Union men that they wanted them all killed and their property confiscated for the benefit of the Confederate Government. They were in favor of hanging those who went to Kansas and joined the Kansas Jayhawkers, as the Kansas soldiers were called. The name Jayhawker was first given to an organization of Free State men in Southern Kansas who, under the Territorial *regime* made retaliatory incursions into Missouri. The name is growing into a nickname for all Kansas people in the same sense as " Hoosier " is applied to Indianians. But several of the men I saw, who were recently thirsting for the blood of the Kansas Jayhawkers, when they looked and knew me, cast their eyes towards the ground, and their countenances changed. They were captured a few weeks ago, having been connected with a band of guerrillas whose operations extended over this county. But they have taken the oath of allegiance to the United States, and given bonds for the faithful performance of their promises. Now that they have escaped the edges of our swords and *seem* to show a disposition to submit to the authority of the Government, I presume no one feels inclined to disturb them, or to cast them into any deeper humiliation. When the rebel army under General McCulloch first came into this section, these men were painstaking in pointing out loyal families that they might be plundered of their property. The war is teaching the intolerant some grand lessons in toleration, and those of one-sided views to study the nature of their opponents' arguments. Men who recently could scarcely tolerate the existence of a neighbor who held opinions on certain subjects different from their own, are now at the mercy of this neighbor. And it is certainly commendable of those who were recently in the minority here, that they do not display a spirit of revenge.

It was at this place in November, 1861, while General Price's army were encamped in the vicinity, that Governor Jackson convened the Rump Legislature, which went through the farce of ratifying the ordinance of Secession. The event was celebrated by the booming of artillery; and great speeches were made to the enthusiastic multitude by the principal leaders.

Their prospects were brighter then than now, and they doubtless thought that Missouri would form one of the stars in the Constellation of the Confederate States.

The town contained about one thousand inhabitants before the war; but the population now is much less, probably not more than half that number independent of the Indian refugees temporarily stopping here. When this section was occupied by the rebel troops, nearly all the loyal families removed to Springfield and Kansas, or to some point within our lines; and since we drove the enemy out, and established posts at nearly all the towns, many of the rebel families have moved south.

A small garrison here could make no sort of defense against an enemy playing upon it with artillery, for there are heights all around the town, except narrow openings to the southeast and north. The brick Court House, however, which stands isolated on the Court

House Square, will hold between two and three
hundred men, who might for several days, hold out
against a superior force not armed with artillery. Our
troops have had several sharp contests with the enemy
here.   About the 2d of July, 1861, some eighty men
of General Sigel's Command, under Captain Conrad
of the Third Missouri infantry, were surrounded in
the Court House and captured by the rebel army
under Generals Price and McCulloch, then marching
up from Camp Walker to join Generals Rains and
Parsons.   And early last spring several companies
of the Seventh Missouri cavalry were surprised by
the enemy and defeated with some loss in killed,
wounded and prisoners.   But since the Kansas Division came into this section, we have chased the
enemy through the town several times, making the
dust fly.   We also killed two or three leaders of local
rebel organizations, who were much feared by the
loyal people.

The Indian soldiers now stationed here, are quartered in the Court House, and have made a number
of port holes for their rifles, to be used in the event
of an attack.   Throughout the State the Militia are
using the Court Houses for quarters and for means
of defense.

One of the desirable features of this place is the Big
Spring in the western part of the town.   It is one of the
finest springs in this section, and would afford a sufficient quantity of the purest water for a city of considerable size.   It has a fall of about ten feet in less than

half a dozen yards, and of course runs out of the bluff like a mill tail. When peace shall spread her beneficent influences over our entire country again, northern enterprise and capital will probably utilize this valuable water-power for manufacturing purposes, and perhaps also contrive some means of conveying a portion of the water to the houses of those who shall make this place their home. With a system of pipes it could easily be done without very heavy expense. Shoal Creek, nearly two miles north of here, is a large stream, and discharges a large volume of water the year round, and in regard to water-power facilities, probably has few equals in the country. At the Grand Falls, sixteen miles northwest of Neosho, it pours over a perpendicular precipice about eighteen feet high. Fine carding and flouring mills at that and a number of other points on this stream, have been in operation for many years. Fortunately, up to the present, nearly all the mills in this section have escaped destruction by the contending armies. It is hoped that no necessity will arise justifying their destruction in any locality.

The country is somewhat broken in this vicinity, and the hillsides are covered with a variety of kinds of what we call "flints." The prairies are quite fertile, but not equal to the creek bottoms, which are scarcely equalled in fertility in any country. My father thinks that his farm of two hundred and sixty acres, which lies four miles north of this place on Shoal Creek, has not its equal in the alluvial plain of the Mississippi

8

valley in point of productiveness. But since the war commenced, the fences have nearly all been destroyed by the rebel armies camping upon it, and only a small portion of it was cultivated last year by a tenant. The first year of the war the Rebels drove away all our live stock, and some of our neighbors who sided with the enemy, even had a discussion among themselves as to what our farm and timbered lands would bring when sold as confiscated property for the benefit of the Confederate treasury, as they were determined to have them.

In regard to the destruction of fences, I may say that as far as my own observation goes, few of those enclosing farms on the public highways have escaped. When we encamped fifteen miles north-east of here last autumn, just before the battle of Newtonia in this county, we burned thousands of rails for fuel, and if we bivouacked on the field at night, we made numerous fires along the roadside. It is almost impossible for a large army to pass through the country in which it is operating without causing more or less injury to the property of friend as well as foe. I have noted, with feelings of deep regret, that the loyal people of this State frequently sustain losses at the hands of our troops because they happen to be in bad company; that is, because they live in communities where the rebel sentiment predominates. Though there were few men in this section at the beginning of the war who were willing to acknowledge that they were abolitionists, yet when it came to choosing between the

Union and rebellion, nearly half of the people chose
the Union, and elected to cast their fortunes with it.
A good many of the wealthiest and most prominent
men in south-west Missouri were strong and pronounced Unionists from the very beginning, and
worked tooth and nail for our success, though they
knew that they took their lives in their hands to do it.
Colonel Harvey Ritchie, of Newtonia, who was State
senator at the breaking out of the war, issued a public address to the people of south-west Missouri, urging them, in the most eloquent language, to stand firm
by the Union and not be led into any secession movement.   This address went into the hands of thousands
of citizens, and no doubt had great influence in keeping many steadfast for the Union, and in opening the
eyes of others to the follies and rashness of secession.
It is therefore painful to hear officers and soldiers
who know very little about the politics of this State,
characterizing all the people alike as rebels, and as
entitled to the same sympathy.   These thoughtless
officers and men sometimes ask, if anyone ventures
to speak a word on behalf of the loyal men of this
section, where are the men ?   But if they would
look around intelligently, they would easily see that
of all the deserted homes, and homes in which there
is no one left but women and children, that the men
are not in every case in the rebel army.   Those who
were with us last fall when we were encamped on Pea
Ridge battle field, must have seen from the head-
boards placed over the graves of the Federal soldiers

that fell on that field, that Missouri troops suffered as severe losses as the troops from Iowa, Illinois and Indiana. The principal body of our troops that were engaged at the battle of Wilson Creek under Generals Lyon and Sigel were also Missouri troops. The First regiment of Missouri artillery alone, lost in that battle killed, officers 1 ; enlisted men 66 ; wounded officers 2 ; enlisted men 210 ; missing officers 2 ; enlisted men 6, or a total of casualties of 292 men. Let those who are blind to these facts, read of the great battles of Fort Donelson and Pittsburg Landing, and see if Missouri did not sustain her *pro rata* of losses in killed and wounded for the Union cause. Probably some of those who are so careless in their remarks in regard to *all* the people of this State being rebels, would not like to acknowledge that Missouri, after furnishing all the men she has for the rebel army, has also furnished more men for the Union army than either of the great States, Iowa or Massachusetts. If this is not the exact truth, it is very near it. If we include the troops called out for active service in this State, there is not a reasonable doubt of it. This State has sins enough to answer for without having to answer for any for which she is not justly chargeable. And I deeply sympathize with those families whose desolated homes lie before them, and whose male members lie on some distant field, or are even now, this very moment, at the front, nobly performing their duties in defense of the old flag and the Union. I have a right to feel touched in this matter, for all the male members of our family, except the two little boys, have been away from home nearly a year and a half. And until our troops came into this section, mother had to endure many hardships in providing food and clothing for the children, for rebel marauders repeatedly robbed us of the best articles of clothing, bed-clothing, etc. I have seen men from the loyal States, whose families were doubtless resting in perfect security, and enjoying the property and good things with which honest labor has rewarded them, who yet appeared blind to the fact that a double sacrifice is put upon the Union soldiers of this State.

The soldier in the field from this State is constantly tortured with the thought that his wife, mother, daughter or sister, is being robbed, insulted or burned out of her home, with no one to look to for protection, and assistance and advice. No doubt, on the tented field, or wherever sweet sleep sits upon his eyelids, he is often awakened by horrible dreams of seeing his house in flames climbing to the sky, and his wife and little children gathered around her near it, with sad expressions, wondering what they shall do for food and shelter and clothing. The picture is not overdrawn and wholly imaginary, as some may suppose who are not familiar with what they would perhaps call unimportant incidents of the war in Missouri; but is an actuality of no unusual occurrence, whether many of the soldiers from this State have such dreams or not. In fact it would be difficult to overdraw a picture

representing the hardships and privation that many of
the loyal families of this State have had to endure since
the war commenced.   But under all these extraordinary trials and difficulties, of desolation and ruin, they
have remained firm in their devotion and loyalty to the
Government.   Their ears, therefore, should never hear
unpleasant and reproachful words in wholly unjustifiable connections from those who should be their
friends.   As far as I am personally concerned, I do not
wish to make even rebel families feel uncomfortable on
account of the position they have taken in regard to
the war.   But when they become, as we sometimes
hear, unnecessarily insolent and troublesome, I think
it might be well to send them south of our lines.
They should always, however, have fair warning before
we resort to such severe measures.   The greatest
trouble we have with rebel families is in the country,
where they harbor bushwhackers.   This guerrilla warfare is so detestable to all honorable minded men, that
those engaged in it cannot justly complain if we adopt
extreme measures to suppress it.   Our losses in this
State by this mode of warfare, during the past year,
would probably foot up, if we could get correct figures,
several hundred soldiers killed, besides perhaps nearly
as many Union citizens.

Since we drove the enemy out of Newtonia last
October, the place has been occupied by the State
Militia.   They are throwing up fortifications and preparing to build a block house there, which when completed, ought to enable them to hold the place against

a large force of the enemy. A number of rebel citizens who have recently taken the oath of allegiance, have been compelled to furnish teams and labor towards constructing these fortifications, of which they bitterly complain. But if they desire the protection of the Government, they should do something in a generous spirit to assist it.

As the Militia are well mounted and furnished with arms and equipments by the general Government, they should be able to keep this section free of guerrillas. Though the Militia force, which now numbers ten or twelve thousand men, are not obliged to go out of the State, yet they are kept in active service, and their service is scarcely less arduous than that of the Volunteer Cavalry in the field. The force under General Brown that fought General Marmaduke at the battle of Springfield, on the 8th instant, as already stated, consisted chiefly of State Militia. And in the engagement, they stood as firm as veterans until the enemy were driven from the field.

To-day, February 2d, Major Foreman had erected on the Court House Square, Neosho, a high flagstaff, and run up our National Flag, and its folds floated to the breeze for the first time since a detachment of General Sigel's men were captured in the Court House here on the 3d July, 1861. Expressions from some of the rebel families in town show that they regard it scornfully, and would, if they dared, trail it in the dust. But as we are just beginning to develop our strength, while the enemy is unquestionably beginning to show signs

of weakness, we will hardly withdraw our troops from
this section again. Those who do not like the sight
of our National Flag, should therefore move south,
and join their friends who carry the Confederate Flag.
As we have occupied all the towns of any consequence
in Southwest Missouri, and as we have about ten
thousand men in the field along the southern border
of the State, I think that nothing short of annihila-
tion of this army, or withdrawal of it to co-operate
with some other army in another section, can endanger our position here, nor indeed any of our posts
west of Springfield.

Yesterday (2d) a party of guerrillas were seen near
Granby, eight miles northeast of this place. It is supposed that they were after a quantity of concealed
lead to make into balls to replenish their cartridge
boxes. Whether there is any hidden lead there, we
have no means of knowing at this moment. Granby,
at the breaking out of the war, contained a population
of six or seven thousand people, nearly all of whom
were connected with the mining business, and many
large smelting furnaces were in operation. It was
probably one of the richest lead mines in this country.
The mining operations continued there until about a
year ago, and of course were of immense importance
to the enemy in the way of furnishing balls for their
small arms. But the eyes of the furnaces have been
blown out, and some of the buildings destroyed, so that
no one has ventured to invest money in the business
again. It is thought by experienced miners that most

of this country is rich in galena ore. When, therefore, peace shall have come to the country, mining operations will no doubt be resumed in this section, and whatever mineral resources it possesses developed.

Last night (3d) a detachment of ten men, with the mail and despatches, arrived here from the *First Division, Army of the Frontier,* now encamped in the vicinity of Springfield. Several of the men belonged to that part of my regiment which left us at Elm Springs, and they informed me that they had just heard from Fayetteville, Arkansas, before leaving camp, that my brother James died in hospital there on the 26th or 27th of January. As the information came through reliable parties, men whom I have known since the regiment was organized, I at once conveyed the sad intelligence to his wife and to father and mother. We were all greatly distressed, and that which increased the burden of our grief was the thought that he should have died from home in hospital, with none of us near him; nor perhaps even of any of the comrades of his own regiment. Father and mother, just before I came here on this few days' leave, had it under consideration to go after him to bring him home, but were told that it would be difficult, if not impossible, to get permission to remove him. Such a task, anyway, in midwinter, would have been attended with much suffering and danger to the patient.

He has breathed out his noble life, very dear to us all, that coming generations may enjoy the blessings which we hope his sufferings and death will help to secure. Just one year and six months before he died, I came from Kansas, traveling at night and on by-roads, and passing hard by the enemy's guards, and guided him and father back there. I little thought then that I should be called upon so soon to mourn his death. Yet when we enlisted into the army I knew that we should have to take the risk of being stricken down by the enemy's bullets the same as other soldiers in time of war. Enlisting into the volunteer force of a State whose people have just cause for not feeling very friendly towards the people of this State in general, we had no influential friends to look to for any favors, even if we had desired them. Offering our services to the Government in a land of strangers, easy, honorable and lucrative positions, or positions comparatively free from dangers and hardships of the war, did not seek us. We were in earnest for the Government, and waited for no special inducements to enlist. Had he been of a disposition to want to shirk the duties of a true soldier, he could easily enough have gone to the hospital immediately after having received the fatal wound in the shoulder at the battle of Coon Creek, on the 22d of last August. Though he knew that the ball had not been found by the surgeons who made a partial diagnosis of the wound, and knowing too that the ball, wherever it had lodged, had had the effect of producing at different times, queer sensations of dizziness and numbness of certain muscles, yet with all these serious premonitions of his approaching end, he preferred to remain with his company as long as he could stand upon his feet. He fell paralyzed at the battle of Cane Hill, at a place where his company was required to dismount and scale the mountain on foot, in order to dislodge the enemy from a certain position. I am perfectly conscious that if these few simple words referred to the sufferings and death of some general officer instead of a private soldier, they would be read by many with greater eagerness, and touch deeper their sympathetic emotions. But he was my brother, and I would be recreant to my conscience, were I not, in passing, to mention that noble devotion to duty which hastened his death. And in speaking of him I speak of thousands of other noble men who have recently laid down their lives in defense of their country.

Only a few days ago, referring to the dangers and hardships of the war, and the intense anxiety she felt for us when in the field, mother said that she looked forward to the time when the war would be over with the profoundest interest, so that she might have all her sons home to sit down together with her at the same table. But alas! her picture of a united family after the war, in whatever manner it may terminate, can now never be realized

Why should I refer to these expressions of grief in our home? Thousands of mothers over this land are this day mourning for their husbands and sons who will never return home from the war, Nor do we see the end of these sacrifices yet, of the noblest and best of our country. And there are doubtless hundreds of families from whom more than one son has been sacrificed in the cause of the Union. We have only a faint realization of the horrors of war until some calamity like this comes to our own doors and invades our family.

CHAPTER VI.

The Author's return to his division at Scott's Mills—Colonel Phillips' popularity with his troops—Rebels returning and taking
the oath of allegiance—Indians make good troops to fight
bushwhackers—Increase of wild game since the war—A detachment of Federal troops worsted in a skirmish with guerrillas—Captain Conkey loses eleven men by capture—Guerrilla chieftains commissioned by the Rebel authorities—Comments on plans proposed by some to break up the guerrilla
warfare—Sickness and heavy mortality among the Indian
Refugees at Neosho—Sick and wounded being removed from
Fayetteville to Fort Scott—The classes of the enemy the Federals have to deal with—Bushwhackers—Guerrillas—Detachments returning to and leaving the State—The regular forces
in our front—Illustrations—Incidents from the Expedition to
Low Jack—The battle of Coon Creek—Concluding remarks
on the Indians.

The 12th of February I joined the Indian division
at Scott's Mills, McDonald County, Missouri, on the
Cowskin river, twenty-two miles south west of Neosho,
and about the same distance north of our old camp
at Maysville. The bottom lands along the stream are
excellent, and there are numerous fine farms, on most
of which fine crops were raised last year. The movement of the division to this place is not regarded as
retrograde or falling back, but simply for the purpose

of more easily supplying our animals with forage and provisioning the refugee families with us. The mills here are in very good condition, and daily turn out large quantities of meal and flour, which will do much to relieve the demands of hunger among the refugees. Since we left Elm Springs as a separate command, Colonel Phillips has steadily grown in popularity with his troops, and we now believe him to be an able and judicious commander. At the end of a month he has made no mistake, but on the contrary has managed the affairs of his District in a manner deserving the warmest commendation.

The active operations of this command, and of the troops at Neosho under Major John A. Foreman, against the guerrillas in this section, are beginning to have a wholesome effect. Scarcely a day passes that a squad of rebels do not come in and take the oath of allegiance and ask the protection of the Government. Those who come in generally express the opinion that many more would come if they knew that they would be protected and allowed to live at home instead of being sent north at prisoners. They are mostly regarded with mistrust, for it has sometimes turned out that those whom we received and treated kindly, soon became dissatisfied with the situation, and went south again and joined the guerrillas. Until we came here, bushwhackers were as plenty as wild game up and down this river, but during the last two weeks, quite a number have been killed by our troops. They will hardly be able to find a safe retreat anywhere in the vicinity of this command.   An Indian seems to me to almost scent a secret foe.   I think this trait or characteristic may be to some extent accounted for by many of them following their natural mode of life—that is of hunting in the woods for game for miles around the camp.

It is well known to every one in the least familiar with this section during antebellum times, that the game in this region, such as deer and wild turkeys, have increased in great numbers the past two years. Many hogs have become wild in the river bottoms and flee from the sight of man like a deer.   When the houses have been burned and the fences around the farms destroyed, as we find here and there, animals like hogs, that live without constant attention from man, soon run wild.   The game that the Indians have killed this winter would probably, if we could estimate it, form quite an item in the way of maintaining their families.

It occasionally happens that, in a contest with the guerillas in this section, small detachments of our troops get worsted.   On the first instant, a detachment from the command at Neosho had a skirmish with a company of guerillas on Burkhart prairie, twelve miles north-west of that post, and had two men badly wounded, without inflicting any loss on the enemy as far as is known.   The commanding officer of the post, Major Foreman, immediately sent out a larger force, about a hundred men, to the vicinity where the skirmish took place, but it returned to its station after having captured one wagon loaded with plunder, and having chased the enemy several miles through the woods.

Captain Theo. Conkey, of the Third Wisconsin cavalry, who has recently been operating along the Spring River, in Jasper County, against the guerillas, had a lively contest a few days ago with Livingston's band, and in the affair, had half a dozen of his men captured. The loss sustained by the enemy, if any, I have been unable to ascertain, as Captain Conkey receives his orders from the commanding officer at Fort Scott. Livingston, we understand, is commissioned by and acting under regular orders from the rebel authorities, and is not accused of killing his prisoners like Quantrell, whose operations are confined chiefly to Jackson and Cass counties, and with whom we had a number of skirmishes last May. But Livingston attacks our supply trains, and his numerous predatory actions about unprotected points have given him considerable prominence during the last year. Whenever our troops come upon him with equal, or perhaps, somewhat superior numbers, he never stands, but soon scatters his men in small squads, permitting them sometimes to return to their homes for a few days. But between Neosho and Fort Scott, a distance of eighty miles, there is no point, except a camp on Dry Wood, fourteen miles south of Fort Scott, where we have any troops stationed. This large space of unoccupied country gives a wide field of operations for such an organization as Livingston's. And until we can estab-

lish more numerous stations along the western border
tier of counties in this State, it will probably be difficult,
if not impossible, to entirely break up such guerilla
bands and also bushwhacking. To accomplish this
object, there are some who favor applying the torch
indiscriminately, to the houses of Union people and
rebels. I can never conscientiously favor such a
scheme ; nor do I believe that the evil requires such
heroic treatment at our hands. I have seen the standing chimneys and smoking ruins of desolated homes
of Union people as well as rebels too often to wish to
see such scenes renewed in a wholesale manner. Nor
do I believe that such acts on our part would remedy
the evil which we wish to extirpate. It seems to me
that the enemy could occupy the desolate country all
the same, and make his incursions into Kansas and
into the counties of Missouri still further to the
east. Though my age and position would not, to the
minds of many, justify my presuming to criticise the
actions of those whose maturer years have given
them more varied experiences, and in many things a
sounder judgment, yet I venture to think that
our officers have too often permitted the indiscriminate destruction of private property, which should not
have been destroyed, thus causing a needless amount
of suffering among those whom we should endeavor
to protect in the possession of their lives and property. I am perfectly willing, however, to do such
officers the justice to believe that they seldom or never
permit such acts, after thinking over the consequen-
9

ces, with such deliberation as I may be able to do when setting down to write on the subject. An officer marching through the country at the head of his squadron or regiment, without the thought of an enemy being near, is suddenly fired upon at a certain place by a party of guerrillas, and gets one or more of his men killed or wounded. His first thought is likely to be, that the family living on the place have been giving the enemy aid and comfort. This may be true or may not. But the chances are that the house will be burned, without making a thorough investigation to ascertain whether those occupying it were in sympathy with, or knew anything about the presence of, the enemy.

Then there are people whose sympathies are divided concerning the issues involved in the war; I mean by this that, taking a large number of citizens such as we have to deal with, their loyalty would perhaps range from slight to complete without qualification. Some again, though they sympathize with the Government, and really wish its success, yet having relatives and friends in the rebel army who are very dear to them, have not the courage to utter their convictions in a strong and positive manner. The question arises, should the slightly loyal receive the punishment or be treated the same as the disloyal who are tooth and nail against us? It will thus be seen that an apparently very simple question, becomes quite involved, when looked at closely. It is therefore useless to suppose that the sturdy soldier will enter into all these hair splitting niceties before giving his orders. He looks at things just as they present themselves to him, and if injustice is done, it may be, that after reflection, no one would regret it more keenly than himself. Taking this view of the matter, relieves in a measure our officers of the charge of permitting unnecessary destruction of private property. In all those extraordinary cases where private property has been destroyed by our troops, that clearly should not have been destroyed, the Government should, and probably will, in time, pay for, provided of course, that the parties to whom it belongs are loyal to the United States. I would not destroy even the property of rebel citizens except in cases of military necessity; and then it is not supposable that any demand will ever be made upon the Government for payment. But let us pass from this question which, in a few years, will doubtless engage the attention of legislators.

Parties coming from Neosho report that there is a great deal of sickness among the Indian soldiers and their families at that place. Taking into account the number of Indians there, and the number sick, the mortality amongst them is considered very high. The prevailing type of disease which is now taking off so many of them, I understand is typhoid fever. The hardships incident to leaving their homes in the Nation, and innutritious food and insufficient quantities of food, together with the poorly clad condition of many, are probably among the causes of this high mortality in some of the families. But of course the

remark in regard to food and clothing cannot apply to
the Indian soldiers, for they are as well fed and
clothed as we are, that is, they have had their regular
allowances during the winter. But the families and
each member thereof have not perhaps had full rations
during the winter. Though great care and interest
have been manifested by Colonel Phillips in looking
after them, yet it has been impossible to make them as
comfortable as at their homes. The want of proper
sheltering has also probably in many cases contributed
to their discomforts and sickness. Home sickness,
from being exiles, also doubtless has a depressing influence amongst some of them.

Such of the sick and wounded at Fayetteville and
in the field hospitals of this division as will bear
removing, are being taken to Fort Scott. The General
Hospital at that place is better provided with everything essential to their proper care and treatment.
The great difficulty is to get them there without increasing too much their suffering. But men convalescing from
the effects of wounds, and placed in ambulances, and
the ambulances driven carefully, should be taken the
distance from Fayetteville to Fort Scott, say one
hundred and fifty miles, without great inconvenience,
except while *en route* they should be struck with
a change of extremely cold weather, or a storm of
sleet or snow. Even then, the heavy woolen blankets
with which every soldier is provided, would enable
them to get through without much suffering. Should

the present fine weather continue a few days longer, they will have reached their destination in good condition.

Yesterday (15th), Colonel Phillips sent a squad of ten rebel prisoners that we recently captured, to Neosho, Missouri, to be held until there is an opportunity of sending them to Fort Scott or Leavenworth.

We have four classes of the enemy to deal with in this section.

First, the bushwhackers, who are unorganized and generally found singly, but, as sometimes happens, in squads of two to half a dozen. They are generally men who stay around in the vicinity of their homes, and fire upon our troops from bluffs or other inaccessible points, or when they see one of our soldiers alone on dispatch or courier duty shoot him off his horse with their rifles, and despoil him of his arms, clothing, money and equipments. Since we came into this region last autumn, we have had quite a number of men who were either with the advance or rear guard, or on escort duty to trains, killed and wounded by bushwhackers. Though of course bushwhackers are all rebels, yet I think that most of them are men of bad blood, men whose natural inclinations and evil tendencies lead them to follow a robber life. They only take advantage of the existing chaotic state of things to show their true characters. Should the war immediately cease, probably only a small percentage of such desperate characters would return to or adopt

an honest mode of life. But putting themselves outside
the pale of civilized warfare, they will likely nearly all
be killed off in a few years. I may be judging them
too harshly, but in the light of such facts as have
come under my notice, I don't think so.

Second, guerrilla bands, men having some sort of
military organization, and whose movements are directed by a leader. Most of the leaders of the guerrillas with
whom we have to contend, I have frequently heard,
hold commissions from the Confederate government,
or the fugitive Governor of Missouri. Livingston
whom I have already referred to, may be cited as an
instance. The function of guerrillas is similar to that
of privateers. While the privateer is commissione d
by the rebel authorities to prey upon our marine commerce, the guerrillas are commissioned to prey upon
our inland commerce, destroy public property, such as
trains, &c., and to impede our movements in every
possible manner. Though as I have mentioned, Livingston is not accused of murdering his prisoners in
cold blood, yet our soldiers feel, and I think justly so,
that their lives would be very insecure in the hands of
most . guerrilla leaders, like Quantrill for example.
We have to be always on the lookout for guerrillas,
and our trains are obliged to be always well guarded,
for if the enemy capture a courier with dispatches, or
a soldier from a scouting party, they may get information that will enable them to concentrate at a given
point and attack our escort and trains from an ambush.
This mode of warfare often enables a small force to

defeat a superior force encumbered with trains. In fact the concealed enemy has a great advantage when he attacks about an equal number of our troops. An enemy of a hundred men concealed in a favorable position, might kill and wound half a company of soldiers the first volley. The rest, if not thrown into confusion by such a sudden burst of destruction, would in such case be unable to cope with the enemy flushed by his success. To guard against such disasters a military commander must be always wide awake and on the alert, and he must know the strength of the enemy in his rear as well as in his front. We now believe that the enemy, in whatever manner he may choose to operate against us, will have to be exceedingly industrious and wide awake to gain a point on Colonel Phillips. His movements on the military chessboard show that he is not likely to be checkmated or broken up by an opponent handling an equal number of men.

Third, rebels returning to their homes in that section of the State from which they entered the rebel army; or rebels leaving the vicinity of their homes in detachments to join the rebel army, or to remain south during the progress of the war. Whether leaving the State in detachments, or returning to it in detachments, they rarely show an inclination to assume the offensive, seeming to prefer to pass through the country unobserved. But those leaving the State, when they find that there is a fair prospect of capturing property that can be taken along without impeding their movements, are not so careful to avoid contact with our troops. Even if their attacks be unsuccessful, and they completely fail in any given design, they can continue their march southward without increasing the danger of being intercepted and captured. Only a few weeks ago, at Neosho, our pickets were fired into one night, as was supposed, by quite a force of the enemy going south, but as they found that we were not to be surprised, decided to make no further demonstration.

The enemy returning to the State may have either of two objects in view. He may be intending to follow a guerrilla warfare, or he may be intending to concentrate at some point designated, to make a combined movement against some place occupied by a given number of our troops. A combined movement of this kind he made against Lone Jack in Jackson county, Missouri, on the 15th and 16th of last August, resulting in the defeat of our troops with a heavy loss in killed and wounded, and the capture of a section of the Third Indiana Battery.*   We marched day and

* The following casualties at the battle of Lone Jack on the Federal side, I have gathered from official data : Second battalion Missouri State Militia, killed, enlisted men, 4; wounded, officers, 1 ; enlisted men, 5 ; missing, officers, 1 ; enlisted men, 5. Sixth Missouri State Militia, killed, enlisted men, 9 ; wounded, officers, 5 ; enlisted men, 35 ; missing, enlisted men, 17.   Seventh Missouri Volunteer cavalry, killed, officers, 2 ; enlisted men, 19 ; wounded, officers, 3 ; enlisted men, 62 ; missing, enlisted men, 11. Two Companies Seventh Missouri State Militia cavalry, killed, enlisted men, 6 ; wounded, officers, 1; enlisted men, 14 ; missing, enlisted men, 6.   Eighth Missouri State Militia cavalry, killed, enlisted men, 9 ; wounded, officers, 2 : enlisted men, 28; missing,

enlisted men, 4. Third Indiana battery, killed, enlisted men, 5 ; Total killed, officers, 2 ; enlisted men, 51 ; wounded, officers, 13 ; enlisted men, 144, exclusive of the Third Indiana battery ; missing, officers, 1; enlisted men, 43.

Major Emory S. Foster, Seventh Missouri cavalry, who commanded our troops in the engagement, reports that he had about 800 men, and that one-third of this force were killed, wounded and missing. This was one of the most gallant fights of the war, for a small force. The enemy had 2,500 men.

night from Fort Scott to Lone Jack, to reinforce our troops, but when we arrived on the ground we were mortified to learn that the battle had been fought the day before. The enemy under Generals Shelby and Cockrell were still encamped on the field ; but when we came in sight, instead of giving battle, as we anticipated they would after their recent victory, they retreated. It was about six o'clock when we came up, and General Blunt immediately commenced to form his troops in line of battle, as the enemy seemed to be making some kind of hostile movements. I was with Colonel Jewell and General Blunt, and some of his staff were near us. We expected every moment that the enemy were going to open fire upon us, for we could plainly see him coming down the road towards us about half a mile off. We could also see, that when they came to a certain point they seemed to file to their left, which was our right, as we had formed in line. We supposed that they were aiming to turn our right, and General Blunt threw out skirmishers to discover their intentions. Our infantry, consisting of the Ninth and Twelfth regiments from Wisconsin,

which had been put into four-mule Government
wagons at Fort Scott, had just arrived, but it was
now getting dark, and an approaching storm, together
with our ignorance of the topographical condition of
that section, made it impossible to commence an immediate attack. The rain came down in torrents, and
it was soon intensely dark. We quickly discovered,
however, that the road half a mile beyond the head of
our column diverged, coming toward us, and that the
enemy, instead of preparing to make the attack, had
taken the left-hand road at the point of divergence,
and were in full retreat. We moved about cautiously
in the darkness of the night, for the country was badly cut up by ditches or wash-outs, and quite a number
of our ambulances, caissons and artillery wagons got
partially or completely upset, and into positions from
which it required much labor to extricate them. The
trail of the enemy was discovered during the night,
and when the dim light of morning came, our advance was just in sight of the rebel rear guard. But
neither the enemy nor our forces had marched many
miles during the dark rainy night, for we were forming
our squadrons here and there, expecting every moment
to run into the rebel cavalry. The entire force of the
enemy, numbering fully twenty-five hundred men,
had moved around us during the night, and now commenced a hasty retreat towards the southern part of
the State. We pursued them day and night, giving
only a few hours each day to ourselves and to our animals to take food and rest, and struck them with our

cavalry about one hundred miles south of Lone Jack at Coon Creek, in which engagement twenty-six men were killed and wounded in the company to which my brother belonged, and, as I have already stated, he was among the wounded. Captain H. S. Green of the Sixth Kansas cavalry was among the severely wounded while gallantly leading his men. We could not hold the rebel force until the rest of our cavalry, artillery and infantry came up, and this affair practically ended the expedition, though a portion of the cavalry continued the pursuit almost to the southern line of the State.

I have entered somewhat into details because we did some extraordinary marching, and also because I wished to point out how an enemy passing us in small detachments, may form in our rear a formidable army.

The *Fourth* class of the enemy we have to deal with, is his organized or regular forces which we expect to find in our front. Whether we shall seek him or he shall us, it may take the approach of spring, or even summer to decide. In the meantime we shall endeavor to hold our own ground in this section, keep our animals in as good condition as possible, and not permit our arms to rust.

We have very favorable reports from Captain A. C. Spillman of this division, who has been in command of the post at Neosho since Major Foreman left there. Captain Spillman is showing himself to be a very competent and energetic young officer. His scouting parties are active in hunting down bushwhackers, and

in making that section an unsafe and an uncomfortable retreat for them. Colonel Phillips has not only
shown sound judgment in the general management of
his division, but also in the selection of officers for
his staff as confidential advisers, and also other officers of special fitness for special duties. Probably few
officers could be found who would make a better Assistant Adjutant General than Captain William Gallaher, or a better Judge Advocate than Captain Joel
Moody. Of Captain Gallaher I can speak from personal knowledge, as I have known him since I entered
the service.

Colonel William F. Cloud, Second Kansas cavalry,
who is now in command of the District of Southwest Missouri, with head quarters at Springfield, was
at Neosha yesterday, 20th instant, with a detachment
of the 7th Missouri State Militia and one company
of his own regiment, having been on a scout of several
days in search of Livingston's band. If the remainder of General Blunt's division, which separated from
us at Elm Springs, is occupying the country around
Springfield, it would seem Colonel Phillips' division
is now occupying the most advanced position of any
of our troops in the west. It would also seem that he
is holding a more important position, and actually
doing more service than any two brigadier-generals
in General Schofield's department. We have here a
few illustrations of the manner in which meritorious
millitary service is too often regarded. It is thought
by some that General Schofield would prefer to re-

ward with promotion an incapable volunteer officer than a really deserving one. I have heard the remark, that "if he could have a division of troops and review them once a week on a level plain in fair weather, perhaps there are few officers who could shine equally with him, but that as an active field officer, who will acomplish deeds such as to win admiration even from the foe, recent experiences show him to be almost a complete failure." It may be, however, that in the light of just and intelligent criticism, his merit would shine with a brighter lustre than it does with us. In some other field, if he goes to the front, it may not be difficult to inspire his troops with confidence. But there are many who think that for the good of the cause for which we are fighting, he should be removed from this department.

The Cherokee Council, which has been in session several weeks, adjourned on the 22nd, *sine die*. Most of the prominent men of the Nation were present, and made speeches in regard to the passage of certain laws touching the interests of the Cherokee people. One of the most important measures which they have had under discussion, has for its object the abolition of slavery in the Cherokee Nation at an early day. While slavery has for some generations existed in the Cherokee Nation, it has never existed in that form which characterized the institution in the Southern States. The Indians have been with us now upwards of six months, and, from what we have seen, it is doubtless true that slavery of the negroes amongst

them has been only in name. They never act towards
the Indians with that reserve and sign of respect
noticeable when they come into our presence. I am
satisfied that the hardships of slavery amongst the
Indians were never comparable to the hardships of
slavery in the cotton-raising States. It would perhaps
be difficult to impress any negro with the idea that
there is as great a distance between him and an Indian
as there is between him and a white man. In some
respects I think myself that there is very little difference, particularly in matters involving social status.
The possibilities of a negro here are probably very
nearly, if not quite, equal to the possibilities of the
Indian, as far as intellectual force is concerned. And
from my own observations I believe that they are, as a
race, more able to stand contact with what we call
high civilization, than the Indians. When I traveled
over several of the cotton-raising States, a year before
the war commenced, from a good many inquiries which
I made, I became convinced that the degrading, and in
many instances even hard life of slavery, had not perceptibly diminished the reproductive powers of the
negroes. Careful inquiries might, however, show, in
certain sections, where both sexes have been worked
very hard on the plantations, that their reproductive
powers have perceptibly diminished. Though it has
been but a few centuries since they were brought to
this Continent, yet when we contrast their peculiar
traits of character with those of the Indian, we are
sure to be led to the conclusion that they will exist as

a distinct race among us, after the Indian shall have disappeared, and shall only be referred to in history as an extinct race. It will probably not be many generations before we shall be contriving means, not how to kill off the Indians, but how to preserve the few which are left. Even should the fifteen to twenty thousand Cherokees amalgamate with the whites, it is not likely that, in the course of a dozen generations, there would be more than a slight trace of Indian blood in their descendants. Amalgamation has already taken place rather extensively, as our Indians here plainly show. Indeed, the half-breeds and quarter-bloods form a considerable part of the population of the Nation. But they are, I have been informed, mostly the offspring of polygamous marriages and unions, such as would not be sanctioned amongst us. We know very well that since this country was first settled by Europeans, traders and adventurers have lived amongst the Indians, and it seems that, by forming temporary unions, and sometimes lasting ones, with the native women, they gain certain rights and privileges that are not accorded to those who will not enter into such alliances. Many of the Cherokee women have very good features, and white men who desire to get wived may perhaps, often be congratulated upon their choice, We therefore frequently see amongst these "half-breeds," "quarter-bloods," &c., men of much intelligence and force of character. It is not unusual, however, for them to display the adventurous spirit of their white fathers, and the fierceness of their native mothers. But these people are capable of making great advances in civilization, before their veins shall have been drained of the last drop of Indian blood.

CHAPTER VII.

The Indian Division moves to Pineville, Mo—Remarks on the
physical aspect of the country and its resources—Few depredations committed considering the general character and
condition of the refugee camp-followers—The President's
Emancipation Proclamation—A good many officers and
soldiers opposed to it—It is a military necessity—It is just
and is warmly commended—The Government will soon have
colored troops in the field—Colonel Phillips' brother wounded
—Colonel Judson's brigade at Mount Vernon—The Indian
division marches to Bentonville, Arkansas—Description of
the country—Rebel prisoners sent to Springfield—They were
brought in by loyal Arkansas troops—A meteor of great
brightnsss observed—Reflections on sidereal worlds and
meteoric displays—The Indian Delegation go to Washington.

THE Indian division struck tents at Scott's Mills and
marched leisurely up the Cowskin river about twenty
miles, and encamped near Pineville, the county seat
of McDonald county, on the 21st of February. We
were several days marching this distance, because, as I
suppose, Colonel Phillips wishes to move at his leisure
to those localities where our animals can be most easily
foraged until spring shall have advanced far enough to
justify a forward movement. As we are to go from
here to Bentonville, Benton county, Arkansas, in a few
days, we are now doubtless taking the first steps

10

towards entering upon the spring campaign.   Our
soldiers seem delighted that we are to turn our faces
to the South, and that we are to re-occupy the section
from which we were withdrawn the first of the year.

This is not much of an agricultural region, as there
is not much soil fit for cultivation, except along the
river bottoms. The Cowskin or Elk river, which flows
in a westerly course, nearly through the centre of the
county, is not perceptibly smaller here than at Scott's
Mills. It differs from our Kansas rivers in this respect,
that it discharges a large volume of water the year round,
while they almost dry up during the summer months
of dry seasons.   With some attention given to its
improvement for navigation, light draft steamers
might run on it between this point and Grand River
several months of the year.   It flows over a gravelly
bottom, and is as clear as a crystal, being fed by per-
petual springs.   Water-power mills have been constructed upon it wherever required.   In this vicinity,
and for ten or fifteen miles above here, a number
of saw mills were in operation before the war, making
lumber. This is the only county in southwest Missouri
in which there are any pine forests.   Hence, therefore,
all the pine lumber used for building and other purposes, in the counties north and east of this, for a
distance of sixty to seventy-five miles, was furnished
by this section. It is quite different from the white
pine shipped from the north, and used in the towns
along the Missouri river and in Kansas. It is known
as yellow pine, and is very heavy, containing large

quantities of resin or pitch. A piece of it lighted
will burn like a torch, to such an extent is it saturated
with the oil of turpentine. Before the war there was
also manufactured in this region considerable tar or
pitch, obtained from this yellow pine. It was used
altogether by the people of south west Missouri and
Arkansas in lubricating the wooden axles of their old-
fashioned wagons. The people of this section do not
use for lubricating purposes, oil, tallow or axle grease,
as we do on our wagons, Perhaps tar would not be
as suitable for iron axles, such as are used in the army
wagon.

From all that I have seen of this county, I think it
is too poor to ever attract to it a very large number
of immigrants. It is possible, however, but not
probable, that these rocky hills contain hidden treas-
ures of immense value, of which we know nothing at
present. I can see how it is possible to utilize the
hilly and poor upland regions to some extent. They
are mostly covered with fine timber, and in the spring,
summer and autumn months, with a fine growth of
wild grass. When all the land which is fit to cultivate along the streams is taken up, large flocks of sheep
and goats and herds of cattle can be pastured during
half the year, at little expense, on the hills and
uplands. But before people can be induced to come
here and adopt such rigid economy, the fertile plains
of Kansas and the richer portions of this State, will
be densely populated.

In some sections of the country now, the destruction

of forests, in getting timber for various economical purposes, is more rapid than their growth. Their destruction must become even more marked, as the population of the country increases and its resources are steadily developed. The time is therefore coming when the forests on these hills will be quite an item of commerce to this section, and a source of profit to the owners.

Out of the great number of fine springs in this section, whose clear cold water is a luxury, particularly during the summer months, it is possible that some of them may possess medicinal properties, which will make them places of public resort, and temporary abodes for invalids from all parts of the world.

As no large body of our troops have been in this vicinity since last autumn, and as we have no troops stationed in this county at all, a good many rebels have returned from the southern army and from Texas and southern Arkansas, and have been living at their homes nearly all winter. Since we came here, some of them have come into our lines and taken the oath of allegiance to the Government, and others have either gone South, or remain in the country endeavoring to avoid capture by our troops. Only a few weeks ago a party of a dozen or so rebels in this vicinity, sent a message to the commanding officer at Neosho that they were willing to come in and surrender and take the oath, but when a detachment of our troops came down here to receive them, they were not found. It is reported that they had some fears of our Indian soldiers,

and went to Mount Vernon to give themselves up to
the proper authorities. From all that I can hear, I
have no doubt but that Colonel Phillips' firmness, tempered with moderation, has had much to do in induc-
ing those who have recently been in arms against the
Government, yet who have realized their mistake and
feel somwhat friendly inclined towards us, to come in
and renew their allegiance to the old flag. Though
he has had a mixed command of Indians and white
men, which probably few officers would be able to
manage creditably, yet he has kept his soldiers under
perfect control, so perfect, indeed, that we nowhere
hear of houses burned, or the useless destruction of
property. This is almost remarkable considering the
great number of refugees and camp-followers of every
condition and color and phase of moral character he
has to keep his eyes upon. While we were encamped
at Maysville some colored male refugees who were
caught committing some unauthorized depredations in
the country, were punished by each being compelled
to carry a log of wood, weighing perhaps thirty to forty
pounds, several hours each day for two or three days.
The punishment of those men has had a wholesome
effect in preventing the reckless and indiscriminate
plundering that would surely have followed, had not
our commander been thus prompt in setting his seal of
condemnation upon it. No one can tell to what
length a mass of unorganized and ignorant men would
go, were not some restraint put upon their actions. It
is safe to say, however, that the lives and property of

no class in the vicinity would be safe, and for myself I should not be surprised to hear of them cutting their own throats, were they permitted to follow their own unbridled passions. Colonel Phillips has no doubt carefully considered and foreseen the result which would naturally flow from allowing refugees, camp-followers, or even his own troops, to commit depredations on their own account. When he sends out his forage trains, he sends them under officers who act under specific instructions. Should the officer in charge of a train go outside of his instructions, and take any property or permit it to be taken by the men under him, with the view of applying it to private use, and complaint be made to headquarters, Colonel Phillips would have him immediatly Court-martialed, and if found guilty of the charges preferred against him, he would be dismissed the service. But while he is prompt in repressing acts that would tend to reflect upon our arms, he is not accused of acting, in any case, hastly and without sufficient cause. I am sure that it cannot be said years hence, when the war is over, that Colonel Phillips, with perfect indifference, permitted the Federal troops under him to rob the women of this section of their jewelry and other trinkets. But should the spirit of justice and moderation that have guided his action, since he assumed command of this division, continue to guide his future movements, and should he be spared a full measure of years, and return to this section, the people will doubtless welcome him with grateful hearts, and point to him as a Federal commander whose military and private life reflected luster upon the cause which he represented.

The President's Emancipation Proclamation, which went into effect on the first of January, and the prospect of immediately arming the freedmen to fight the enemy, their late masters, are just beginning to be warmly discussed by officers and soldiers and citizens. We hear from Neosho and other sections of the State, that returned rebels and many democrats regard these new measures of the Government with a good deal of bitterness, and predict that they will weaken our cause throughout the country. They pretend to think that it would be a great disgrace to the Government to permit negro soldiers to go into the field and fight by the side of white soldiers of the Union armies. But these guardians of propriety and advisers of the Government, see no objection to the negroes of the South raising supplies for the rebel armies, building their fortifications, acting as servants for officers, and in contributing in various ways, directly and indirectly, to strengthening the backbone of the Confederacy. They wish to see the Government compel the negroes to continue forging the chains intended to keep them bound in slavery for ever. Even some of our officers and soldiers seem to think that nothing but evil can come out of these measures, and denounce President Lincoln for inaugurating them. They understand very little about how difficult it is to resist the progressive spirit of our time, and would ignore the fact that the war has forced the Government to adopt certain

measures which it was not desirous of adopting at the
beginning.   They like to repeat with some emphasis
that they did not enter the service of the Government
for the purpose of abolishing slavery, but for the purpose of saving the Union.   And this general statement now being made by many in the army, I think
represents their true sentiments.   Had they known that
the war would have so soon brought about the abolition of slavery, a great many men now in the service
would probably never have enlisted.   But I think that
those who take this view of the matter, occupy a very
inconsistent position.   We might ask, would they
keep a portion of our army busy returning runaway
slaves to their rebel masters?   Or would they have
large pastures or mess houses to keep all the slaves in
that run away from their masters and come into our
lines?   Or would they carefully investigate each case
to ascertain to whom the man, woman or child belonged, and then put a tag around the individual's
neck so that he could be returned to the proper owner
when the war is over.   To my mind any other position
than that taken by the Government would not only be
absurd, but impractible.   The rebels brought on the
war, and that their leaders were too short sighted to
foresee the results is now plain to every one.   They
must make the best of their own mistake.   They
gloried in being blind to the probable future destiny
of slavery.   While the war was not at first ostensibly
carried on by the Government for the purpose of abolishing slavery, matters have now taken such a turn

that the freedom of the slaves has become a public necessity. Though perhaps most of our people will temporarily deplore the necessity, there are others, a large minority too, who will hail this opportunity which the Government has, of wiping out a national crime, with delight. It is a great victory for the latter class,—a victory that many never dreamed of realizing during their lives. This class shall no longer be considered a contemptible minority of fanatics and disturbers of the peace, because we have advocated that all men should have equal rights, to life, liberty and the pursuit to happiness. In the future history of the Republic those noble men of this generation, who have stood firm against great odds in advocating the abolition of slavery, will be regarded as among the saviors of the country. The taunts, and insults, and sacrifices which they have endured, have not counted for nothing. The judicial murder of John Brown will make him a martyr to freedom to the future generations of this country; and his name is already woven into a war song, which is sung throughout all our armies.

And now the slaves are going to help pay the price of their freedom by supporting the strong arms of their deliverers, instead of being a burden to them. How much better this is than if they do nothing, for their descendants can then say with conscious pride, "our fathers, by their manhood and valor, and by their blood and sacrifices, contributed to our freedom." It would be unnatural for the late slaves to remain idle in this great conflict. Now is their time to striκe, and they will not fail to do it. We have already heard that a colored regiment is being organized in Kansas from the negro refugees from Missouri and Arkansas. If properly officered I have no doubt that they will march to the front with firm steps and brave hearts, and meet the enemy like men who are conscious that they are fighting for their liberty and their lives.

Lieutenant Maxwell Phillips, of the Third Indian regiment, was wounded in a skimish with bushwhackers on Pea Ridge a few days ago. Though a brother of the Colonel, he has had to share equally with other officers the dangers and hardships of the field. His wound is quite serious, though it is not thought that with careful attention, it will prove mortal. He has been sent to Neosho in an ambulance; but will probably soon be taken to Kansas to stay until he recovers. He has been an active and efficient officer during the winter, and this division cannot well afford to lose his services.

Colonel Judson's brigade is encamped at Mt. Vernon, about thirty miles west of Springfield. The cavalry is obliged to keep constantly moving in order to find sufficient forage for the animals. The troops in the vicinity of Springfield do not seem to be making any preparations for an active spring campaign into that section of Arkansas occupied by the enemy. I should like to hear of our victorious troops of last winter carrying their arms into the ranks of the enemy, instead of spending the season in inactivity along the border counties of southern Missouri.

From near Pineville, Missouri, we marched to Water's Mills, about three miles north of Bentonville, Arkansas. Nothing occurred on the march worth mentioning, except that the country we passed over was rough and hilly, as in the vicinity of Pineville. We could see the pine forests on the distant hills, but there were none directly on our road. Our advance guard saw several flocks of wild turkeys. There are great numbers of them in a part of the region that we passed over, for it is very thinly settled with a house here and there, miles apart. And from what I saw I think that the acorn-bearing oaks must have produced immense quantities of acorns last year, thus furnishing abundant food for the wild turkeys and pigeons of this section. We encamped at Water's Mills only a few days, and moved to Bentonville on the 27th of February. We shall probably stay here several weeks. Bentonville is a small town, and perhaps never contained a population of more than three or four hundred. For agricultural purposes this county is even poorer than McDonald county, Missouri. Considerable tobacco, however, was raised on the small cultivated tracts before the war. The hills around here are not quite so rugged as along Elk river and Sugar Creek some twenty miles northeast of us.

Yesterday morning, March 1st, Colonel Phillips sent a scout in the direction of White river, almost east of this place, for the purpose of discovering a party of rebels reported to have been seen in that vicinity a few days ago; but it returned about midnight without having found them. Our cavalry will probably be kept busy for awhile in endeavoring to free this section from bushwhackers, for they have had almost full sway since we passed through here last October, just before the battle of Old Fort Wayne. When we came here, only three days ago, the dust raised by their horses' heels had scarcely settled. As a general thing the bush-whackers in this section are mounted upon fine ani-mals, and if they get the start of us beyond the range of our Sharp's carbines, we are rarely able to over take them. In the battalion of the Sixth Kansas cavalry there are some good horses, and in a chase a trooper may now and then be able to dash ahead of his com-rades and bring down his enemy by a well directed shot from his carbine or army revolver. But the animals upon which the Indians are mounted are mostly ponies, and of course not conspicuous for fleet-ness as compared with some of our more carefully bred horses. For many years before the war the horse fan-ciers of Missouri delighted to trace the genealogies of their horses back to the celebrated fine stock of Kentucky. The Indian ponies, however, are very hardy, and stand the service remarkably well. An Indian looks awkward seated upon one of our fine cavalry horses, so thoroughly have Indians and ponies become associated in our minds together.

A portion of the first Arkansas cavalry stationed at Fayetteville, twenty-five miles south of this place, brought in yesterday about thirty rebel prisoners, recently captured in the direction of Van Buren.

They are to be sent to Springfield, Missouri, in a few days, as we have no facilities for holding prisoners of war in safety. As all the available men of this division are required for active service in the field, none of them can well be spared for guarding prisoners, even temporarily. The military prisons north are the proper places for such of the enemy as we capture, instead of marching them from station to station with us.

The turning over of these prisoners to Colonel Phillips by the loyal Arkansas troops is noted with much satisfaction, for I remarked several months ago that there were enough Union men in northwestern Arkansas, if organized into regiments and battalions, to contribute largely in holding this section. The First regiment of Arkansas cavalry, commanded by Colonel M. La Rue Harrison, has now nearly completed its organization, and most of the men have received their arms, bright new uniforms and equipments. It is reported that some of the men were conscripts in the rebel army, and no doubt met us on the field at Prairie Grove. But that they have voluntarily come in and enlisted in the Union army, is all the evidence of loyalty that we require. Since they have thrown off their butter-nut clothing and put on the Federal blue uniform they look much improved in personal appearance, and no doubt will make good soldiers, and if they hold Fayetteville, their valor will probably be tested before the summer shall have ended

It is now a settled fact that we shall move into the Cherokee Nation in a few weeks, and then these Arkansas troops at Fayetteville will be much isolated, unless, however, some of the troops about Springfield shall move southwest in this direction. It is the intention to immediately commence the construction of some sort of fortifications at Fayetteville. If this intention is carried into effect it will enable the troops there to temporarily repel any force of the enemy likely to be brought against them. But the works about to be constructed would not enable Colonel Harrison to stand a siege of many days, unless he is better provisioned and supplied with water than is probable.

Last night (2d), about half past nine o'clock, an unusually bright meteor shot across the sky from the northeast to the southwest. It was so bright that it seemed to almost cast a shadow, and to illuminate our camp. It left a track for quite a distance through the atmosphere, which must have lasted for several seconds. Several soldiers a few yards distant, who had not yet retired, but who were standing about their camp fire, talking over their adventures and fighting some of their battles over, also saw it. It changed their conversation and the current of their thoughts. I caught some of their remarks in regard to it. They thought it a strange phenomenon, as it was so much brighter than ordinary meteors, and wondered if it had any significance in relation to our future movements. One of the party was able to recall to his mind that just before some important event in his life, a great storm and extraordinary thunder and lightning had occurred, or the sky had presented a peculiar and

unusual appearance. There are many people yet who
believe that natural phenomena of this kind have
special reference to human affairs, to such an extent
are their minds unemancipated from the gross and ir-
rational errors of less enlightened times. Many will
remember that those who are always looking for signs
of some extraordinary future event, referred, almost
with delight, to the great comet of 1858, as foreboding
war. It was once thought by our ancestors, and is
still thought by some uncivilized races, that eclipses of
the sun and moon had some connection with the affairs
of men; but we have got past that, and regard the
notion as absurd. It is likewise absurd to suppose
that a comet in the heavens, or a meteor passing
through our atmosphere, has any connection with
human affairs. To all inquiring minds, extraordinary
natural phenomena have always been a stimulus to investigation. The beauties of the heavens on a clear
night are fascinating studies not only for the astrono-
mer, but also for many who have had very little scientific training. In the southern heavens, during the
earlier part of the night, the Constellation Orion and
the Great Dog (Canis Major) are conspicuous objects
of interest. Sirius, in the latter Constellation, is the
brightest star in the heavens, and has guided the
actions of men in war and in peace, long before the
dawn of written history. When alone admiring those
far off worlds of the universe, to us mere scintillating
points—what strange thoughts come rushing through
the mind. If they are suns, as we are taught, like our

sun, have they planets revolving around them like the planets that revolve around our sun? And if they thus have their systems of planets and satellites revolving around them, are any of those planets inhabited by beings something like those on this earth? But the nightly procession of the Constellations across the heavens will continue eternally, and we shall get no answer to our questions.

On the 3rd the Indian Delegation left for Washington on business pertaining to their own interests. While they have no representative in Congress, the Cherokees, Creeks, &c., deem it expedient to keep at the Capitol of our Government during the Sessions of Congress, representatives to confer with the authorities, and to prepare such measures as it may be thought desirable to bring before Congress. Not a year passes that Congress is not called upon to pass certain laws in regard to the affairs of most of the Indian tribes. Their forms of government are simple, but as we have to deal with each separate tribe as an independent nation, the department of Indian Affairs is getting to be quite complicated. The Government must listen to the complaint of each tribe, with a patient ear, investigate the alleged cause of complaint in each case, and as far as possible, under treaty stipulations remove every cause of irritation.

CHAPTER VIII.

Colonel Phillips invited to address a Mass Meeting of the Union
Citizens of Northwestern Arkansas, at Fayetteville—The great
difficulty in getting Forage—A Scouting Party returns from
Van Buren—The Indian Division encamped on the edge of the
Battle Field of Pea Ridge —An account of the Battle from data
collected on the Field and from Eye Witnesses—Rebel raid
on Neosho and Capture of Negroes—A Deserter from the
Enemy gives Position and strength of their forces—The Enemy's wounded from Prairie Grove at Cane Hill still—Great
Mortality among them— Skirmish with Bushwhackers—Arrival of Forage Trains from White River—Horses eat each
others Manes and Tails off—The Small-pox among the Indians—Very few of them Vaccinated —Only a few cases among
the White Soldiers—Remarks on the Disease—The Government should stock with Animals to furnish Vaccine Virus for
the Army.

On the morning of March 4th, Colonel Phillips,
with an escort of one hundred men, set out for Fayetteville. The Union citizens of Washington county,
have called a mass meeting to be held at that place,
and as that county is in his district, have invited him
to be present, and to address them on current issues,
and concerning their future prospects. Of course I
have no means of knowing what advice he will give
them, but it is easy to imagine that he will advise

11

tnem to enroll every able-bodied loyal man in defence of their homes, to be vigilant and take every precaution against surprise by the enemy, to see to it that the troops shall not display a spirit of lawlessness in any section in which they may be operating, and lastly that the citizens who are in sympathy with the Government shall, as far as practicable, co-operate with the troops. While I do not know anything about the Colonel as a public speaker, I do know that he is able to express his thoughts with ease and elegance upon paper, for he was for a number of years, before the war, a staff correspondent of the New York *Tribune* in Kansas, and wrote the first History of Kansas under the territorial *regime*. I do not know that we have a more forcible writer in the State, and if he keeps his official garments clean, and gets through the war alive, and returns to Kansas, I cannot see why he should not be one of our leading men, and why the people should not feel proud of honoring him with the highest position within their gift. Though a man's present conduct and character may be such as to win our admiration, and justify us in speaking of his prospective bright future; yet in these times, when there is so much tripping among great men, it is hardly safe to draw such a future picture of a man as his present career would seem to warrant. He may or he may not follow our imaginary paths, and obstacles may be thrown in his way which no one can foresee. Though it is unquestionably the duty of every officer and soldier in our armies. to work earnestly and faithfully, until we shall compel the last man of the enemy to lay down his arms, and return to his allegiance to the Government, yet we know that already, during the progress of the war, there have been instances in which officers through jealousy, and to break down the reputations of their colleagues, have failed to co-operate with them, thus causing a useless and criminal destruction of the lives of our troops, and a prolonging of the contest. So it may be that obstacles will be interposed to prevent the deserved promotion of Colonel Phillips.

It is getting to be more difficult every day to find sufficient forage for our animals. They are really beginning to feel the pinch of hunger, and I fear will be much reduced in condition before spring opens, so that they can live by grazing. Our forage trains are sent almost two days march from camp, and then frequently return with most of the wagons empty or only partly filled with wheat straw. This, under ordinary circumstances, we use for bedding for our animals, but now we are obliged to use it largely as a substitute for hay and fodder. We cannot understand why we are not able to get all the corn and oats from Kansas that may be required for the command, for we hear that great quantities have been contracted for and are stored at Fort Scott. If our animals are permitted to run down in flesh and to become weak, we shall be obliged to content ourselves with less aggressiveness. It is possible, however, that before we shall have reached our usual radius of fifteen to twenty miles, some neighborhood will be found that can furnish us corn, oats, hay and straw for several weeks.

A scouting party from this division has just returned
from Van Buren *via* Fayetteville, having been absent
about a week. While they were in the vicinity of
Van Buren, Captain Fred Crafts, the commanding
officer of the detachment, sent a spy into Fort Smith,
who returned and reported that the enemy had only
about three hundred men stationed there. It is therefore evident that we have no organized enemy of much
consequence directly in our front for at least one hundred
miles south of us. Since our expedition to Van Buren
last December, the rebel authorities have not ventured
to keep a regular station north of the Arkansas river.
After an army becomes so demoralized as were General
Hindman's forces last winter, it takes some time to
reorganize it for effective operations. Unless the
enemy receives reinforcements from east of the Mississippi, which is not at all likely at present, I think
it will be impossible for him to organize another such
an army as that which he had at Prairie Grove. It
looks now as if the enemy would require all his available forces in the west for the defense of Vicksburg,
which is being invested by our forces under General
Grant. It would probably be difficult for the enemy
there to either receive reinforcements from the west
or to send out troops to the west, so tight are our lines
being drawn around them.

One year ago to day, the 6th, the battle known as
"Pea Ridge" commenced on this very ground. On
the 6th the enemy, under General Van Dorn, attacked
General Sigel's division at this place, and he retreated,

contesting every inch of ground, until he formed a
junction with the other divisions of our army under
the command of General S. R. Curtis, twelve miles
northeast of here, between Pea Ridge and Cross Hollows. I have heard it said that General Van Dorn
made the remark, that had his forces attacked General Sigel twenty minutes sooner, he would have captured the entire division of five or six thousand men.
Twenty minutes more would probably have enabled
General Van Dorn to have thrown a strong force between Generals Curtis and Sigel, and to have fought
them separately. A short distance east of this place,
on the line of retreat, in looking over the late scene of
operations, I noticed a number of trees still bearing
marks of shot and shell and small arms. General
Curtis' forces not only drove Sterling Price's army
out of Missouri into Arkansas, attacking it first at
Springfield and then at Sugar Creek, but pursued them
to Fayetteville, twenty miles south of here. Some
sixteen miles south of Fayetteville General Price met
the combined forces of Generals McCulloch, McIntosh
and Pike. General Van Dorn, who had recently been
appointed by the Confederate authorities to the command of the Trans-Mississippi Department, had just
arrived when the rebel forces formed a junction. He
at once assumed command of the combined forces,
numbering about thirty-five thousand men, and some
sixty pieces of light artillery, and marched rapidly to
attack General Curtis. Our cavalry and some light
artillery that were in advance, and had occupied Fay-

etteville, fell back on our infantry as the enemy advanced in force. All our troops, except General Sigel's division, were on the main road leading from Springfield to Fayetteville. His division was on the road leading from Bentonville to Fayetteville, which, as already stated, at this point is about twelve miles west of the Springfield and Fayetteville road. His position was therefore a critical one, and had General Van Dorn succeeding in cutting him off from the main army under General Curtis, he might have been easily beaten, and his division destroyed or compelled to surrender. I have been informed by parties who were with General Sigel on his march from this place, that he was sometimes almost surrounded by the enemy; that during four or five hours, and until he received re-inforcements from General Curtis, he was obliged to fight the enemy in his front, on his flanks and in his rear. But he continued his march, and was able to form a junction late in the afternoon with General Jeff. C. Davis' division, about two miles west of the Springfield road at the west end of Pea Ridge. Our forces, however, were still divided into two separate armies, but in supporting distance of each other. During the night of the 6th, General Van Dorn moved his entire army around to the west of ours, and on the morning of the 7th had his line of battle formed north of us in our rear, thus cutting off any hope of retreat. General Curtis was therefore obliged to make a change of front; that is, his line of battle must now front north instead of south. General Sterling Price's forces occupied the Springfield road directly north of General Curtis' camp, and the divisions of the enemy under Generals McCulloch and McIntosh held positions directly north of General Sigel, some three miles west of Price. On the 7th the battle opened on our right, and raged furiously during the entire day with varying results. When night came our right wing had been driven back nearly a mile, but our left wing, under Generals Sigel and Davis, had defeated the right wing of the enemy, killing Generals McCulloch and McIntosh. During the night of the 7th the enemy's forces formed a junction on the ground held by his left wing, which was a strong position.

By moving around and taking up positions north of our forces, it was evident that the rebel generals felt sure of being able to destroy our army or compel it to surrender. Therefore on the morning of the 8th, at sunrise, the battle was resumed with even greater fierceness. But General Curtis and his division commanders had not been idle during the night in arranging their troops and batteries for the impending struggle. Our left wing, under General Sigel, was first furiously assaulted by the right wing of the enemy, but maintained its position with great firmness. After several hours hard fighting General Sigel ordered into position about thirty pieces of artillery, which, soon getting the range of the enemy's guns, silenced battery after battery. Our infantry then, under cover of our batteries, crept forward, and when within a short distance of the enemy's lines the order was given to charge them. The troops that made this gallant charge were composed of Illinois, Indiana and Missouri regiments. The enemy's right wing was now pressed back in a good deal of confusion. Soon after this fierce contest our right wing forced back with great stubborness the left wing of the enemy. His lines now formed a kind of crescent, with the convex part of it turned toward us, and the horns directed from us, and our right and left wings cross-fired him with terrible effect. General Curtis, quickly seizing the situation, now ordered the charge all along our lines, and in a short time the enemy were completely routed at every point, and fled in great disorder in every direction, leaving their dead upon the field.

The federal losses in killed and wounded during the three days was upwards of twelve hundred men and officers. We did not lose any general officers, while the enemy had two general officers killed,— Brigadier Generals McCulloch and McIntosh. The enemy's losses of enlisted men, killed and wounded, also exceeded ours, besides General Curtis captured nearly a thousand prisoners.

That this sketch might be as accurate as possible, I spent three days last October, when we were encamped on the battle-field of Pea Ridge, in ascertaining the positions of different divisions of the two armies. A gentleman who was with General Curtis during the three day's struggle accompanied us over the field, and was able to point out nearly all the places of interest, and I made memoranda of them; besides, I have recently gone over a part of the field. It was easy to judge where the battle had been fiercest by the number of newly-made graves. At points where considerable numbers of our soldiers were killed, long trenches were dug and the men placed in them side by side, and a head-board placed over each man, giving his name, regiment, or battery. The places pointed out to us as the graves of the rebel dead, indicated that they had been buried in heaps; and we were told by our guide that such was the fact. I did not see a single head-board placed over any of their graves, although General Curtis gave General Van Dorn permission to bury his dead; and rebel-burying parties were on the field several days under a flag of truce.

About a quarter of a mile north of Elk Horn tavern, on the brow of a hill a few yards west of the Springfield and Fayetteville road, I counted thirty-three graves close together, the head-boards showing that the men who fell on that hallowed ground belonged to the Ninth Iowa infantry. Upwards of two miles southwest of Elk Horn tavern, where the battle also raged with great fury, the head-boards showed that the men who had fallen in this locality belonged to the Second, Twelfth and Twenty-fourth regiments Missouri infantry, and Eighth and Twenty-second regiments Indiana infantry, and Thirty-seventh regiment Illinois infantry. At other places on the field the federal dead had been buried in smaller groups than at the points mentioned above. When we were encamped on the battle-field in October, the traces of this great battle still most visible were around Elk Horn tavern. The trees in the orchard and the small undergrowth in the woods near by were much scarred and cut to pieces by small arms and by grape and canister of the two armies.   About half a mile south of Elk Horn, on the west side of the high road, and just north of the large field in which the federal trains were parked, the timber, covering a space of perhaps half a mile square, was dreadfully torn to pieces by shot and shell. I saw trees, probably eighteen inches in diameter, torn and split as if they had been struck by lightning.   The storm from the federal batteries that burst over this part of the field must have been terrific.   It was mostly the work of our batteries on the 7th, after the repulse of General Curtis' right wing around Elk Horn. The federal forces occupying the large field above mentioned, could easily bring their artillery into posi-tion to play upon the heavy-timbered woods.

I have now conducted the reader over the battle-field of Pea Ridge, commencing at this place, pointed out to him the position of our forces, and the points where our brave men fell in greatest numbers.   I hope that before many years shall have elapsed after the war is ended, the country, for whom these noble men offered up their lives, will erect at least two monuments upon the ground where they fell, to commemorate their heroic deeds; and that this ground shall be hallowed to the generations who shall succeed us.   I could not pass this first anniversary upon this field without add-ing a word to the memory of the two hundred patriot soldiers who rest in their graves only a few miles from our camp.* This night no doubt the thoughts of hundreds of those who lost husbands, fathers, brothers or

*The Federal army that fought the battle of Pea Ridge was divided by General Curtis into four divisions, as follows:

The First Divison, commanded by Colonel P. J. Osterhaus, Twelfth Missouri infantry, was composed of the following organizations: Illinois—Twenty-fifth, Thirty-sixth, Thirty-ninth and Forty-fourth regiments of infantry. Missouri—Third, Twelfth and Seventeenth regiments infantry, two battalions Benton Hussars and two batteries, A and B, six guns each, Second regiment light artillery.

Second Division, commanded by Brigadier General A. Asboth, consisted of the following organizations: Missouri—Second and Fifteenth regiments infantry, and Fourth and Fifth regiments of cavalry, and flying battery, six guns, Ohio Second battery light artillery.

Third Division, commanded by General Jeff. C. Davis, consisted of the following organizations: Indiana—Eighth, Eighteenth and twenty-second regiments infantry; Illinois–Thirty-seventh and fifty-ninth regiments infantry; Missouri—First and Ninth regiments cavalry, and Colonel Phelps' regiment of infantry, and two batteries, one of four guns and another of six guns,

Fourth Division, commanded by Colonel Eugene Carr, Third Illinois cavalry, was composed of the following organizations: Iowa—Fourth and Ninth regiments infantry, and Third cavalry, and first and third batteries Light artillery; Illinois—Thirty-fifth-regiment infantry and Third cavalry; Missouri—Twenty-fifth regiment infantry and Bowen's battalion cavalry.

General Sigel commanded the First and Second Divisions, which formed our left wing, General Davis our centre, and Colonel Carr our right wing.

The Federal losses were as follows: First division 144, Second division 119, Third division 329, and Fourth division 701, making a total of 1,351 killed, wounded and missing. The total killed in the four divisions was 203, according to official reports.

sons at the battle of Pea Ridge, turn to this field, and their minds are filled with unspeakable grief on account of the cutting short of the lives of those whom they loved so dearly. Not only will they call to mind this first anniversary of this great battle, but they will likely call to mind each succeeding anniversary of it while their affections last, for the dead heroes buried upon this field. Nor is this all. Hundreds of our brave soldiers who were wounded in this battle, still bear scars and unhealed wounds that will remind them probably of the anniversary of the bloody field of Pea Ridge as long as they live. The ides of March of each succeeding year will bring vividly before their minds the bloody scenes they have passed through on this field. They will recall with great vividness the sufferings from cold and fatigue, and the hopes and fears of those three eventful days. When they recall the charges in which comrades fell by their sides, and of others who were left on the field mortally wounded and in the agonies of death, shadows of sadness will pass over their countenances. Though these brave-hearted men in the discharge of their duties could plunge the cold steel into the enemy, yet their hearts are full of tenderness and affection; and the sufferings of a comrade from having nobly performed his duty, often causes the warm tear to roll down the cheeks of the stern soldier.

Information was received from Neosho this morning (9th) that a force of rebels under Livingston made a raid on that place a few nights ago and captured about twenty

negroes and a number of horses and mules. There was
not much of a skirmish, for the rebel leader did not
venture near where our troops were quartered, and
they did not attack him because he had left before
they had fairly got into position It seems that
guards were not posted upon all the roads leading
into town; or if they were, that they got captured, or
reached the post but a few moments ahead of the
enemy. A couple of soldiers posted on a road several
miles out, by the time they had halted and ascertained
whether the approaching force was friend or foe, would,
if the latter, have few chances of escape, if it were at
night. If Livingston's men are mounted upon as
good horses as they are reported to be, they could
move more rapidly than an Indian guard mounted on
a pony. In a few weeks the Indian soldiers and all the
refugee Indian families will leave Neosho and join us
in the Nation, and then it is the intention to have stationed there several companies of the Missouri State
Militia, who generally have good horses, and will
probably be able at least to hold their own with the
guerrillas of southwest Missouri.

A deserter came into our lines to-day from Colonel
Carroll's Arkansas regiment, which is now stationed
below Van Buren on the Arkansas river. He does
not think that the enemy in that section contemplates
an immediate movement northward, as they have not
a force sufficiently strong to meet our troops in the
open field. Nearly all the rebel troops in Arkansas,
he thinks, are in the vicinity of Little Rock, at any

rate, that there is not a large force in the western part
of the State.   We have no reason to doubt this latter
part of his statement, for our reconnoitering parties
are ever now and then returning from the vicinity of
Van Buren, and in each instance report no enemy in
force.   Captain John Rogers, of the battalion Sixth
Kansas cavalry, with a detachment of two hundred
men, returned yesterday evening (13th) from beyond
Cane Hill, in the Boston Mountains, and reports having met with no signs of the enemy.   He saw, however, at Cane Hill a large number of the rebel wounded that were taken to that place last December from
the battle-field of Prairie Grove.   We have heard that
a large percentage of the rebel wounded—probably
nearly as many as General Hindman left on the field
—have died in the hospitals there during the past
winter.   It may be that the mortality is not unusually
high for the number wounded.   If they have been
furnished with ample medical supplies and attention,
and sufficient fuel, covering and clothing, one would
naturally think that the winter would be more favorable for the healing of gunshot wounds than the
warm weather of summer.   It has now been upwards
of three months since the battle of Prairie Grove, and
it is a little surprising that the rebel authorities should
not have removed all their wounded to Fort Smith or
to some point within their lines, by this time

A detachment of about twenty-five men from this
division had a fight yesterday, some fifteen miles from
camp, with a party of bushwhackers, and killed six of

them. Two of our soldiers were wounded. This was the liveliest skirmish our foraging parties have had for several weeks.

Two companies of the Third Indian regiment came in this evening from Maysville, where they have been stationed for some time. That place is now abandoned, and the small fort that was constructed there during the winter, as a temporary defence, has been destroyed. As we exhausted that section of forage and commissary supplies before leaving it, it will now hardly afford any special attractions for guerrillas to return to until spring shall bring grass sufficient for grazing purposes.

This evening (14th) a train of upwards of one hundred wagons came in, loaded principally with corn. The corn and forage thus brought in was obtained in the vicinity of White River, east of here, and the expedition has been absent five days. This forage will afford great relief to many of our hungry animals that have been rapidly losing flesh of late on account of short rations. In a good many instances, horses that have been fastened to young trees, have gnawed the bark therefrom as high as they could reach, so keenly have they felt the pinch of hunger. I have seen some horses, too, that have even lost their manes and tails by their fellows chewing them in the absence of something more nutritious. When the demands of the appetite are not satisfied, men as well as animals resort to almost anything they can chew for food.

Several days ago one or two members of a refugee

family were reported to be down with the smallpox From inquiries which have been made to-day, it appears that quite a number of other cases have broken out among the refugees and Indian soldiers here.   A small pox hospital has been established about half a mile outside the limits of our camp, where all small-pox patients are taken as soon as their disease has been determined.   Three or four patients have already died, and fears are expressed that the disease will spread considerably among the Indians, as it does not appear that many of them have been vaccinated.   It may also take off some of our white soldiers, though I do not find that any of them are in the hospital yet. They have generally been vaccinated within the last two or three years, so that they do not manifest much dread of the disease.   It is not likely, however, that if some of their friends should be taken to the Small-pox Hospital, they would display much affection for them for a month or so.   Though the white soldiers of Captain Hopkins' battery and the battalion of the Sixth Kansas Cavalry camp near together, yet there can be very little isolation, as by guard and other duties white and Indian soldiers are daily thrown together.   If the disease shows a tendency to spread, and to assume a serious form with a high percentage of mortality, Colonel Phillips will not probably permit the air of our camp to become much infected with its germs, before moving to another locality.

This is surely a strange enemy to attack our army. Silently as Apollo's arrows it comes to those who are not armed against it, and the chances are somewhat less than one in ten of its taking off its victim. We are thus reminded that we should not only guard against attacks from the visible foe whom we seek, but that we should also guard against attacks from the invisible foe whom we do not seek, and which may be lurking in the very air we breathe. An invisible portion of the small-pox virus introduced into the blood of a person who has never been vaccinated, nor had the smallpox, sets up a kind of fermentation, which goes on until it has entirely changed the molecular constitution of the blood, and in some way or other affects all the tissues of the body; or invisible germs, floating in the air and inhaled into the lungs, produce similar changes. But that we are able by vaccination to ward off, in a great measure, the dangers from this loathsome disease, is surely a great blessing. Were it not that many of us feel shielded from its attack, we should not likely be moving about here daily with such perfect composure of mind while others are suffering from its effects only a few hundred yards off.

There are some who have a dread of vaccination, and I have no doubt that there is often just cause for such dread, for there have been many instances in which bad results have come from using virus obtained from unhealthy persons or animals. The very greatest caution should therefore be exercised in regard to obtaining the virus from only perfectly healthy persons or animals. Speaking not as a medical practitioner,

12

but as I think from a common-sense point of view, I should say that the virus intended for use, ought not be obtained from anyone whose blood has been poisoned by immoral practices, or anyone having a consumptive or scrofulous diathesis, or anyone either of whose parents or grandparents died of consumption or were scrofulous. Anyone who would ignorantly or willfully trifle with the lives and future health of his fellows, is a criminal and justly deserves our execrations. It is possible, however, even after one has used his most deliberate judgment, to be sometimes mistaken or deceived. From such information as we have on the subject, I think it is generally regarded as safest to use the virus obtained from the cow. If animals were raised for this special purpose, kept isolated and in good condition, and properly inspected, then there should be only an infinitesimal danger in using the virus obtained from them. If individual enterprise cannot find it renumerative enough to go to this trouble, I think that, in time of war, the Government would not go outside of its legitimate functions to stock a farm or farms with animals, for the purpose of furnishing virus for its soldiers and sailors and citizen employes.

Our Medical department will, no doubt, after proper inquiries, be able to vaccinate most of those who have not already been recently vaccinated, and thus do much to prevent the spread of the disease. The approach of spring and a warmer season, will also, perhaps, be more favorable towards stamping it out.

CHAPTER IX.

The march to Camp Moonlight—Captain Mefford, Sixth Kansas
Cavalry, defeats Livingston's band—Grass sufficient for grazing purposes about Fort Gibson—Supply train reinforced—
A bushwhacker killed near camp—The people should be
better informed by proclamation of the Federal purposes—
Officers for the Fourth and Fifth Indian regiments report to
Colonel Phillips—No such regiments exist—Criticisms concerning the matter—Near Rhea's Mills again—Two loyal Arkansas regiments organized—After a battle the people show
on which side their sympathies are by their expressions—The
people of a less haughty spirit than in Missouri—Reconnoissance returned from Dutch Mills—Women and children raise
their own foodstuffs—The soldiers exchange their surplus
rations for butter, eggs, &c—The Army ration—A party of
Union men arrive from Texas—They were hunted by the
enemy with blood hounds.

On the morning of the 17th of March we struck
tents, left Bentonville, and marched fifteen miles southwest to Big Springs, at the head of Flint Creek. This
is a more desirable section than around Bentonville.
The spring here is one of the finest in Northwestern
Arkansas, and furnishes an abundance of excellent
water for ourselves and animals. It arises out of the
earth almost like a fountain, and runs off in a strong,
swift current. This would be a delightful spot for a

village, for, at a small cost the water from this spring could be conducted through pipes into the houses for the convenience of families. Our camp is called Camp Moonlight, in honor of Colonel Thomas Moonlight, of the Eleventh Kansas infantry, who was General Blunt's Chief of Staff during the campaign in this section last fall. He is a brilliant officer, and, in personal appearance, one of the finest looking officers we had in the division. He is a Scotchman by birth, and is about six feet two inches in height, well proportioned, and his presence, though commanding, is not too stern, and altogether is likely to produce a favorable impression. I remember him during the fall of 1861, as commanding Moonlight's battery, the first light battery raised in Kansas. I think he was also on the staff of General James H. Lane when he marched the Kansas brigade through Missouri to join General Fremont's army at Springfield. No officer has been more active in organizing and fitting out our Kansas troops for the field; nor has any officer been more active in the field than Colonel Moonlight. His sound judgment and counsel no doubt contributed largely to the success of our campaign in this section last winter.

Captain David Mefford, Sixth Kansas cavalry, a few days ago had a skirmish with Livingston's band about sixteen miles north of Neosho, and got three of his men badly wounded, but succeeded in killing and wounding seven of the enemy, and putting the remainder to flight. Captain Mefford is an experienced officer, and a better one could not be selected to deal with Livingston's guerrillas.

Several persons who have just arrived from Fort Gibson report that grass is coming up in sufficient quantities on the Arkansas River and lower Grand River bottoms for grazing purposes. While Indian ponies might live there on the grass now, it will probably be two or three weeks before our cavalry horses can live on wild grass, and perform the service required of them. It is necessary that they should have such strength-giving food as corn and oats, if the cavalry arm of the service is to be very effective. But all the approaching signs of spring increase the anxiety of the Indians to get into the nation. They have not, however, as yet displayed any impatience, but are content to be guided by the judgment of Colonel Phillips. As soon as transportation can be had to remove the Refugee Indian families from Neosho, they will leave that place to join this command in the nation. It is not likely, however, that the transportation will be in readiness before the first of April. And perhaps it would not be advisable for them to leave there at an earlier date, as in this latitude there frequently occurs some severe weather the latter part of March. As the season is always about a week further advanced at Fort Gibson, there will be no unnecessary delay in their removal.

Information was received here yesterday evening that a rebel force of one hundred men were seen the day before in the vicinity of Cane Hill. Colonel

Phillips immediately sent out a detachment of cavalry under Captain Fred Crafts to discover the movements of the enemy, but the force returned here this evening without being able to ascertain anything definite in regard to the enemy. It is not very likely that such a small force would remain many hours at any place within twenty miles of this command. This was probably a scouting party of the enemy sent our from the rebel camp below Van Buren, to discover something if possible in regard to our movements. A detachment of seventy-five men under Captain H. S. Anderson, Third Indian regiment, were sent out to-day to overtake and reinforce the escort to our supply train which left here yesterday morning *en route* to Fort Scott. It appears that Colonel Phillips has information leading him to believe that the rebel force which was seen a few days ago in the vicinity of Cane Hill, has gone north, possibly with the view of attacking our train.

A man was found dead to-day just outside the limits of our camp. Upon investigation the fact was disclosed that he was a bushwhacker, and had been killed the day we arrived here by some of our advance guard. A detail of men were sent out to bury him in the spot where he had fallen. As decomposition had commenced when he was found, no efforts were made to ascertain whether he had any effects about him that would give any information concerning his name and where he lived. While I have no inclination to make a funeral oration over him, yet I will venture to remark that

there is a sad thought connected with his lonely and
obscure grave, for he has fallen in a cause that can
never receive the sympathy of men fighting for justice
and equal rights, without distinction of race or color.
His misguided actions may have resulted, not from
a natural evil and perverse disposition, but from asso-
ciations and connections over which he had no control.
He may not have delighted in shooting our soldiers
from concealed positions, and he may not have fired at
them at all. If, when on the march, our troops see a
man on the highway or in the woods, and he starts to
run and does not stop when they cry "halt!" they are
sure to fire upon him. We are constantly hearing of
men who, after having acted for a while with the enemy,
became tired of the rebellion and returned to their
homes, but were afraid to come in and surrender to
the Federal authorities. We are also told that some
of these men, when our troops come into their neighborhood, take to the woods, but without any hostile intentions towards us, and that they are fed by their
families clandestinely. Lieutenant Masterton of the
Second Indiana battery, was assassinated by just this
class of men when we were encamped near here last
fall. A number of other officers and soldiers of our
division met a similar fate, and we feel that men who
flee from us are our enemies, and not to be trusted.
No doubt many of the people of this section have exaggerated notions of our troops, particularly Kansas
troops and Indians. That the people might not be
kept in ignorance of our purposes and actions, I have

sometimes thought it should not be regarded as exceeding his duty if our military commander should issue a proclamation to the people of the section we occupy, defining our duties, and setting forth the treatment that will be extended to all who may wish to come in and surrender and renew their allegiance to the Government. If such proclamation were made, and some pains taken to have it put into the hands of all the people of this section, I believe that there are many who would seek our protection and friendship, that are now avoiding us. At any rate every opportunity should be given them to return to their allegiance to the Government.

Colonel Phillips, with a detachment of one hundred cavalry, started out to-day in search of another convenient place for pitching our camp. There is very little forage in this vicinity, our troops having well-nigh exhausted the supply when we were encamped near here last fall, before the battle of Cane Hill. When we leave here we shall march to Illinois river, twelve miles south.

To-day, March 23d, a number of officers who have recently been appointed by the Secretary of War to positions in the Fourth and Fifth Indian regiments, reported to Colonel Phillips for duty. As the Fourth and Fifth Indian regiments are purely imaginary organizations, as far as any one here knows, it is difficult to see what duty Colonel Phillips can assign them to. If these gentlemen were anxious to serve the Government at this critical time, the authorities at Washington might have given them permission to go into the Nation to recruit their own companies and regiments; and then as fast as a sufficient number of men were enlisted into each company to entitle it to a company organization, their commissions could have been sent to them.   I do not know what report will be made to higher authorities in regard to the matter, but I feel very sure, from inquiries and general information, that there cannot be enlisted from amongst the loyal portion of the Cherokees, Creeks, and Seminoles, more than enough men to keep the present three Indian regiments up to their maximum strength.   This seems an unusual proceeding, to issue commissions to officers for organizations that do not exist and probably never will exist.   These officers I suspect, from what I have heard, are nearly all relatives or favorities of high officials of the Government, and perhaps not in a single instance has an appointment been made on account of merit, that is, on account of bravery displayed on the field, and ability to handle troops in action.   If the Washington authorities really desired to organize one or more Indian regiments, it would have been very little trouble to have sent out here for a report showing the number of Indians that could probably be enlisted into the service within a specified time.   Colonel Phillips no doubt could make such a report in a few weeks, which would be approximately correct.   If there had been vacancies to fill in the Indian regiments, it would, in my opinion, be much more just on the part of the Government to have filled them by appointments from lists of non-commissioned officers of regiments that have seen service on the border. It is not very pleasant to those who have been in active service since early in the war, to have their services unrecognized, and to see green and untried men given important appointments by their sides and over them. Nearly all the orderly sergeants of the three Indian regiments of this division, are white men, appointed from Kansas regiments, and should be promoted to fill any vacancies that may occur in their respective regiments. In the event of raising another Indian regiment or battalion, or in the case of Colored regiments which are now being organized, it would be quite easy for the Department Commander to call on commanding officers of regiments to furnish him lists of non-commissioned officers and privates whose general intelligence, bravery, and knowledge of a particular arm of the service, would make them efficient and useful officers in the event of promotion. Out of these lists should be selected the best qualified and most deserving, who should be recommended to the Secretary of War, or appointing power, for promotion. Such a plan, however, is not likely to be adopted at present. There are too many who, if they must enter the service, must be furnished with honorable positions without regard to fitness to fill them. The class of men, too, who receive important appointments without having first earned them by service in the field or showing some special qualifications, generally have influence enough to get detailed on special duties where there is very little danger from the enemy's bullets. These officers here without commands will probably draw their salaries for a few months, or until the facts are reported to the War Department that there are no men enlisted for the Fourth and Fifth Indian regiments, all the same as if they were fighting, skirmishing and marching every day.

The Indian division left Big Springs or Camp Moonlight on the morning of the 24th, and marched to Illinois River twelve miles south. This brings us within ten or twelve miles of Rhea's Mills, where the *Army of the Frontier*, under General Blunt, was encamped during the month of December.

Colonel Phillips has named our camp here Camp Pomeroy, in honor of Senator Pomeroy, of Kansas. Should a Post office be established at this place after the war, it will probably take the name of our present camp.

On this river there are some fine tracts of land, and the farmer is no doubt well rewarded for his labor The opening of spring, and the fact that our army was all over this section last fall and the early winter, will make it difficult to obtain forage, except in very small quantities, for our animals. But we are gradually moving south with a prospect of holding the country. Two loyal Arkansas regiments belonging to Colonel Phillips' division are stationed at Fayetteville, fifteen miles east of us, and co-operation of the two forces in case of emergency would not be difficult.

A report comes from St. Louis that General Curtis

has been removed from the command of the Department of Missouri for some cause not yet fully known to the public. It is suggested, however, that his removal has been brought about because he cannot give satisfaction to the two political factions in Missouri. The people of Missouri and Kansas, I think, as a general thing, feel kindly towards General Curtis since he won the great battle of Pea Ridge, and saved those States from invasion by the rebel armies, and are not likely to be hasty in passing judgment upon his alleged short-comings in the administration of his department. We do not want a Commanding General with no decided policy, and who will be continually hampering the movements of troops in the field.

A party of dispatch bearers and mail carries just arrived from Neosho, state that a report came therefrom Springfield, that General Hunter has captured Charleston, S. C., after very hard fighting. While we should be greatly delighted to hear of the fall of that rebel stronghold, we are not inclined to credit the report as true. It is amusing to notice the effects that good reports and bad reports have upon the countenances of our men. A report like the above circulated through the camp, even though some doubt is felt in regard to its truthfulness, lights up the countenances of every loyal heart. The prospect of the early closing of the war, the thoughts of carrying our victorious arms and banners into all the rebel strongholds, and of the Stars and Stripes floating over all the cities of the South; and the imaginary scenes of returning

home, after having passed through many hardships
and dangers, are enough to make visible smiles play
over their countenances. But let the news of defeat of
any of our great armies in the east reach us, as sometimes happens, and the sunny countenances of our
soldiers change, and a shadow of disappointment min-
gled with stern determination, may be noticed. On
whichever side our sympathies are on any great question, they are generally clearly displayed on all extraordinary occasions of victory or defeat. In marching
across the country just after a great battle has been
fought by any of our armies, and the news of the result of the battle has preceded us, it is generally easy
to judge on which side the sympathies are, of those
whom we meet of the noncombatant class. If they
are rebels they may sometimes, as a matter of policy,
endeavor to put some restraint upon their feelings,
but such restraint does not usually conceal their real
feelings. We can generally tell that there is some
bitterness of feeling behind a sardonic smile.

From what I have seen, I do not believe that there
is so much of that haughty and defiant spirit among
the noncombatant classes of this state, as in Missouri.
This may be due to the fact that there was much less
wealth and luxury here than in Missouri before the
war. We nowhere see in this section farms containing a thousand acres of land in unbroken tracts, and
inclosed with stone or hedge fences, and stocked with
great numbers of horses, mules and cattle, as might
have been seen in most of the western counties of

Missouri a few years ago. The people of Missouri, with
their slave labor and abundance of everything, acted as
if they felt their superiority to the people of any other
section. Though no one desires to humble their proud
spirits, the war will probably teach them a keener
sense of justice than they have hitherto shown towards those who differed with them in regard to
slavery.

A party of seven guerrillas was seen yesterday
evening less than a mile from our camp, but they soon
disappeared in the thick woods. Whether they are
prowling around intent on some mischief, or whether
they have unintentionally come upon us while passing
through the country to some other locality, is not
known. But as the soldiers express it, it will hardly
be safe for them to roost in this vicinity. It is possible that they have been sent by the rebel commanding
officer at Van Buren or Fort Smith, into this section,
for the purpose of ascertaining whether our whole
force is moving south, or only a reconnoitering party.
In a few days the organized forces of the enemy north
of the Arkansas River will find it convenient to retire
to the south bank. There is now no prospect of Colonel Phillip's progress being checked this side of Fort
Gibson.

Yesterday morning (28th) a detachment of thirty
men were sent to Neosho with the mail for the North,
and instructions to the commanding officer at Neosho,
in regard to removing the troops and all the refugee
Indian families from there to the nation. By the time

they will be able to join us, their ponies can live by grazing on the grass of the river bottoms. They will no doubt be delighted beyond expression that the time has come for their return to their homes from their long exile.

Captain N. B. Lucas and Lieutenant W. M. Smalley, of the battalion of the Sixth Kansas cavalry, with about two hundred men, returned last night from Dutch Mills, a small place a few miles west of Cane Hill, and right on the line of Arkansas and the Cherokee Nation. We were sent out two days ago with the view of ascertaining as far as possible any contemplated movements of the enemy, as information had been received here *via* Fayetteville, that a rebel force of a thousand men, under Colonel Carroll, were encamped at Van Buren on the 24th, and were intending to move north on the state line road. From all the information we could get there is no reason to believe that Colonel Carroll's force will make any effort to operate north of the mountains for several weeks. If Colonel M. LaRue Harrison, the commanding officer at Fayetteville, is a good fighter, he should be able to hold that post against three thousand men. He has probably better facilities for keeping himself informed in regard to the movements of the enemy south of him than Colonel Phillips has, for many refugee families are constantly coming into that place from all over the western part of the State. A good many of the families of the men of the two regiments stationed there, have not left their homes. An almost constant communication is therefore kept up between the troops at Fayetteville and such of their families as still remain on their homesteads. The loyal families living at a distance from Fayetteville probably feel such a deep interest in the command to which their male members belong, that doubtless, in many instances, they would spare no effort to convey information to it which may be useful to it in guarding against surprise by the enemy. Many of the women of this section are perfectly at ease in horse-back riding, and in a matter in which they felt great interest, would perhaps not hesitate to perform a journey of several days. But admitting that the wives and daughters of our troops at Fayetteville are disposed to keep them advised of the movements, as far as practicable, where would they get animals to ride. That indeed would be the great difficulty; but I think that very many families, both loyal and disloyal, keep some kind of animals on their premises; blind horses, knock-kneed mules, or even something better, so that they will not do for army service. Very few first-class horses and mules were left in this section after our army moved north last winter.

Arrangements are being made to remove all the sick of this division to Hilterbrand's Mills, about thirty miles west of here, in the Cherokee nation, on the first of April. We know now that we shall move across the line into the Nation in a few days. The peach trees have been in bloom for several days, and the swelling buds on the forest trees are ready to burst, and display their young leaflets, and we see a good many wild flowers of early species by the wayside. Some of our detachments which have just come down from Missouri and Kansas, say that the season is nearly two weeks further advanced here than there. But Spring will not bring that renewed life and activity. of which it is significant, among the people here, that it will North. Of the hundreds of farms all over this region, very few can be cultivated this season, for the fences around most of them have been destroyed, burned as fuel by the armies, and there is nobody left to cultivate them except women and children, cripples and old men. Here and there these classes may find rails enough left to inclose a few acres, and cultivate them, with the assistance of such animals as have not been taken for use in the army. Mothers and daughters who, before the war, never dreamed of having to work in the fields, and who knew nothing of the hardships entailed upon many families by the war, will have to raise their own sustenance in this section this year. Of course in those families where sons are growing up, and are in their teens, the hardships will not fall so heavily upon the female members. The uncertainty of being able to use or to get a just and fair equivalent for what they raise under all these disadvantages, must fill the minds of many with discouragement. Their own necessities, however, prospective want, prompt them to make the best of the situation. We have seen some plowing and preparations for planting and sowing garden stuff; and Colonel Phil-

13

lips has exercised great care in not permitting depredations on the premises of the people, on the line of our march, and in the neigborhood of our camps. We have been obliged to forage on the country during the past winter, but I think, as a general rule, families have been permitted to keep undisturbed their supplies of provisions, such as flour, meal and bacon. The rations issued to this command, with the exception of fresh beef and pork, have all been transported from the North. We have had full rations all winter, for which we are indebted to the untiring and cautious judgment of Colonel Phillips. The army ration is good, substantial food, and is all any man, not a glutton, needs to keep himself in excellent condition. And our men are in excellent condition, and I think it probable, that since they have become inured to the service, they had never enjoyed better health at any time before their enlistments. Each company accumulates quite a surplus of rations every month.. The company commissary sergeant is generally authorized to exchange some of these surplus rations for articles not issued by the Government, as butter, eggs, chickens, &c. Our excellent coffee is in great demand among the people of this section, as many of them have not used the genuine article since the first year of the war. In some families brown corn or wheat has been used as a substitute. Corn coffee is a quite common expression in this section, but the next generation may never hear of it. We sometimes hear the remark, that a cup of "Yankee coffee" will make even a rebel lady smile. To many the flavor of pure coffee is more agreeable than the bouquet of a fine wine. Rebel as well as Union families, do not hesitate to offer their commodities for exchange. Our tea, sugar, molasses, and even salt, may also be exchanged to good advantage by our soldiers, as these articles cannot now be obtained in this section by purchase.

I have generally issued to the regiment to which I belong, from one-fourth to half of the bread ration in hard bread, or "hard tack," and the remainder in flour; and about the same proportion of the meat ration in bacon, and the balance in fresh beef. Hence when detachments are sent out on scouting expeditions for several days, they are furnished with hard bread and bacon, a food that is strength-giving and much relished after one has been marching all day and night. When in camp we always have fresh bread and fresh meat, beef, pork or mutton. Perhaps no government has ever had a better system of providing for the comforts of its soldiers than ours, during the present war.

Eleven men came into our camp to-day (31st) from southwestern Arkansas and northern Texas. J. R. Pratt, a staunch and prominent Unionist from Texas, is the leader of the party. He lived in Missouri at the breaking out of the war, and moved to Texas to keep out of it, but soon found that it was not a suitable place for a man whose sympathies were with the Government. These men represent a dreadful state of things in the sections which they have recently left. Mr. Pratt states that in northwestern Texas, there are

many Union families, and that the Union men have
made several attempts to organize, but that such attempts have resulted disastrously to all those whose
names were connected with any loyal demonstration.
He also represents that a good many Unionists have
been hung—sixteen in one town, and that others have
been persecuted and hunted down with the assistance
of bloodhounds; that Union men could not then conceal themselves in the woods and mountains in the
vicinity of their homes, as rebels do in this section,
for the bloodhounds would soon be upon their tracks.
They could find no resting place until they left the
State, Such cruel and relentless treatment as these
men appear to have received at the hands of the rebel
authorities, we might expect from savages, but not
from civilized men. For upwards of two hundred
miles they had a toilsome journey, often finding it
difficult to work their way through mountain passes,
guarded by the enemy. Men of pronounced Union
sentiments no doubt have a hard time of it, where they
are so unfortunate as to live in localities in which the
rebel sentiment largely predominates. Perhaps few
of us fully realize what it costs to be a Union man in
the South. But let those who love the Old Flag of their
fathers, stand firm in its defence, for if the signs of
the times are not at fault, the day of their deliverance cannot be very distant.

CHAPTER X.

April Fool's day—Seven Pin Indians killed at Park Hill, C. N.,
by the enemy in federal uniform—The march to Cincinnati
on the State line—War paint and yelping of the Indians when
they start out—Commendable conduct of the Indian soldiers
while in Missouri and Arkansas—The division crosses the
line into the Indian country—On the march to Park Hill—
The country becomes more inviting and the vegetation more
advanced—Rebel scouting party near Fayetteville—Arrival at
Park Hill and meeting of the Indian refugee families from
Neosho—Great manifestations of joy and affecting scenes—
Stanawaitie commanding the rebel Indians—Colonel Phillips
sends out a strong reconnoissance—Webber's Falls—He
drives the enemy into the Arkansas River and takes Fort
Gibson—Description of the place—Its importance—The
beautiful Grand and Verdigris Rivers.

THIS is April Fool's day, but no one has come to me
all aglow with excitement and asked me to prepare to
meet the enemy charging down the road. Nor have
I heard that some adventurous spirit, amongst us, in a
dream last night, commenced to kill all our animals,
thinking he was slaying the enemy like mad Ajax.
Probably not one in a hundred of our soldiers here
thinks of the first day of April in connection with the
custom associated with it in nearly all the large cities
of Christendom.

A detachment of this division just arrived from Park Hill, Cherokee Nation, reports that seven of our Indians, known as Pins, were killed at that place a few days ago by a party of rebels wearing the federal uniform. By this deception and dastardly act the enemy were permitted to approach within a few yards of the Indians, and, by a well-directed fire, shot them down before they had time to offer any resistance. This is not the only instance during the past year of small detachments of our troops having been entrapped by the enemy who were dressed in the federal uniform. Orders were issued early in the war in regard to the punishment to be inflicted upon rebels caught wearing the federal uniform. Every one captured wearing it should be tried by a drum-head court-martial, condemned and immediately shot. Should any of our soldiers go within the enemy's lines and practice a similar deception, and get captured, they would hardly expect any leniency from the confederate authorities. Such a method of carrying on war cannot be too strongly condemned, nor those caught engaged in it too quickly punished to the extent of involving the death penalty. On our side we do not wish to let the war degenerate into a form that would put us on a par with the lowest savages. One would think that the confederate leaders, who like to boast of their chivalry, would not tolerate practices so much at variance with the usages of modern warfare among civilized nations. In the end such treachery and cowardice can avail them nothing, besides it will leave a stain upon their arms that history cannot wipe out.

The Indian division left Camp Pomeroy on the Illinois river, on the morning of the 3d, and marched twelve miles southwest to Cincinnati, a small village on the State line. The place may have contained a population of a hundred people before the war, but probably nearly half the families have moved away—particularly those of known Union sentiments. In peaceable times the few business establishments here perhaps had quite a traffic with the Indians from the Cherokee Nation. It is the intention to remain here only a few days, when we shall pass into the Indian territory, which will probably for some time be the centre of our operations.

Lieutenant Joseph Hall, of the battalion of the Sixth Kansas cavalry, with a detachment of one hundred men, came in to-day from Dutch Mills, where he was sent several days ago to fetch out a number of Unionists who have been concealed in the mountains to escape capture and destruction by the enemy. Colonel Phillips has shown a disposition to do everything in his power to afford protection to the loyal people of this section. The appeals for protection and assistance in various ways are quite numerous. One day a report comes in that a Union family, some thirty miles distant in a given direction, has been robbed by bushwhackers of everything they possessed, are in destitute circumstances, and desire to come into our lines until they have an opportunity of going north with our supply trains and escorts. Another day the news comes to us of a loyal family in distress in some other direction. A detachment of cavalry and one or more mule teams are sent out to bring in the men, women and children, and their effects.

Last night, just as a scouting party were going out, an Indian soldier was instantly killed by the discharge of a musket on the shoulder of a comrade in front of him,—going off accidentally. The muzzle of the gun was so near him that the ball tore away nearly the whole anterior portion of the skull. The Indian troops are armed with muzzle-loading muskets, whose calibres range from 69 to 72, requiring balls weighing upwards of an ounce. They do not always sling their muskets to their shoulders so that the muzzles point directly downwards, as we do our Sharp's carbines. Nor are their arms as effective as ours. We can perhaps, on an average, load and discharge our Sharpe's carbines a dozen times while an Indian loads and discharges his musket once. Our small arms have been already greatly improved since the war commenced. The troops that have been longest in the field are generally supplied with the most improved models. But the Indians are generally good marksmen, and when rapid firing is not required (as on the skirmish line) their muskets may be used quite effectively.

The Indians are rather amusing as soldiers, particularly in regard to their war-paint and yelping when starting out on a scouting expedition or on the march. They seem to prefer to march in single file; but our

officers have drilled them in the regular manual, so
that there is now very little difficulty in having them
march by twos, fours, and by platoons, as required.
But no matter in what order they are marching, when
they start out and the head of the column has got far
enough from camp for the rear to get in motion, the
war whoop commences at the head of the column and
runs back to the rear. This is generally kept up for
some time. When the air is more resonant than
usual, I have heard the woods fairly ring with their
yelping. During the campaign in this section last
fall, Colonel Phillips' Indian brigade was often a mile
or more from us, but we knew every morning, unless
it was stormy weather, just when it started out, by
this yelping or war whoop, which generally lasted fifteen to twenty minutes. There is a strong contrast
between the Indian and our white soldiers in this respect. Ten thousand of our white troops may start
out on the march every morning, and manifest such
silence that they could not be heard a hundred yards
away, except as to the tramping of their horses and
the ratting of their artillery carriages.

Though our Indian troops have been in Missouri
and Arkansas since early last autumn, I believe that
they have committed fewer unathorized depredations
than the same number of white troops, had they occupied the same localities. The non-combatant classes
seem to have an almost instinctive fear of the Indians,
yet it has been a very rare thing to hear of complaints
being made against our Indian soldiers for having

committed unauthorized acts. Much credit is due to Colonel Phillips for the splendid discipline he has maintained without having to resort to severe measures. No military commander could have discharged his duty in a more commendable manner. We pass now into the Indian country, and bid a temporary adieu to Arkansas.

Early on the morning of the 6th we left Cincinnati and marched to Dutch Mills, twelve miles south, on the State line. At this point we took the road leading into the Cherokee Nation towards Park Hill, but marched only a few miles west when we pitched our camp, and called it Camp "Jim Lane," in honor of Senator James H. Lane, whose name is familiar to every one acquainted with the history of Kansas. At eight o'clock on the morning of the 8th everything was in readines to move, and from Camp "Jim Lane" we marched to Park Hill, twenty-two miles west, and encamped near the residence of the Chief, John Ross. After we left Duchtown every mile of the country we passed over became more inviting. For agricultural and grazing purposes it is certainly much superior to Arkansas. We crossed the Illinois river again, a few miles to the east of us on the march here. It discharges a larger volume of water than when we crossed it in Arkansas, and its bottoms are much wider, and its course changes toward the south. It does not, however, go rushing along in such a rapid and impetuous current, but is now a placid and gently flowing stream. Every day's march to the southwest brings us into a region where the vegetation is more advanced than where we were the day before, the wild flowers are more beautiful, the birds sing sweeter and have brighter and more elegant plumage, and altogether one feels happier. We believe that even our animals show a more hopeful expression. Grass and wild onions in the river bottoms are up an inch or so in height, and animals not required to work can live without any other food. The country here is not so broken and hilly as in nortwestern Arkansas; in fact we are right on the border of the prairie region.

A detachment of the battalion, the Sixth Kansas cavalry, who came in from Fayetteville this morning, report that a rebel scouting party of about one hundred and fifty men, were within seven miles of that place on the 6th instant. Our soldiers came near running into the main body of them, so near, indeed, that they captured one of their men who had fallen behind, and brought him a prisoner to our camp, using him most of the time as a guide. This considerable force of the enemy's cavalry, so near our troops, indicates his intention of displaying greater activity as the season advances. Now that we are getting so far away from Fayetteville, about fifty miles, and as we shall probably have our own hands full very soon, Colonel Harrison will have to depend upon his own resources to hold his station. We are unable to understand why so many of our troops are kept in the vicinity of Springfield, as we have heard of no threatened invasion of Missouri by the enemy directly south or southeast of that place. The State Militia could probably preserve order in that section if our volunteer troops should occupy a more advanced position, and prevent the invasion of the State by the organized forces of the enemy.

The refugee train arrived to-day (9th) from Neosho, having been ten days *en route* to this place. The train, which was about a mile long, came in sight about ten o'clock. It was a lovely spring morning, the air soft and balmy, and everything looking gay and cheerful. Some of the Indian soldiers went out several miles to meet their families, but many waited until the train had approached near our camp. I watched them with a good deal of interest. Such manifestations of joy on the meeting of husbands and wives and children, I have never before witnessed. There were, perhaps, nearly a thousand families brought down, and in many instances husbands have been separated from their wives and children for nearly a year. Their joy was, no doubt, increased with the thought of being able to meet one another in their own country and near their own capital. The restoring to their homes an entire people who have so long been exiles, will surely be an event in their history that should not be passed over without mention. If they were as emotional in their natures as the French, I know they would cry with one voice, *viva la* Phillips. But their unbounded confidence in him shows their strong regard for him, and is probably as keenly appreciated by him as noisy demonstrations. That he should have provided for the safety and comfort of their families during the winter, and restored them to their homes so early in the spring, is enough to set them rejoicing,with hearts full of gratitude towards their deliverer. Tahlequah, the capital of the Cherokee Nation, is about seven miles northwest of here, but it has never been a place of much importance in a business point of view. It never contained a population of more than a few hundred inhabitants, and a dozen good buildings. Some of the buildings will probably soon be used for hospital purposes for the sick of this division, particularly the small-pox patients.

A skirmish took place yesterday, the 10th, at Fort Gibson between a battalion of our Indian soldiers and a small force of Standwaities' Rebel Indians, resulting in the capture of half a dozen prisoners and the killing and wounding of five of the enemy, the remainder having made their escape by swimming across the Arkansas river. It may now be said that we have undisputed possession of all the Indian country north of the Arkansas river. If there are any forces on this side of the river they will doubtless plunge into it rather than to cross swords with our troops.

Colonel Standwaitie, who has commanded the Rebel portion of the Cherokees, is himself a Cherokee, and seems to have a wider fame than his valor and military skill entitle him to. We have heard a good deal of him ever since we came into this country last June, but have been unable to meet him. When we have had a skirmish with any of his Indians, it has always turned out that he was not with them. We do not quite regard him as a mythical character, but we do not believe him to be such a brave and dashing Indian as he has often been represented, and as the frequent use of his name in connection with predatory actions would indicate. He has never boldly attacked even a detachment of our troops. Our Indians say that his name is not appropriate at all, that he does not stand and wait for us, but that he is always on the run as soon as our troops seek him. We shall, however, doubtless have occasion to try his valor before the summer is over.

Our entire division is to move to Fort Gibson in a few days; but before setting out, Colonel Phillips has deemed it expedient to thoroughly reconnoitre the country between here and that place, and for that purpose to-day sent out a party of the Second Indian regiment and one company of the battalion of the Sixth Kansas cavalry, under Colonel David B. Corwin. Every precaution is being taken that our trains, artillery, and thorough organization shall not be endangered by ambuscade or surprise. We are now so far away from any other troops from whom we could expect assistance, that a defeat might prove the complete demoralization of this division. Colonel Phillips has carefully considered the probable consequences which would be sure to follow any reckless action of a military commander occupying his position.

Major Foreman, of the Third Indian regiment, who was sent out from here on the 8th instant with about three hundred men, to make a reconnoissance in the direction of Webber's Falls, on the Arkansas river, some twenty-five miles south of us, returned to-day, having captured nearly three hundred head of cattle, and killed six of the enemy, including one captain and one sergeant. He also brought in a number of prisoners, who thought that their last day had come. The action took place near the mouth of the Illinois river, and the enemy were so completely surprised that they made very little resistence. We had only three or four men wounded.

On the morning of the 13th the troops and trains of our division left "Camp John Ross," and marched to Fort Gibson, eighteen miles southwest. We passed over a lovely country, probably the finest in the Cherokee Nation. It appears to have been very well settled before the war, with many good farms under cultivation. The line of march was mainly over rolling prairies, though there was some timber on several small streams which we crossed.

Now that we have pitched our tents at Fort Gibson, and as this place will probably be the centre of our operations during the spring and summer, we may look around a little with the view of finding something worth setting down. This is quite an old post. It was established as a military post by the United States before the Cherokees left their Tennessee and Georgia homes and emigrated to this Territory. There are now two or three persons living here who say that they have a distinct recollection of Jefferson Davis, a

Lieutenant of Dragoons, when he was stationed at this post as far back as 1832. It does not appear that any defensive works were ever erected here, except a couple. of block-houses, and they are useless now. There are two good substantial stone buildings which have been used for quartermaster and commissary store houses. Their roofing is made of slate, and they will be very valuable in storing our quartermaster and commissary supplies, as they are transported by trains from Fort Scott. They are large enough to hold supplies for this division for upwards of thirty days. And they stand on a bluff overlooking Grand River to the west. The officers' and soldiers' quarters are wooden structures, and built on a plazza or public square, similar to the Court House squares of country towns. They are about two hundred yards south of the stone buildings above mentioned, on the slope of the hill, and are beginning to look old and dilapidated, although the interiors of the officers' quarters are in good condition, having been more expensively and elegantly finished up than the soldiers' quarters. They are different from the officers' and soldiers' quarters at Fort Scott, Kansas, in this respect: They are all single storied buildings, while at Scott the officers' quarters have two stories with attics, and the soldiers' quarters are two stories. There are several unfinished stone buildings on the bluff near the quartermaster and commissary store houses, which before the war the Government had under contract to be finished up for permanent quarters for officers and soldiers of the Regular Army.

The location here is a lovely one for a military post, and perhaps for some future city of considerable importance. Looking to the east from the bluff where the stone buildings stand, you see in the distance, some ten miles off, the western terminus of the range of mountains which run north-eastward through Arkansas. Turning to the south, you overlook the Arkansas river three miles distant, and your eyes rest upon the opposite heights, and the prairie country beyond. Some places the heights are obscured by the heavy timber along the Arkansas; at other places you see them as through a vista. Turning to the west and south-west, you see at the distance of two miles, the western heights of Grand River. Further to the south-west may be seen a prairie region with a strip of timber running through it in a south-east direction. This strip of timber marks the course of the Verdigris River, which empties into the Arkansas River some five or six miles above the mouth of Grand River. The junctions of these three rivers, the Arkansas, the Grand and the Verdigris, being within a few miles of each other, and the three being nearly of the same size, will be favorable for the building of an important city somewhere in this vicinity when the country comes into the possession of the whites, as it probably will sometime in the future. The Cherokees, however, have made such progress in civilization, and have also been such staunch and reliable friends of the whites for nearly a century, with one or two unimportant exceptions, that they are not likely to be disturbed in the peaceable

14

possession of their country under the existing order of things. As a people, they might have been regarded as wealthy before the war. When we came into this section and the country above here last July and August, we saw fine herds of cattle and ponies grazing upon the prairies, or standing in the cool waters of shady and peaceful flowing streams, the very pictures of rural life in a beautiful and happy country. The pictures were of course incomplete, for we nowhere saw in the background or foreground happy maidens tripping along and attending to their dairy or household duties. Nor did we hear happy voices or see any of those desirable features of country life, familiar to those whose earlier years were passed on the farm.

But let us return to things as we now see them. This has been a central position from which the Government could easily communicate with a number of Indian tribes. Supplies for the troops stationed here, and annuity goods for distribution to the Indians, have been brought up by river transportation, ever since this post was established. Every season during the spring rise of the Arkansas River, light draft steamers have not only run to this point, but sometimes for nearly a hundred miles above here on the Grand River. I saw an inscription on a tombstone yesterday, that a Lieutenant of the Regular Army was drowned at the mouth of the Neosho river in 1836, from having fallen overboard a steamboat at that point. The point where the military road to Fort Scott crosses the Neosho river is nearly a hundred miles from Gibson. But I have heard from those who have lived here for many years, that there has been very little steamboating above this place. There has been no great inducements, no great commercial interests involved, to make it worth while to keep the river in a navigable condition. It requires a considerable rise in the Arkansas to enable boats to pass Webber's Falls. Below that point light draft steamers can probably run on the river the greater part of the year. How far it is possible to remove the obstacles to navigation at Webber's Falls, can be determined only after a careful examination by an experienced and competent engineer. Navigation on the Arkansas will always be troublesome between this place and Fort Smith, on account of the river constantly shifting its current, caused by the formation of sand bars. It is turbid and treacherous, and contrasts strongly with the Grand River, which is perfectly clear except during the season of heavy rains, and flows over a gravelly or pebbly bottom. Both rivers abound in fish, and those of our soldiers who are fond of the sport of angling will doubtless, when off duty, try their skill at it while we are stationed here.

From the bluff we can see a portion of the territory of the Creeks and Seminoles, Chickasaws and Cherokees. We have not as yet had any loyal Choctaws and Chickasaws join us, though we hear there are a good many among them who would prefer to cast their fortunes with the Union if they could have any reasonable assurance of protection. As we have come here to stay, they will probably have ample opportunity of manifesting their loyalty and devotion to the Government by coming in and surrendering to Colonel Phillips.

CHAPTER XI.

Fort Gibson the Key to the Indian country—The enemy showing signs of activity—The troops at Gibson commence to
build bake ovens—Anxiety for the supply train—Creek
Indians coming in—The enemy concentrating at Webber's
Falls—Celebrating the event of hoisting the United States
Flag at Fort Gibson—A sad accident—Arrival of supply train
from Fort Scott—Part of Neosho burned—The enemy attack
Fayetteville and are defeated—A young man as a spy caught
dressed in a woman's suit—The troops commence to throw up
fortifications at Fort Gibson—Strength of the Federal position—Engagement at Webber's Falls—Capture of the enemy's
camp—Assassination of Dr. Gillpatrick—They are on business
in connection with exchanging of prisoners—Arrival of rebel
officers under a flag of truce—Reconnoissance of Colonel
Schaurte to the Arkansas line—Colonel Harrison abandons
Fayetteville—Colonel Phillips reviews his division.

The importance of this position is not likely at first
glance to be fully appreciated. It is really the key to
this entire Indian country, and great credit is
due to Colonel Phillips for having seized it before
the enemy received reinforcements. By throwing up
breast works and constructing fortifications, we can
hold the place against a force of the enemy twice as
large as our own, unless he should be better supplied
with long-range artillery than we are. I think that

we have also gained an advantage in regard to obtaining our supplies from Fort Scott. While we are further removed from our base of supplies, the distance to Fort Scott from this post by the old military road being about one hundred and sixty miles, our supply trains after they leave the southern line of Kansas will move all the way down on the west side of Grand river, and therefore doubtless be freer from attacks by the enemy than if they were obliged to come down the State lines of Missouri and Arkansas. From about this time in the spring until the summer is considerably advanced, it is frequently difficult for cavalry, artillery and infantry to cross Grand River, for a distance of seventy to eighty miles above here, without pontoon trains, which neither the enemy nor our army in the west possess. Such large trains as ours, are unquestionably coveted prizes, which the enemy will probably organize expeditions for the purpose of capturing or destroying. As our trains will require strong escorts, it is easy to see that our troops will have no time to spend in idleness. We can of course depend upon the country here for nothing except fresh beef, and in a few weeks, grass for our animals. Since the enemy can hold no position north of the Arkansas River, we have already seen indications that he is not going to remain inactive in this region during the spring and summer.

Our troops to-day (14th) commenced building bake ovens, which indicates clearly enough Colonel Phillips' intention of permanently holding this place. These will be the first ovens we have put up in the field. They will not only economize the expenditure of fuel, but also enable the companies to save more from their flour ration than they could do by baking their bread by the old process; besides the bread is better and considered healthier. We have men with us who were engaged in the bakery business before enlistment. Hence we shall probably have as good bread as is usually made at city bakeries. But we shall miss the butter and eggs which we were able to get quite often while in Missouri and Arkansas. If, however, we manage to keep on hand full rations we shall have no cause to complain about our fare.

A detachment of ten men of the Battalion Sixth Kansas cavalry, and about fifty Indian soldiers, were sent out to-day (15th) in the direction of Maysville to meet our commissary train now due from Fort Scott. As it was expected to join us at Park Hill, and has not yet been heard from, some uneasiness is felt for its safety. We have been almost constantly on the move recently, and it is possible that the commanding officer of the escort has stopped it at some point this side of Fort Scott for a day or two, for more definite instructions as to where to join us. If instructions had been sent forward for it to join us here on the 13th, it would have come down on the west side of Grand River, instead of *via* Maysville on the State line road. We do not believe that there is a force of the enemy north of us of sufficient strength to venture to attack the train. A flag of truce came in to-day from the

Creek Indians concerning tneir coming in and joining our army. About fifty have already come in since we arrived here, and they express their willingness to do all in their power to establish law and order and com plete obedience to the authority of the United States, in their country. Those just in think that many others will come when assured of protection. Though I have not heard what kind of speeches Colonel Phillips makes to them, yet I suppose that he informs them that he has come here to afford protection to all those who are disposed to be friendly and loyal to the Government, and to make war even to the knife and from the knife to the hilt against its enemies; that we are here not for the purpose of seeking vengeance and paying off old scores, but to establish justice and the harmonious relations of the people to the Government. They are no doubt informed that to offer further resistance to the Government is sure to bring further desolation to their country and additional miseries to their homes. In his speeches to the different Indian delegations that have waited upon him, he has endeavored to give them good advice, which they will find it to their interest to carefully consider.

We have information to-day (16th,) from a source deemed reliable, that the enemy are concentrating a force of four or five hundred men at Webber's Falls, about twenty-five miles below this post. As the point where they are gathering is on the south side of the Arkansas, and as it is not fordable below the mouth of Grand river, we may not be able to disturb them for a few days. With a river as large as the Arkansas between them, two opposing forces may continue as neighbors for some time. But barring this obstacle there would certainly be either a "fight or a foot race" very soon with an enemy not superior in numbers to our command, encamped so near us as Webber's Falls.

Yesterday, the 17th, was given to festivities in celebrating the event of hoisting the Union Flag at the military post of Fort Gibson, that it may float from the flag staff where it was hauled down in foul dishonor soon after the breaking out of the war. This is the first time that the Stars and Stripes, the emblem of our nationality, have been hoisted on the post flag staff since the enemy took possession of the Government property here, and there were many whose affection for the Old Flag was so strong, that when its folds floated to the breeze they shed tears of joy. The Star Spangled Banner and other national airs were sung by half a dozen ladies and gentlemen—several of the ladies being wives of officers on a visit to their husbands. As an improvised choir they did well, and their voices sounded sweetly, the balmy air of spring being peculiarly favorable for music, instrumental or vocal, to produce a good effect. The solos, duets, and choruses were real treats, as we have had no music of any kind recently. Last autumn and winter when General Blunt's division was all together, we had two or three excellent bands and good music every day. The Ninth Wisconsin infantry, a German regiment, had perhaps the best band in the division, and as they frequently encamped near the Sixth Kansas cavalry, I have often listened to it much delighted.

It becomes my painful duty now to mention a serious accident that occurred during our celebration yesterday. While Major Henry Hopkins' battery was firing a national salute of thirty-four guns, one of the pieces just after it had been swabbed and the blank cartridge rammed home, went off accidentally before the rammer was fully withdrawn, and while it was still in the hands of the gunner. One of his arms was blown off above the elbow, and the other hand was almost torn off, and is now in a dreadfully mutilated condition, and will probably have to be amputated in a few days. He was for an instant enveloped in a flame of fire and smoke, and is therefore badly burned about the body. The gun was pointed south, and I picked up, nearly two hundred yards from it, two fingers and several tendons. It is not likely that the poor fellow will recover from these injuries. An Indian was also fatally injured by a piece of the rammer.

From my own observations during the last two years I am under the impression that the number of accidental injuries in an army will foot up a larger percentage than is generally supposed. Few days pass that we do not hear of some soldier of this command receiving a serious accidental injury incident to the service. Human foresight can never completely guard against accidents, even of the simplest kind.

We hope that the National Flag that we reverence

and look upon with such devotion, will never again be hauled down from the flagstaff at this post, by the enemy. A general, whose soldiers had mutinied, is said to have expressed the belief that if he could only look the leaders in their eyes, he thought that they would return to their allegiance. So I believe that there are many rebels who, if they could but look upon our beautiful flag of the Union as its folds gently float to the breeze, would gladly return to their allegiance to the Government.

The Creek Indians still continue to come in, and are generally anxious to enlist into our army. While the estimated number that will probably come would not make a regiment, nor even a battalion; they might be enlisted into the service and assigned to the three Indian regiments of this command until they shall have been filled to their maximum strength. There is reason to believe such a course will be adopted by Colonel Phillips. As most of the men in the First and Second regiments are Creeks and Seminoles, it is likely that all recruits belonging to either of these nations, would prefer to be assigned to one or the other of these regiments. Their preferences will no doubt be respected as far as possible.

A party of about a dozen white men who claim to have recently deserted from General Marmaduke's command, came to our pickets this morning, and were brought into camp to day. They represent that the rebel leaders in Arkansas are displaying a good deal of activity in organizing their demoralized forces for

the spring and summer campaigns. They say that
General Cooper will have command of the rebel forces
in the Indian Territory, and that General Cabell will
be assigned to the command of Western Arkansas,
but that they will co-operate with each other as far as
practicable. This all corresponds with the information
which our spies have recently brought in.

Our commissary train of one hundred and twenty-
five wagons arrived this morning (20th) from Fort Scott.
The slight anxiety felt by some of our troops will now
be at an end. It is estimated that the supplies received
by this train will ration this command for upwards of
a month. On account of some rumors that have been
afloat for several days, a detachment of two hundred
cavalry was sent out to escort it into camp. It will
now be the business of the troops here to keep the
country open between this post and the southern line
of Kansas. And we feel satisfied that Colonel Phillips will not be unmindful of his duty in this respect.
Colonel C. W. Blair, the commanding officer at Fort
Scott, will probably furnish escorts strong enough to
guard our trains to Baxter Springs or Neosho river.
Should the enemy at any time throw a force between
this post and either of those points, with the view of
attacking a train, Colonel Phillips will reinforce the
escort by troops from this division. But the main
body of his troops will be required for active service
in this vicinity in contending with the enemy in front
and around us.

This last train came down *via* Neosho, Missouri,

but will return on the old Military road, which runs
along on the west side of Grand River.

Those who came down with the train from Neosho,
state that a large portion of the town was recently
burned. It was not definitely known whether the
fire was started accidentally, or by an incendiary. It
was discovered after night, and had make such progress
that it could not be checked with the means the people
had at hand. Two companies of the Missouri State
Militia have been stationed there since Colonel Phillips
withdrew his Indian troops; but one cannot easily
believe that there could be found among them an individual who would deliberately attempt to burn a
town of his own State; a town, too, which he is paid
to protect.

The report which reached here two days ago, that
Fayetteville had been taken on the 18th instant by a
rebel force of fifteen hundred men, under command of
General Cabell, turns out to be untrue. Until more
definite information reached here, some apprehensions
were felt for the safety of that post. Dispatches have
now been received, stating that our troops there under
Colonel Harrison had a sharp engagement with the
enemy under General Cabell, on the 18th instant,
which lasted two hours. The enemy were unsuccessful in the attack and compelled to retreat, leaving most
of their killed and wounded on the field. From such
information as I have been able to obtain, our losses
were about thirty men killed and wounded, while the
losses of the enemy were probably very nearly fifty.

Our troops had some slight advantage, as they fought part of the time from behind fortifications, and were on the defensive. The loyal Arkansas soldiers are represented to have acted with distinguished bravery throughout the contest. Having defeated the enemy in this first important engagement, they will now feel confident of their strength, and in any future contest they may have, defend their position with greater stubbornness than if they had been unsuccessful.

A spy was caught to-day (23d) near camp, dressed in a woman's suit. He is a young fellow with light hair, fair complexion, of a rather prepossessing appearance, and I should think not over sixteen years of age. When I saw him in the Provost-marshal's tent he seemed to be badly frightened, in fact almost frightened out of his wits. Two or three officers were putting questions to him in regard to his visiting our camp in disguise, but his excitement had not sufficiently subsided to enable him to give rational answers. He seemed ready to confess anything asked of him. He showed that he was unaccustomed to being goaded with questions of such a serious nature. From ancient times to the present day, it has been the practice of commanding generals of armies to hang spies immediately after being caught, so as to make it impossible for the enemy to gain any advantage from the information which they may have obtained. What disposition will be made of this young man, has not yet been determined. Colonel Phillips, as commanding officer of troops in the field, has authority to order him tried by a drum-head court martial, and, if found guilty, hung within the next twenty-four hours. It is possible that his youthful age may save him from the death penalty at present, and that he will be turned over to the Department commander, for such punishment as he may deem proper. He claims to have been sent here by General Cooper, who is now encamped near Webber's Falls, for the purpose of getting information in regard to our strength and intentions in the near future.

It was by the merest accident that he was detected. When several of our Indian soldiers first saw him near the limits of our camp, they thought that he was a white woman, although there are now very few white women in this country. They also noticed that his movements were peculiar, and not like those of a woman, and when they came towards him, he started to run, but in the chase they soon convinced him that his only safety lay in his absolute submission. His garments were probably an impediment to his flight, but as our Indians are generally quite fleet of foot, they would have soon overtaken him anyway.

If I were going as a spy into the enemy's camp, to dress in a woman's suit would be about the last method I should think of adopting, even if I had as marked feminine features as some young men, which I have not. And as to the *time* for making such an adventure, I should prefer the night to broad daylight, particularly if there was any one in the enemy's camp likely to know me.

The engineers have surveyed and laid off the

ground for the new fortifications at this post. A line
of breastworks is to be thrown up to encompass the
stone buildings on the bluff, commencing on the north
side and extending around to the south side. The west
side is a steep bluff running down to the water's edge
of the Grand River. The area to be inclosed on three
sides will be about ten acres. Details of men have
been made from all the troops here, and ordered to report to the officer in charge of the works in the morning, with picks, shovels, &c. When there does not appear to be any immediate danger from attack, soldiers
do not usually like to work on fortifications. As the
enemy are making no threatening demonstrations, an
expression of dissatisfaction may now and then be
heard from the men in regard to slinging the pick and
shovel. The weather is beginning to get warm, and
such arduous labor is not coveted.

The picks and shovels have now been flying for
three days, and the line of breastworks are rapidly assuming their proper form. In examining the position
to-day, I came to the conclusion that there is not an
elevation so high as the one on which our works are
being constructed, within a less distance than two
miles of us. To the east and southeast, we could
easily sweep the plain with our artillery. To the north
and northeast, the enemy's infantry, should he make
an assault, would have a better opportunity of approaching near our works through the dense woods
and broken ravines. But as we shall have an *abatis*
over a portion of this ground, we would be able to thin

the ranks of the enemy, should he make an attack
from this quarter, before he got through it, by pouring into his advancing columns, a constant stream of
grape and canister. The heights on the west side of
Grand River are too distant for an enemy to shell us
with much effect with ordinary field artillery. In a few
weeks therefore our position can be made quite a strong
one. But the presence of General Cabell in the vicinity of Cane Hill a few days ago, with upwards of a
thousand cavalry; and the force under General Cooper
near us on the opposite side of the Arkansas River, in
the vicinity of Webber's Falls, looks as if Colonel
Phillips will be required to display great firmness and
activity, to enable us to maintain our position here.
As the enemy have two generals operating to the south
and east of us; and as we may suppose that each General commands at least two brigades, we have the prospect of being matched by superior numbers in a few
weeks. According to a reasonable estimate we may
conclude that they could, in case of emergency, concentrate a force not much short of seven thousand men.
This is fully twice the strength of our troops at this
point.

On the evening of the 24th, Colonel Phillips took a
force of six hundred men, composed of details from
the three Indian regiments, and the battalion of the
sixth Kansas cavalry, and crossed the Arkansas River
several miles below this post, and making a night's
march, reached Webber's Falls early Saturday morning, and at once commenced a vigorous attack on the
15

enemy's camp. They were taken by surprise, and fired but few rounds when they fled in disorder towards Fort Smith and North Fork town, where General Cooper's main force is encamped and organizing. We did not pursue them a great distance, as our animals were much fatigued from the night's march. The action was sharp for a few minutes, when the enemy broke, leaving on the field fifteen killed and as many wounded. We had one Indian killed and ten men wounded. But our most serious loss was the killing, or rather assassination of Dr. Gilpatrick, a special agent of the Government, who accompanied us on this reconnoitering expedition. After the skirmish was over, he was called upon by a rebel woman to dress the wound of a rebel soldier, who had fallen a hundred yards or so from where we halted. While performing this duty of mercy for a fallen foe, he was shot by a rebel from a concealed position, and he died immediately afterwards. We all felt indignant that he should have been thus basely entrapped. We brought him back with us, and he is to be buried on Sunday with military honors.

We captured a large quantity of camp and garrison equipage, flour, bacon, &c., and completely destroyed their camp. As it was not quite day-break when we charged into them, a good many fled in their night clothes. They perhaps thought that we would not venture to cross the Arkansas, as it has not been fordable for many days, and even to-day came well up to the sides of our horses. It was a bold dash, and Colonel Phillips deserves great credit for planning and successfully executing the movement. This expedition will have a demoralizing effect upon the enemy, and perhaps retard his organizing to take the field against us. To that extent it is important.

While we were absent on the reconnoissance to Webber's Falls, two rebel officers came into our camp here, under a flag of truce from General Cooper, in regard to exchanging prisoners. They were detained until our return.. We perhaps hold a few more rebel prisoners than they hold of Federal prisoners. They are authorized to offer for exchange a certain number of our officers and enlisted men, for an equal number of their officers and enlisted men. These officers have been kept in close quarters since their arrival, and will be blindfolded when they are conducted beyond our lines. This precaution is deemed necessary to prevent them from gaining any information in regard to the strength and disposition of our troops at this post.

The same day we left for Webber's Falls, Colonel Phillips sent out Lieutenant-Colonel F. W. Schaurte, second Indian regiment, with about five hundred men, in the direction of Ivansville, a little town on the Arkansas line. Major Foreman, with four companies of the Third Indian regiment, a detachment from the battalion Sixth Kansas Cavalry, and a section of Hopkins' battery, joined Colonel Schaurte beyond Park Hill. Colonel Harrison, commanding at Fayetteville, was also expected to join Colonel Schaurte near the State line. These troops were to attack the enemy

near Cane Hill, if he seemed disposed to give battle.
But after nearly a week of hard marching, the expedition under Colonel Schaurte returned to this post, having had only a slight skirmish with the enemy. The
troops were much fatigued and hungry when they
came in. The last three days they were on less than
half rations. The enemy under General Cabell, when
they heard of the approach of our troops, immediately packed up their baggage and camp equipage, and
retreated towards Van Buren. They will, however,
doubtless return again shortly, as our troops have now
been all withdrawn from that section. They will not
only return, but they will probably return and carry
their arms still further north and west until they meet
with resistance from our forces.

Colonel Harrison, instead of joining Colonel Schaurte
at the State line, abandoned Fayetteville, and retreated
to Cassville, Missouri, a small town on the main road
leading to Springfield. It is much regretted that
Colonel Harrison did not display a little more nerve,
and that he has felt the necessity of abandoning his
post, for it leaves the Union people of northwestern
Arkansas without any protection whatever. If his
supplies were running too short to enable him to stand
a seige of a week or so, and if he could get no assurance of reinforcements in the event of a seige, then
there may be some justification for his action. The
enemy have been reinforced since the engagement at
Fayetteville on the 18th instant, and he may have felt
that there was danger of being cut off from our troops

in Missouri. We hope that his withdrawal will be only temporary, and that he will shortly return, and wipe out this apparent blot upon his military record. A good many Union people in the vicinity of Fayetteville had commenced to cultivate such tracts of land as their means permit, and without the protection of the Federal troops, they will hardly for the rest of the season be able to give proper attention to their crops.

On the 30th, information reached this post, that the enemy, considerably reinforced, returned to Webber's Falls, two or three days after we left, and are now driving out all the Indian families in that vicinity suspected of being in any manner friendly to the Union cause. A number of families have just come into our lines for protection, and they state that the rebels have burned their houses to prevent their returning to them. We might in the eyes of many justly retaliate by burning the property of rebels in the territory occupied by our troops, but this is not our purpose, to unnecessarily increase the hardships of women and children, nor to destroy private property, except in cases of absolute necessity. Such cases have been extremely few as far as this command is concerned.

We feel here that the Department Commander should not have permitted our troops to leave Fayetteville, while there were several brigades in southern Missouri not very actively employed.

On May 1st, Colonel Phillips reviewed his troops, on the open grounds near the Fort. He had in line upwards of two thousand men. The Indians, having recently been furnished with new uniforms, made a creditable appearance. But with their long, black hair, there is a marked contrast between them and our white soldiers, who generally have their hair cut rather short, besides it is several shades lighter than the Indian's hair. The Indian soldiers are in good condition, and though their arms are not the best, yet if handled to the best advantage, may be made quite effective, turned against the enemy.

CHAPTER XII.

The author sent with dispatches to Colonel Harrison at Cassville,
    Missouri—The first night's march in a storm of thunder and
    lightning—The next morning on the battle-ground of Locust
    Grove—Account of the battle and of the capture of Colonel
    Clarkson's command—Passing over the ground of an exciting
    chase of last year—Camp in the forest—On the look out for
    the enemy—In Missouri—Arrival at Cassville—Detention
    at Cassville—The troops there daily expecting to be at.
    tacked—Large number of troops, including the State militia,
    in Southwest Missouri—Activity of the militia—The First
    Kansas colored infantry organized, and at Baxter Springs—
    Remarks on arming the freedmen—Many small tracts being
    cultivated in Missouri—By whom—On the march to Fort
    Gibson—A fight with Guerillas –Stopping in a lonely re-
    treat—Return to Fort Gibson.

I have already mentioned Colonel Harrison leaving
Fayetteville with his troops and marching to Cassville,
Missouri. When the information first reached us, I
suspected that Colonel Phillips was not entirely satisfied with the movement. It has been generally understood here that the troops at Fayetteville belonged
to Colonel Phillips' districts, and would not be expected to leave that station without his orders.

Friday evening, May 1st, Captain William Gallaher,
Assistant Adjutant General of the division, sent for

me, and stated that he had an important service which he wanted me to undertake. He made out an order for my detail, and also for eight men to accompany me, and sent it to the commanding officer of the battalion Sixth Kansas cavalry. We were directed to report at headquarters at nine o'clock for more difinite instructions. Captain Gallagher then stated that he had important dispatches which he wanted taken to Colonel Harrison, at Cassville, Missouri,—a distance of about one hundred and fifty miles by the route we would be obliged to travel. He also said that we might consider ourselves in the enemy's country from the time we left Fort Gibson until we reached Cassville, as we had no troops stationed anywhere in the region through which we would be obliged to pass. We filled our cartridge-boxes with ammunition for our carbines and revolvers, and our haversacks with hard bread and bacon for five days, and put some shelled corn in the nose-bags for our horses, and reported at headquarters as directed, to the second. Captain Gallagher delivered to me the packages, gave us a few words of caution, and suggested that it would be safest to follow the road along the east side of Grand River until we came to Lewis Ross's place near Grand Saline, some thirty miles above Fort Gibson. He then bade us good night, and we were soon beyond the limits of the camp, wending our way northward, on the road above mentioned. It was cloudy when we started out, and, during the night, thunder and lightning and rain banished sleep from our eyes.

Some of the great flashes of lightning seemed to fairly light up the woods as if they had been on fire. The heavy rolling of the thunder, with now and then a sharp clap, was grand; but some of the men thought that they should prefer to witness and hear it all in camp. The night was so dark and the road so dim that we gave the reins to our horses, and were guided by the general course we were marching. None of us had been over this path before, and there was no pole star to inform us how far, at any time, we were deviating from our proper course. But when the storm clouds of the night had passed over and daylight came, we found that we had kept the most direct route, and that we were near Locust Grove, where we had a fight with Colonel Clarkson's command, the 2d of last July, and captured him with one hundred and ten of his soldiers, nearly all of whom were white men. We also captured his baggage and supply trains, in all upwards of one hundred wagons and about three hundred animals. Colonel William Weir, Tenth Kansas infantry, who commanded the expedition, marched us two days and nights, and we struck the enemy just at dawn—some of the brightest stars were still shining—and we had him surrounded before he knew of our presence. We reached their camp right on the heels of their pickets, so that they had no time to form in line and prepare for battle. It was a warm night, and only a few of them seem to have slept with even their trousers on, as they did not suppose we were within forty miles.

In the engagement they lost about thirty men killed and wounded. Most of the killed and wounded were among those who attempted to pass through the openings where our lines had not quite closed up. We had only eight men wounded. After this affair the troops of the *Indian Expedition* had no organized force to oppose north of the Arkansas river. The prisoners were sent to Fort Scott, and the train and animals taken to our camp on Cabin Creek, a few miles from here on the west side of Grand river.

The salt works near here have made this locality one of considerable importance for many years. Before the war large quantities of salt were taken from this place to various points in southwest Missouri and northwest Arkansas, and sold or exchanged for goods which the Indians required. We passed several of the salt wells this morning, and they were flowing like fountains, the column of salt water in one instance extending five or six feet above the ground. The wells we saw were bored like artesian wells. We took a few moments to examine them, as it would afford our horses an opportunity to refresh themselves by rest and grazing. Judging by the openings and the columns of water, we estimated that the bore was not more than three or four inches in diameter. If the supply of saline water is inexhaustable, this will likely be an important point some day.

The country is perfectly delightful in this vicinity. The forest trees and the whole face of the landscape are robed in green. The sun shining above the van-ishing storm-clouds, has inspired the birds to singing all the morning in an exceeding happy mood. We saw a number of species, some having very elegant forms and beautiful plumage. They can have matters all their own way in this region if they can avoid their enemies of the hawk tribe, and some wingless enemies among the lower animals, for there are now very few Indian families living in this section. When we halted this morning on a secluded spot near Locust Grove, to graze our horses and to allow the men to refresh themselves by a short nap, we had not passed more than three houses with occupants, since leaving Gibson. The country seems as silent as a graveyard, except as to the songs of birds and the humming of insects. No sounds are heard from people plowing in the fields, or the yelping of hounds chasing the deer, or of chickens cackling in the barnyard. As soon as it was light this morning we carefully examined the dim road for fresh horse tracks; but we saw none, which satisfied us that the enemy had not crossed or been on our path since the rain. We did not know but that the enemy had sent out scouting parties to watch the movements of our trains, and that we might run into a detachment unless we were very cautious. As there is a good crossing of the Grand River near Grand Saline, and as it is always fordable after a rise in the river, before any other point for miles above or below, we thought it would be the favorite point for the enemy to strike, should they have serious intentions of attacking our trains.

When we left Grand river at Grand Saline, we marched across the country in a northeast direction, with the intention of passing into Missouri near Scott's Mills, on the Cowskin river, in the southwest corner of the State. Our route for the greater part of the day was over a rough, hilly country, uninhabited by Indian families. When night came we encamped near Lynch's Mills on Spavinaw Creek, about sixteen miles below Standwaitie's Mills. At this place we saw one of our loyal Indians, who was at home with his family. He told us that, about a week ago, a party of ten loyal Indians, of whom he was one, had a fight with about an equal number of rebel Indians, a mile below this place, and that they killed half of the rebel party, but got four of their own men badly wounded in the affair. He spoke very good English, and seemed to be telling a straightforward story. A grain of allowance, however, should, perhaps, be made for exaggeration. But from the information which we receive from time to time, there is no doubt but that such bloody contests are quite common in different parts of the Nation.

We were in this section last June with Colonel Jewell, of the Sixth Kansas cavalry. An incident occurred near here, which is worth mentioning, now that were are on the ground again. While we were enencamped on Cowskin prairie we received information through our scouts that Colonel Standwaitie, with a force of four or five hundred Indians, was in this vicinity. Colonel Jewell, with about three hundred cavalry, was directed by Colonel Weer to make a re-connoissance to this point. We made a night's march, and late in the afternoon of the following day we heard that Standwaitie, with a small party of men, had just passed along the road we were on, only about an hour before. We pushed along with the hope of over-taking them, and had not marched many miles when we caught sight of him. He had stopped at a house on the road to get dinner, and some of the party who had not dismounted, having heard the tramping of our horses' feet, gave the alarm, and they mounted their horses and galloped away just as we were coming in sight Colonel Jewell directed our bugler to sound the gal-lop, and we chased them several miles, but we soon found that it was useless to keep it up further, as our animals were too much jaded to overtake their fresh horses. Standwaitie was on his way to join Colonel Clarkson at Locust Grove, and was taking it leisurely. But, as we continued our march, we reached Locust Grove first, and captured Clarkson before he had time to receive reinforcements.

Sunday morning, May 3d, as soon as the earliest rays of the sun streaked the east and the stars were disappearing, we were up and on the march. The day was lovely, but the country seemed like a vast wilder-ness, as no sounds greeted our ears or objects met our sight, which indicated that we were within the limits of civilization. We reached Scott's Mills just before sundown, having met with no one during the day. When we struck the State line road, a few miles fur-

tner south of the Mills, we examined carefully again
for horse tracks.   We saw some tracks, but they
seemed to have been made early in the morning, or,
perhaps, the day before.   The tracks showed that the
horses were shod with shoes different from those which
we use.   The locality of Scott's Mills has been noted
for bushwhackers since our troops have occupied southwest Missouri, and I thought it best to use such vigilance as would leave no opportunity for the enemy to
surprise us.   We did not stop at the Mills, but continued our march up the valley of the Cowskin River
until ten o'clock, when we turned aside from the main
road into a thick woods, and dismounted, and picketed
our horses on a small open spot where there was fair
grazing.   After having spread our blankets upon the
ground, and left two men on guard, we threw ourselves
down and slept soundly for five hours.   Monday morning, May 4th, we were on the march about three o'clock.
Nothing occurred during the day, except that we
passed a good many more houses with families living
in them than the two previous days.   We were constantly on the lookout, however, feeling that we might
be fired upon from the woods or bluffs at almost any
moment.   But we were not.   We encamped a few
miles east of Pineville, and on the evening of the 5th
we reached Cassville, and delivered the dispatches and
packages to Colonel Harrison, commanding the post.
From conversations with some of the officers and soldiers of the First Arkansas cavalry here, it does not
appear that he has any intention of returning to Fayetteville soon.

We find that we shall be obliged to remain here
perhaps a week to await dispatches from Springfield.
Colonel Harrison will probably endeavor to justify
his action before the Department Commander. We
think that he has laid himself open to charges and
specifications and a trial by Court Martial. But the
detention is fortunate for us in some respects; for if
we should start back immediately, it is doubtful
whether all our horses would be able to make it
through to Fort Gibson. A week's rest, with such attention as we shall endeavor to give them, will enable
them to recuperate considerably, and we hope sufficiently to carry us through when we get ready to
start back.

The troops here are daily expecting to be attacked
by the enemy, but from what I can hear I don't believe
that the officers have such definite information in regard to the strength and movements of the enemy, as
to warrant the belief that any immediate danger need
be apprehended. As we have just passed over
a region of one hundred and fifty miles unoccupied by our troops, it is perhaps safe to say
that it is also unoccupied by any forces of the
enemy other than bands of guerrillas and bushwhackers. Colonel Harrison, it would seem, is need-
lessly nervous, and his nervousness may be slightly
contagious.

I find that we have a good many troops in Southwest Missouri. Colonel T. T. Crittenden, of the
Seventh Missouri Militia cavalry, has eight hundred

men and two pieces of the Second Indian battery, stationed at Newtonia, twenty-five miles northwest of Cassville. From all accounts he is an active and energetic officer, and is doing good service for the State. There are also fortifications and a block house at Newtonia, so that the principal part of the cavalry force stationed there can be kept in the field. Two companies of the Eighth Missouri State Militia cavalry, are stationed at Neosho, under Captain Milton Burch, one of the most efficient officers in Southwest Missouri. There are also several companies stationed at Mount Vernon, thirty miles northeast of this place, and at Springfield there are probably between three and four thousand effective troops.

The Missouri State troops are well armed, mounted and equipped, and should be, and I believe are, effective troops in the service of the State. They could, no doubt, maintain order in this State and suppress guerrilla warfare, if our volunteer forces would take more advanced positions and prevent invasion of the State by an organized army of the enemy.

It was reported the day after our arrival, that Colonel Cloud, with a force of two thousand men and a battery of light artillery, was to leave Springfield immediately for this point. But he has not put in an appearance yet. He has probably marched in some other direction. There does not seem to be any hope of being able to accompany our troops as far as Fayetteville on our return.

We hear every day of the Militia scouting the

country and skirmishing with bushwhackers. At a
distance one might think that they have very little to
do. But they are constantly moving. The commanding officer of a post, for instance, receives information
of the presence of a party of guerrillas in a certain
locality so many miles to the southeast, and of another
party at another place so many miles to the southwest. A detachment of cavalry must at once be sent
out in each case. They may or they may not find
the enemy.

Thus they are kept employed, performing a great
amount of service with very small results, if we take
into account the operations of the troops from only a
single post. If, however, we look at the operations of
the Militia forces over the State, we find that the results are not trifling. Taking into account the number of men in active service, it is claimed that their
percentages of losses in killed and wounded, are as
high as the percentage of casualties among volunteer
troops in the field. While this may not be quite true,
I have no doubt that their annual losses foot up a high
percentage.

Information has been received here that the First
Kansas Colored regiment has completed its organization, and is now stationed at Baxter Springs, under
command of Colonel James M. Williams. Kansas
now has the honor of organizing the first Colored regiment for service in the war. This is highly gratifying
and in perfect harmony with the spirit and tradition
of her people, who have ever been on the side of jus-

16

tice in regard to the question of slavery. It is surely fitting that they should take the lead in organizing the late slaves for the defence of the Government and for perpetuating their own freedom. It will now not be many months before we shall hear of the organization of Colored regiments all over those sections of the South occupied by our troops. I have no doubt but that they will give a good account of themselves when they come to meet the enemy on the field. The *impropriety* of arming them against their late masters may be talked of by those who would fight the enemy with kid gloves, and without trying to hurt him; but not by those who are in earnest about carrying the war through to a successful conclusion, by every legitimate means recognized by civilized nations. There will perhaps always be in society, even of the most advanced type, a conservative party that will reluctantly take a step forward in the moral and social progress of their time. Its function is a proper one, and it is no more than we should expect, to find this spirit of conservatism displayed at such a time as the present. But the great common sense of our people must relegate that phase of it which opposes the arming of the freedmen to the region where all the barbarisms which we have outgrown, are buried. Many of us may live to see the day when many of those who are now doing their best to keep social and moral progress from breaking over ancient landmarks, will wonder how it was that they held such views.

But to return to the colored troops at Baxter Springs.

Though they may be of some service at that point in
affording protection to our supply trains, it is to be
regretted that they were not sent on to Fort Gibson,
as the situation is getting such that they are much
needed there. It is also reported that they are building
a small fort at Baxter, and that they have already had
several skirmishes with Livingston's band of guerillas,
whose operations are chiefly confined to that section.
Stationed inside of fortifications properly supplied with
water and rations and ammunition for a month, two
companies of infantry ought to be able to hold the
place against any force of guerrillas likely to attack
it. The guerrilla leaders in that section declare that
they will not take the colored soldiers nor the officers
under whom they are serving, as prisoners of war. If
the enemy really intend to murder all colored soldiers
and their officers who fall into their hands, they cannot
justly complain if the colored troops retaliate the first
opportunity, which might not be long delayed. Men's
evil actions frequently return upon them with com-
pound interest, when least expected. And so it may
be in this case. The enemy may be inventing the
means of his own destruction. Seeing that it is possible that they are turning their swords against their
own breasts, and that they may suffer most by the
barbarous acts which they propose to put into effect,
they may reconsider the matter.

In addition to the infantry, there should be two companies of cavalry stationed at Baxter to scout the country thoroughly. The enemy, it is not likely, will care

much for a small infantry force at that station, as they can play around it even in sight, so long as they keep out of range of the infantrymen's muskets

General F. J. Herron's two divisions of the *Army of the Frontier*, which were with us at the battle of Prairie Grove, have been ordered to join General Grant's army now besieging Vicksburg. These troops, during the last three months, have been operating along the southern counties of Missouri, but recently they moved to the vicinity of Rolla. General Herron is a gallant officer, and commands troops that have already made a glorious record. They are now entitled to have Prairie Grove inscribed upon their victorious banners, and in a few months they will probably have Vicksburg added.

A detachment of the State Militia had a skirmish with a squad of guerrillas on the 9th at Gad Fly, a small place about half way between Cassville and Newtonia, resulting in the wounding of three of the enemy, and the capture of their horses, saddles and equipage, together with two negroes. Slavery is unquestionably getting to be an expensive and troublesome luxury, when the masters are obliged to take their slaves around with them through the woods and over the hills, as they move from place to place. When it comes to this any man of sound mind ought to know that slavery is dead. There are not many grown up negroes in this section, who are not half idiots or old and infirm, who will not likely soon relieve their masters of the trouble of pulling them around from place to place, by running away and joining their friends. Nearly all the negroes of this section gained their freedom when our troops came through here a year ago. A few, particularly old ones, and children who had no parents, however, are still with their master's families on the homesteads.

Since we came into Missouri I have noticed that a good many farms are being cultivated. Of course there are very few families that will be able to till all the land which they once had under cultivation, for they cannot keep the animals and get the hands neces-sary to do it. They have, in many instances, used the rails not destroyed by the armies to inclose such tracts as they will be able to put under cultivation. We saw a number of fields the other day where the corn was coming up and was an inch or so high. There will be very little wheat raised in southwest Missouri this season, for during the season of sowing last autumn, the country was too much overrun by the armies to permit the people to work in the fields. On most of the farms the people have not finished planting their corn yet. In nearly every case where we saw them at work, the daughters or mothers were dropping the corn, as they call it, and the boys too young for the war, were plowing it in or covering it with hoes. If the season is good, a surplus of corn will be raised, particularly in the neighborhoods of posts garrisoned by our troops. As no family is permitted to keep much stock, very little of their corn will be fed to their own animals. But all they have to spare will

doubtless bring a fair price if sold to our troops, provided it is not taken before being sold.   Fruits are
quite an item in the foodstuffs consumed by the people
of this country; and there is good prospect of an abundant yield of apples, peaches, pears, &c., this season.
When our division was encamped near this place last
October, many of the company messes exchanged their
surplus rations of coffee and tea for dried apples and
peaches, honey, &c.   Nearly every family formerly had
from half a dozen to several dozen stands of bees.

The women of southwest Missouri surely deserve
mention for their noble conduct in sticking to their
homesteads and maintaining themselves and their children in the absence of their husbands and fathers and
brothers in the war.   If I were gifted with elegant
expression, nothing could afford me greater pleasure
than to pay them the highest possible tribute for their
truly womanly characters under the most trying circumstances.   With their youthful sons and daughters
they raise their own foodstuffs, and in many instances
spin and weave and manufacture most of their own
clothing.   A good many raise small patches of cotton,
from which they spin and weave their cotton goods,
and keep a few sheep, the wool from which they make
their woolen clothing.   There are men now and then
found of loquacious tongues, who speak disparagingly
and lightly of these people because they wear "home-
spun clothing," and do not appear quite so polished as
those brought up in polite society.   In all this I see a
grand simplicity and beauty, for the women are

extremely modest. Their fair races are set well back under their sunbonnets, and no one who loves to speak the truth would claim that they are forward and bold in their actions. It is often remarked that they are so shy of strangers that they will not ask our officers for pay or receipts for forage, horses, or commissary supplies taken from them. They generally have pleasant, honest expressions, but often bearing a tinge of sadness. Though surrounded by adversities of every kind, they endeavor to preserve their complexions. Probably no section containing the same number of women, would show a larger proportion who possess as good figures and features and complexions. I have observed them closely, for often on scouting expeditions and on the march, I have, in company with others, rode up to the well or spring to fill our canteens with water, or to the gate to make enquiries. Hence I have seen them as they appeared at home in their every-day life.

Well, this is 13th day of May, and the last day we shall lounge around the old brick Court House at Cassville. The dispatches and mail have arrived from Springfield; our horses have rested and fared moderately well in regard to forage, and we now leave for Fort Gibson. We have found the loyal Arkansas soldiers very clever; have had full rations while stopping with them, and our haversacks replenished for our return. When we arrived here, we felt sure that four days on hard bread and bacon had not quite kept us up to our usual standard of strength and activity.

Going without the good strong coffee which we have in camp, no doubt had a depressing effect upon our nervous systems. Though we each took a quantity of ground coffee in our haversacks, we did not take the trouble to kindle a fire every day and make coffee on the route. Every soldier has perhaps noticed how a good cup of coffee, after a night's marching, tones up his nervous system and makes him feel a livelier interest in everything around. We sometimes fill our canteens with coffee before starting out on a reconnoissance of several days; but it is not satisfactory to drink it in this way. We miss that fine flavor or bouquet which we get when it is taken fresh from the camp kettles.

There is no further talk of the enemy attacking the troops at Cassville, nor do they propose to return to Fayetteville until they are reinforced from Springfield.

Nothing of interest occurred the first day of our return march, but the second day, between Pineville and Scott's Mills, we saw eight or ten armed men on horse-back coming towards us, dressed in butter-nut suits, whom we supposed were bush-whackers. As soon as they saw and carefully observed our blue uniforms, they fired a volley at us from their shotguns, making the brush rattle around us, and then instantly wheeled about and galloped back a hundred yards or so and took a road which crosses ours at nearly right angles. We threw our right hands to our carbines and raised them, and discharged a volley at the flying horsemen, but as they were upwards of a hundred yards away when we fired, we could not determine whether the balls from our carbines took effect or not. Upon firing we dashed forward, but when we came to the point where the road they took crossed ours, they had disappeared in the dense woods. We continued our march, kept our eyes open, but did not exert our horses, as we were desirous of preserving their strength in case of an emergency, as a long journey yet lay before us. After passing Scott's Mills we did not take the same path through the Nation that we came up on, but one about ten miles to the South of it, as it would shorten our route considerably. We then struck Grand River about eight miles above Grand Saline. The grass had grown astonishingly since we came up, and we had no trouble in getting good grazing for our horses wherever we stopped.

On the way up and returning, we made it a rule to stop in some lonely retreat at about ten o'clock, and rest and graze our animals for two or three hours, and then resume the march and stop again at five o'clock for two hours, resume the march and halt again at ten at night, and start the next morning between three and four o'clock. Our animals stood this long and tedious journey quite well, and in the course of a week will be able to take their places beside other cavalry horses on the march or on the scout. We arrived at Fort Gibson on the afternoon of the 16th, having been absent upwards of two weeks. It was a real pleasure to see the familiar faces and shake the hands of our comrades. We were congratulated on our safe return, as the enemy have moved up in sight of the Fort, and are getting quite bold of late.   There will be a hiatus in my account of the operations of this command during the last two weeks; but nothing has occurred particularly worth mentioning, and we have had an opportunity of glancing at operations along the border.

CHAPTER XIII.

The enemy occupying the heights south of the Arkansas River in
sight of Fort Gibson—Picket firing across the river all day
long—Strength of General Cooper's force—He is preparing to
capture Colonel Phillips' supply train—Name of post of Fort
Gibson changed to Fort Blunt—Colonel Phillips contending
single-handed with two Generals of the enemy—Hard service for the cavalry—Capture of horses and mules from the
enemy—Activity in the enemy's camp—The enemy kill the
Federal pickets, and capture a good many animals—The battle—Enemy driven from the field and pursued—Recapture of
some animals—Large force of the enemy cross the Arkansas
River, and march to meet the Federal supply train—Convalescent soldiers coming in from Tahlequah—The troops move
inside the fortifications at Fort Gibson—The engagement at
Rapid Ford, Sunday afternoon—Colonel Phillips intended the
movement only as a demonstration.

After returning to my post of duty at Gibson, I
found that the enemy had become much bolder than
when we left on the night of the first instant. They
have moved all the forces from the neighborhoods of
Webber's Falls, North Fork and other points in the
Indian Territory to the heights on the south side of the
Arkansas River, nearly opposite the post, and not more
than five or six miles away. During the entire day,
at intervals of a few minutes, we heard the firing be-

tween their pickets and ours across the river. This
skirmishing between the picket lines of the two armies
has been going on several days. Three or four of our
soldiers have been killed and wounded, and it is believed fully as many of the enemy, as we have the best
arms. The heavy timber on both sides of the Arkansas affords both parties a convenient shelter from the
effects of each other's arms. A man cannot show
himself many seconds without being fired upon. His
chances of being struck depends upon the distance
which separates him and the foe, the marksmanship of
the party firing, the gun and its range. Our carbines,
by raising the sights to the outside limit, will carry a
ball to the mark about a thousand yards. The Arkansas River is not quite that wide at any point within
ten miles of here. The enemy, therefore, after they
get the approximate range of our carbines, will not
likely very often venture inside of this range. If they
do they are sure to be brought down. General Cooper
seems to have command of all the rebel troops operating against us, and they are reported to be composed
mainly of Texans and Indians, estimated at from five to
seven thousand men, with one or two batteries of artillery. Our scouts report that some two days ago they sent
out two strong reconnoitering forces of cavalry; that
one of these forces crossed the river below here for the
purpose of going up on the east side of the Grand
River, and that the other force crossed the Arkansas
and Verdigris Rivers, some seven or eight miles above
this post, for the purpose of going up on the west side

of Grand River, with the view of forming a junction near Cabin Creek, and attacking our supply train, which is expected down from Fort Scott in a few days. If the force really went up on the east side of Grand River, we must have passed very near it some time yesterday when on the way here with dispatches and mail from Cassville. Everything indicates that we shall have a lively time about here in a few days. Whether very large forces of the enemy have crossed the river yet or not, there are certainly strong reasons for believing that they are making preparations to attack our train at some point above here. The heavy firing along the river the past few days is doubtless intended as a *feint*, to occupy our attention, and to prevent us from reinforcing the train's escort. But they will find that Colonel Phillips is not so easily to be thrown off his guard.

The name of this post has been changed from Fort Gibson to Fort Blunt, in honor of Major General James G. Blunt, our division commander of last winter, but who is at present commanding the District of Kansas. If Fort Blunt is not to be abandoned almost as soon as named, the General should use his influence in getting reinforcements sent down here at once, and in having Colonel Phillips made a Brigadier General. After the Colonel has, by continual skirmishing with the enemy, marched his forces down here and *took* possession of this country, and held it against such odds, and so much further in advance of all other Federal troops in the west. it would be manifestly unjust to send an

officer down here who would rank him.   Nor do we believe that if the War Department could see the present state of things in their true light, that it would
permit him to be robbed of his hard-earned honors;
but that it would send him reinforcements, and a com-
mission appropriate to his command.   The command
to which he has been assigned is really a recognition
of his ability and merit.   I have already mentioned that
since he captured this isolated station in the enemy's
country, he has had two of the enemy's generals to
contend with, one of whom may be a Major General.

The active service during the winter and spring,
with inadequate forage, has put our cavalry horses in
bad condition for the service now required of them.
All the animals in camp we are obliged every day to
send out on the prairie, in the vicinity of the Fort,
under guard, to graze.   They are generally sent out
in several herds to different localities.   The plain is
now pretty much denuded of grass for a mile or so of
camp, so that the horses must be taken somewhat beyond this limit.   They are taken out every morning
at daybreak and driven in at night.   Perhaps nearly
half of our cavalry horses are kept out in this way,
while the other half are used by our troops in watching the movements of the enemy, on reconnoissances,
&c.   While animals will fatten on grass when they
get it in sufficient quantities and are not annoyed by
flies, it alone does not afford such nutritive and
strength-giving qualities as will enable our horses to
do hard service, such as is required of them.

A detachment of about four hundred of our cavalry which were sent on a reconnoissance on the 18th, in the direction of the Creek Agency, on south side of the Arkansas, captured about sixty head of horses and mules from General Cooper's command. This bold movement of our troops on the south side of the river, will probably prevent the enemy from sending as large a force as he had intended to attack our supply train. Should they leave their camp guarded by only a small force, Colonel Phillips might take it into his head to take a force of cavalry and cross the Arkansas at the Rapid Ford five miles below this post, and make a dash on it, with the view of capturing or destroying it. Though they probably keep a small force near the ford, we could probably shell them out, and cross without serious loss. But we cannot afford to make a movement that will endanger our train. From the roof of one of the buildings inside our fortification, with a field glass, we can see very near the enemy's camp. The clouds of dust that we saw this afternoon, at several points on the opposite heights, clearly indicates that he is making some important movement. A large cavalry force was in motion, but we could not determine the direction they were marching. The river is now quite low, and there are several points, both above and below us, where they can ford it. It is, I suppose, difficult for Colonel Phillips to determine the nature of their present activity; whether it means to attack us here, or to go up the country west of us, and attack our train due in a few days from Fort Scott.

To-day, the 20th, I have been out nearly all day with our troops. This morning, just before nine o'clock, several of our men came in as fast as their horses could carry them, and reported that the enemy were firing upon our pickets, and had killed several of them, together with a number of herders, and were driving away one or two herds of horses and mules. The bugles were instantly sounded, and in a few momments Colonel Phillips had nearly all his force, consisting of cavalry, dismounted men, and two guns of Captain Hopkins' battery out on the plain, about a mile east of the fort. He immediately formed his line and sent out a detachment of cavalry to the northeast of his position as skirmishers, and soon discovered that the enemy, in considerable force, had formed under cover of a rather dense woods, about a half-mile almost directly east of us. The section of artillery brought out from the fort was directed to open fire upon the enemy. After a half dozen rounds of shells had been thrown into the woods where we first saw them, and our cavalry had opened on the left, I could see from our position, near the section of artillery, that, from the clouds of dust raised in the timber, that the enemy were in rapid movement. We moved forward with the two guns and dismounted men, and our cavalry pressed them on the left. In the meantime all the horses and mules not captured had been driven into camp, and our cavalry was being rapidly reinforced. When our cavalry was sufficiently strengthened by the arrival of troopers from the fort, mounted on horses just brought in, the line on the left was formed, and the bugles sounded the charge. At the same time the artillery, which was supported by the dismounted men, had moved up nearer the timber, and opened with shell. The enemy had no sooner drawn our first volley at a short range than they fled in the direction they came from. We heard that a shell from one of our guns burst in the midst of a body of rebel Indians, killing and wounding quite a number, and throwing the others into a panic. It is often remarked that Indians have a greater dread of artillery than white troops. Our cavalry followed them beyond Greenleaf Prairie, ten miles southeast of the fort, and recaptured a good many of our horses and mules which they had captured in the morning. Their rear was exposed to the fire of our cavalry during the entire afternoon, and they must have suffered considerable loss in killed and wounded. They left on the field only eight men, but we have understood that they took a number along with them who were mortally wounded. We lost fourteen men killed, and had about as many wounded. The engagement lasted about an hour and a half, but some time was consumed on the skirmish line before we ascertained the exact position of the enemy in the woods. They had taken up a position near the road leading to Greenleaf Prairie, and probably intended to draw our troops into an ambuscade. But Colonel Phillips was not to be deceived, by rushing headlong after a pretended flying party of the enemy, to be fired upon by a massed force in the woods. It was entirely

17

due to his coolness and skill in handling his troops that enabled us so quickly to put the enemy to flight. It is a time now that our movements should be conducted with great caution, as the enemy have not only a larger force than ours, but it is composed mainly of white troops.

That he should have succeeded in coming so near us unexpectedly is due to the fact that they killed most of our pickets along the road they came in on. They killed, captured, or cut off all our men on the two outside picket stations, but when they came to the third, not more than three miles from camp, our picket guard hurried to the fort and reported the approach of the enemy. It is supposed that they crossed the river near Webber's Falls and made a night's march. With General Cabell's division operating along the Arkansas line, and General Cooper's force directly in our front within four or five miles of us, it is impossible for Colonel Phillips, with the force at his disposal, to guard all the approaches to this post, except within a radius of a few miles. This raid of the enemy has cost us heavily in animals. Our loss will not fall much short of three hundred horses and mules, and perhaps even more, including the losses of the Indian soldiers. The four companies of the battalion of the Sixth Kansas cavalry lost probably nearly half of their horses. As the men of these companies owned their horses as private property, and have been paid for their risk and use by the Government, the loss to each individual owner will be quite a hardship. Though they may soon be in funds, as the paymaster is expected to come down with the supply train to pay off the troops of this division, it will be difficult for them to find in this section suitable animals for remounts. Indian ponies could perhaps be had, but in my opinion they are only suitable for Indians, and would answer only as temporary remounts for the white soldiers.

One of our Indians, a herder or picket, who was killed by the enemy, had his clothing set on fire and his body burned to a crisp. He was brought in this afternoon with the other killed and wounded, and he presented a ghastly sight. It was a barbarous act on the part of the enemy, and we had supposed that the rebel troops operating against us were commanded by officers who had too high a sense of honor to permit such an outrage. I am unable to see what object they had in view in perpetrating such fiendish treatment on the dead. If they think that such acts will make our men regard them with greater terror, they are mistaken. It was probably done by the rebel Indians. Our pickets at the Rapid Ford five miles below the fort, reported to-day (22d) that the enemy fired wooden balls at them from the opposite side of the river nearly all day. This would indicate that they want to keep up a noise to occupy our attention, and that they have more powder than lead to waste. We can see very clearly that they desire to draw our attention to points on the river below here as much as possible, while their most important movements, are directed to another quarter, to the west side of Grand river, for the purpose of capturing our commissary train

On the 22d our scouts brought in information that a large force of the enemy crossed the Arkansas above the mouths of the Grand and the Verdigris rivers, and are believed to be moving northward. Whether it is their intention to continue their march northward until they meet our supply train, or whether they intend to take up a strong position above here and await its arrival, to make the attack, is not definitely known. Colonel Phillips is watching their movements closely and will use his force here to the best possible advantage to prevent the capture of our train. He has to-night sent out nearly all of his available cavalry to meet the train which is due here Sunday night, the 24th. The enemy seem to be almost as well-informed of its movements as we are, from the preparations they are making to effect its capture. The clouds of dust we saw again to-day west of their camp shows that they are displaying great activity. There is not now a reasonable doubt but that we shall have to fight to get our train in. But as our troops have not yet been defeated, we will not give it up without a hard contest.

A number of our sick and convalescent Indian soldiers who have been at Tahlequah for some time, came in to-day, fearing an attack from the enemy at that place, since it is known that rebel scouts were recently seen in that vicinity. It is provoking that we have not a larger cavalry force in this section. The enemy, however, would not likely attack a hospital, but they might go there and take away with them the convalescent patients, unless those in charge of the hospital should spread the report that a number of small-pox patients are still there, which I am under the impression is a fact. I don't know that we have had any troops stationed there since we came here; and there must be some good reason why the enemy has not shown himself in sight of that place, as it is about twenty-five miles from this post. But he would just about as likely wish to capture a herd of horses with glanders as a hospital filled with small-pox patients.

Sunday, May 24th, was a day of considerable excitement and activity with us. We knew that the threatening movements of the enemy during the last four or five days, meant something; and that the time had come when we must act or suffer inglorious defeat. Colonel Phillips is not an officer who can remain inactive while the enemy are displaying activity about him.

On Saturday (23rd) our pickets along the banks of the river, having first ascertain the range of our carbines and carefully estimated the distance across the river, fired upon and killed three of the enemy's patrol guards on the opposite bank. Our soldiers managed to fix up some cartridges which contained a little more than the usual quantity of powder. At any rate the charges were sufficient to send the balls flying over the river and right into objects at which the carbines were aimed. There is not a better cavalry arm in the service than Sharp's carbine. We have some adventurous spirits in the battalion of the Sixth Kansas cavalry, and I believe that if it were possible they would contrive some means to send a ball two miles, if nothing but a river separated us from the enemy.

There was an alarm in camp Saturday night, caused by a detachment of the enemy making an attempt to capture our pickets at one of the outside stations. In view of the situation and to guard against a possible surprise, Colonel Phillips ordered all the troops encamped on the southern and eastern slopes of the hill, inside of the fortifications. We took our tents down and packed everything up, and in less than two hours were inside the fortifications. Some few of the soldiers thought it useless, while most of them were perfectly satisfied to trust to the judgment of our commanding officer, as he was in a position to know very nearly the exact situation. The thought of being somewhat crowded, it is true, was not a pleasant feature; but nearly every one was willing to forego a little freedom of movement for the sake of greater safety. So this morning when the sun had climbed the mountains, which, from our more elevated position, looked lovely fringed with green, the parapets were bristling with the guns of Captain Hopkins' battery. Various rumors were afloat all the morning concerning the movements of the enemy, but nothing was definitely known. As he is known to have received considerable reinforcements recently, some thought that he might feel strong enough to divide his force into two divisions, one to attack our train, and the other our troops here in the fort. Colonel Phillips, who no doubt comprehends the situation, at three o'clock this afternoon took about five hundred men, infantry, cavalry and one section of Hopkins' battery, and marched down to the Rapid Ford, five miles below here, with the view of making a demonstration against the enemy's camp. I desired to witness the action, and also went along. We marched leisurely, and reached the ford about four o'clock. There had been no firing between the pickets during the day, though it is not likely that they had kept quiet on account of religious scruples. We saw the enemy on the opposite bank in considerable force. They did not seem alarmed at our presence, and were quite willing to show themselves some distance back in an open space. As the river bank on the north side, as well as on the south side, was thickly clothed with brush and woods, they did not see the section of the battery when we commenced forming in line. While they were surveying the situation, Captain Hopkins estimated the range, and in a moment more, bang went a shell from one gun, and then from the other, right into a small group of the enemy. The place became too hot for them. We could plainly see the shells burst near the party, and their instant scattering; but we could not see whether any of them were struck or not by pieces of bursting shells. A number of men were seen near a small house, on the road, several hundred yards beyond the opposite ford. Two or three shells were thrown near them, and they immediately disappeared. Presently, for a hundred yards or so above and below the ford, they opened fire from behind fallen trees and the thick woods, but the balls from their small arms fell spent near us or dropped into the river. We returned several volleys, aiming at the places where we saw the smoke rising from their discharged muskets. I fired a dozen rounds from my Sharp's carbine, waiting every time for the smoke to rise, from some point on the opposite bank. Captain Hopkins now commenced shelling the woods along the opposite bank, and the enemy's firing ceased. They sheltered themselves from our shells by getting behind the trunks of fallen trees. Colonel Phillips, now at the head of his cavalry, followed by the infantry, filed along down into the river, with the apparent intention of marching right across. The river bed on the north side was perfectly dry, the channel running near the opposite bank. We continued to move forward until we reached the middle of the stream, when the enemy opened a volley upon us, wounding two or three men. We returned the fire, but with not much advantage, as we had to guide our horses in the strong current which was now flowing up to their flanks. The heavy volleys of musketry made a good many horses unmanageable. The infantry, however, who were still on the sand bar, returned the fire vigorously, and with better effect, so that the enemy kept back a few yards from shore. Colonel Phillips presently turned back, and we occupied for some time the dry river bed on the north side, and kept up a steady firing for half an hour. In the meantime our twelve pounders had been steadily throwing shot and shell into the woods.

After this demonstration, which lasted nearly three

hours, the whole force, except a guard left at the ford, returned to the fort. We shall probably know in a few days what effect the demonstration has had with the rebel forces. Colonel Phillips displayed great courage and coolness in his exposed position. The enemy's bullets flew around him as thick as hail.

CHAPTER XIV.

The enemy makes a night attack on the Federal supply train—
    Gallant charge led by Colonel Phillips, and total route of the
    enemy—Only a sutler's wagon partially plundered—The
    enemy had another force which failed to co-operate—The pay-
    master paying off the troops—The Government should adopt
    a system to enable officers and soldiers to send their money
    home—Activity noticed in the enemy's camp again—The
    Arkansas River rising—Friendly conversations between Fed-
    eral and Rebel Pickets—The Federal supply train returns to
    Fort Scott with a heavy escort—Engagement between Living-
    ston and the colored troops at Baxter Springs—The enemy
    anxious to know if the colored regiment is coming down—A
    woman takes one of the enemy's horses and comes into the
    Fort—Colonel Phillips to be re-inforced—Skirmish near Park
    Hill—Standwaitie's Indians in the northern part of the nation.

After returning from the Rapid Ford yesterday
evening, and getting our suppers, and resting a few
hours, we started out again to meet our train. While
marching along during the night on the old military
road upon which the train was coming, we saw several
fresh trails, the prairie grass having been tramped down
flat by horses' feet, showing that the enemy were moving in several divisions, doubtless with the intention
of attacking simultaneously from several quarters,
the front and flanks, or front and rear of the escort.

Several of us got off our horses and carefully inspected one trail, and easily distinguished the directions they had marched. Some ten or twelve miles out our detachment formed a junction with the troops guarding the train. The train probably had about two hundred wagons in all, and moving in the closest order possible, stretched out a distance of more than a mile. From the time we joined it the road ran over a broad prairie, until we should get within three or four miles of the fort. We marched with a detachment of about one hundred cavalrymen, say a quarter of a mile in advance of the escort just in front of the train, with detachments of cavalry at convenient distances from each other on both flanks, and with a strong rear guard. Skirmishers were also kept out a half mile on each side of the road, with instructions to keep up with the advance guard. We were moving along quietly, and approaching the timber on Grand River about five miles northwest of the fort, and, perhaps, nearly an hour before day-break, when we heard the report of a musket, and then three or four more shots. We saw the flash from the musket before we saw the enemy or heard the report. It was then silent for a moment, but the next moment we saw our skirmishers and advance guard falling back. Closely following them we saw, by the dim light of the stars, the long lines of the enemy filing over a ridge in the prairie a few hundred yards off. Orders were immediately given for the teams to change to two abreast, as this would shorten the line of wagons we were required to defend. In-

structions were also given to teamsters not to leave
their teams under any circumstances. The enemy
continued to advance, and when some two hundred
yards off, seemed to occupy nearly all the visible horizon upon the prairie, south, east and west of us. One
thousand cavalry, when not marching in close order,
cover a large field, particularly at night, and are likely
to be overestimated in numbers. Our lines were
quickly formed, and when the enemy approached
within a hundred yards of us, we opened fire upon
them. They promptly returned a volley. We continued to pour into their ranks volley after volley, which soon threw them into considerable disorder.
They soon rallied, however, and made a few feeble
efforts at charging us, but did not come nearer than
fifty yards of the troops with whom I was acting, for
our firing was conducted with great caution and deliberation. Several other divisions which they sent to make
attacks at other points, were equally unsuccessful. It
was a grand sight to see the flashes from the long
lines of muskets and carbines. Colonel Phillips formed
his troops into a kind of oblong square,which inclosed
the train. The two short sides of the square were
made quite strong, and when the enemy made an effort to break either of the long and weak sides, we
cross-fired him, and all his efforts were fruitless.
Nearly half of our troops fought dismounted, which
enabled them to fire with greater precision. We held
the enemy in check in this manner for upwards of
an   hour,   and   until   towards   daylight, repul-

sing him in every attack, when Colonel Phillips determined to take the offensive, and at the decisive moment ordered the bugle sounded and led his troops to the charge. We moved forward with a shout, and in a few moments completely routed the enemy all along the line. The main body we pursued several miles in the direction of the Verdigris River, firing into their rear every opportunity. Other detachments fled in other directions. They left twenty-six dead on the field. Our loss was seven or eight men killed, and perhaps twenty-five or thirty wounded. As soon as the enemy had been driven from the field, the train was set in motion, and arrived at Grand River opposite to the fort just after sunrise. During the day one or two wagon loads of the enemy's dead were brought in for burial near this post. We heard through our pickets along the river, that the enemy boasted of their intention of getting their Monday morning's breakfast out of our rations. If this really was their boast, and they brought no rations with them, they must have returned to their camp hungry and disappointed. They did, however, capture and plunder one sutler's wagon. The teamster for the sutler seems to have got frightened and left his team, which became separated from the train and wandered about on the prairie.

We received information through our scouts, that the enemy had another strong force above us on Grand River, which failed to co-operate with the force that engaged us in the morning. So far as we can find out, demonstration at the Rapid Ford, Sunday evening, in front of General Cooper's camp, caused him to change his plans in regard to the point where he had intended to attack our train. The force which fought us in the morning, either returned to defend and save their camp after starting out, or remained in camp longer than they had intended on account of our threatening attitude in that direction Sunday evening, thus preventing them from carrying out the pre-arranged plan of forming a junction with the force north of us at a certain point and at a certain hour Monday morning. It does not seem reasonable, and we do not believe, that the enemy deliberately planned to attack our train within sight of our fortifications, where we might quickly reinforce it with nearly all the troops of this post. Colonel Phillips certainly deserves great credit for the able manner in which he has baffled and defeated the enemy, who have made such great preparations for capturing our train— a prize which they would have highly valued.

It would be difficult to point out a finer movement in military manoeuvers, as having actually occurred, than that which Colonel Phillips executed to save his trains; and were he in a section where military correspondents are swarming around headquarters like they are around the headquarters of our eastern armies, he would be lauded as a real hero. Less brilliant achievements and less distinguished bravery than he has shown on several occasions during the last week, have been considered sufficient in the cases of other officers to earn them promotion. He has shown himself to be remarkably fertile in resources in an emergency. At such times most men lose their heads.

The enemy are reported to have had upwards of fifteen hundred men in the engagement, but I am inclined to think that they had at least two thousand white soldiers and Indians, composed of Texans, Choctaws and Cherokees. Though they seem to have been well-informed in regard to the movements of the trains, perhaps through Livingston's guerrillas, operating in the vicinity of Baxter Springs, they were disappointed in the strength of the escort. Had they succeeded in capturing or burning the train, we should have been obliged to abandon this post, as we could have issued full rations only for a day or so longer. Indeed, of some articles we have already been obliged to issue less than the full allowance. This country could afford no subsistence, except fresh beef; and all our other supplies would be exhausted before we reached the Kansas line.

The paymaster, who came down with the train, commenced on the 27th paying off the troops at this post. Many of the officers and soldiers here have not been paid for eight months, and, of course, payment at this time will be quite acceptable to everyone. A good many of our white soldiers, who have families, generally find some means of sending nearly all their salaries home soon after pay day. Many others would,no doubt, send their money north were it not for the danger of losing it. If a soldier puts his money in an envelope and seals it, and sends it by a friend to his family, his friend may get captured, or killed, or lose it, or be subjected to some great delay. And down here, where we are so much isolated from the rest of the world, the mail is not regarded as a fit and proper medium for the transmission of valuable packages, such as money. A soldier can ill afford to lose five or six months of his small earnings. It would be a great convenience to the officers and soldiers of our armies if the Government should adopt some system by which those desiring to do so could send their money to their families by check. When men carry their money around in their pockets, and have the slightest disposition to gamble, they are liable to be drawn into this immoral habit again—particularly when they have little else to occupy their minds. Since quite a proportion of our white troops lost their horses by the recent raid of the enemy, and by being worn out in the service for want of forage, we have an unusually large number of men subject to continuous camp life. And several times, while taking a stroll on the outskirts of the camp, I have noticed more than a half dozen small groups of men, in pleasant, shady spots, engaged in playing " Chuck Luck." They were all betting, generally in small sums of money A gum or rubber blanket is usually spread upon the ground, and three or four men sit down upon it, with dice and dice-box, and bet on the dice thrown. This affords excitement and kills time, which is a burden to men, who, for months, have been actively employed in scouting and marching. Loaded dice are now and then heard of, and when discovered generally result in a row. Other parties bet on games of cards. Some of those who are rather sharp gamblers, claim to have fleeced their comrades and some of the Indians out of more money than a soldier receives from the Government for six months' salary. The gambling cannot be easily broken up, for parties caught in the act of playing may claim to be playing for amusement.

We have noticed again to-day, from the roof of the large stone building on the bluff, with a spy-glass, unusual activity in the enemy's camp. What it means we do not yet know; and at present we do not feel any great anxiety in regard to it. We are now in a condition our troops would rather like them to attack us; and unless they come with an overwhelming force we should fight them outside our fortifications. But they doubtless know that it would be useless to attack us here, since we were able to rout them the other morning in an open field, when they had an opportunity of choosing the position and time of attack, and were free to maneuver as they pleased.

On the 28th the Arkansas river commenced rising rapidly, so that the enemy will not likely be very active on the north side for perhaps a week or so. They have no steam ferry boats, nor any other kind of boats fit for crossing the river, that we have heard of, between Fort Smith and their present encampment. And since we destroyed their steamboats at Van Buren last December, it is not probable that they have had much

18

river transportation on the Arkansas above Little
Rock. Though this is the season when navigation on
the river is best, neither party is able to use it to advantage. A steamboat plying on the river in the service of one party would be a target for the artillery and
small arms of the other. Below Fort Smith, for, perhaps, nearly two hundred miles, the enemy might ply
steamboats with comparative safety from attack by
our forces. But over that section they have very little
to transport, as the main army is in the neighborhood
of Little Rock.

The present rise is due almost entirely to the flood-
gates having been opened in the mountains. Such local rains as we have had recently have not, probably,
peceptibly affected the volume of water flowing in
the Arkansas, above the mouth of Grand river. The
spring rise of the Arkansas is almost as regular as the
rise of the Nile.

If we had pontoon bridges now, since our troops
are buoyant with life and confident in their strength,
and have full rations for nearly a month, we could annoy the enemy and doubtless drive him from his present position. To have full rations and know that the
larder is well filled, or that the commissary has abundant supplies on hand, gives strength and courage to
the soldier. It takes good food and plenty of it to
keep up a strong vigorous current of blood through
its natural channels.

The enemy's pickets and ours along the river are
getting more tolerant of each others' presence. They

agreed on a temporary truce on the 28th, and approached each other at a narrow point on the river, and talked across the water in a quite friendly manner. They had another conference on the 29th instant, and talked over the engagement of Monday morning pleasantly, and inquired of each other about friends in the two armies. But while parties are talking to each other under truce at one point on the river, they are firing upon each other at some other point. As nothing substantial can be gained by this continuous firing across the river, it will probably cease altogether soon. It has now been going on until there is getting to be very little novelty in it.

Our commissary train started back to Fort Scott on the evening of the 30th, and crossed Grand River twelve miles above this post, on account of its being too high to ford in this vicinity. Nearly all the cavalry here have been ordered to escort it as far as Baxter Springs or Neosho River. When this duty shall have been performed, the troops belonging to this division will return to this station. While it is not likely that the enemy would make a very great effort to capture or destroy our empty train returning, they would doubtless make some effort to destroy it, if they found that it had only a feeble escort. And we, from information received through Indians who have been gathering whortleberries in the mountains, are not sure that they have not already a considerable force above here on a kind of expedition of observation.

Information also came from Baxter Springs on the

31st of May, that a portion of the colored regiment stationed there under Colonel Williams, recently had a hard fight with Livingston's guerillas, and lost about twenty men killed. It seems that Livingston made a raid on the place, for the purpose of driving off the horses and mules kept at that station, and was in a measure successful. The animals, it is stated, were being herded on the prairie near the post where grazing was best, by a small number of colored soldiers, who were suprised when the rebels dashed upon them. When we first heard of the colored infantry being stationed at Baxter Springs several weeks ago, I remarked of the great need of a cavalry force at that point. One company of infantry is worth just about as much there as an infantry regiment, in contending with the guerillas of that section under Livingston. And very few animals can be kept there unless they shall be fed within the limits of the camp. And none are required at the station, except mules for the regimental teams.

A scouting party of the enemy was seen on June 1st, near Green Leaf, about eight miles east of this post. They are supposed to be a part of Standwaitie's rebel Indians, and to be moving in the direction of Tahlequah and the northern part of the Cherokee Nation. As all that part of the Nation adjacent to Arkansas is unoccupied by our troops, they may be permitted to remain in it several weeks undisturbed. Our cavalry is now so much occupied with escort duty to our supply trains, and in watching the movements of the enemy in this immediate vicinity, that Colonel Phillips is unable to send out a force to pursue every detachment of rebels moving northeast of us.

A negro man came into our lines on the 2d, from the rebel camp on the opposite side of the river, and he says that they claim to have upwards of six thousand men. He was taken prisoner on the 20th ultimo by the enemy, when they made the raid and drove away so many of our animals. They were much elated over this affair, but much disappointed in not being able to capture or destroy our supply train. They questioned him a good deal about the strength of our force, and wished to know if the colored troops were really coming down as reinforcements. He says that the thought of having to meet on the field, and on equal terms, the colored soldiers, makes them quite indignant. But a man is a man, black or white, and his being black does not prevent him necessarily from being valuable on the field. They affect to think that our government is hard pressed for soldiers when it feels the necessity of accepting the military service of the recent slaves. But we may observe that the enemy will perhaps find out, before this contest is over, that the recent slaves will feel as much interest in fighting for their freedom as our white soldiers have in fighting to maintain the integrity of the government. It may also be remarked that there are many of us who believe that there can be no permanent union without the permanent freedom of the late slaves. Many who at first scouted this idea, are beginning to take a similar view.

It seems Livingston wrote General Cooper just before our supply train came down, that the colored
regiment would accompany it as an escort from Baxter Springs. He urged that preparations be made for
capturing the whole outfit. The enemy, therefore,
when he attacked the train near here on the 25th ultimo, were somewhat disappointed in not finding it
guarded by an escort of colored troops; and now
affect to believe that we have no colored soldiers enlisted into the service. Before the summer is over,
and we continue to be as near neighbors as at present,
they will likely become abundantly satisfied on this
point—that is, that we have a regiment of soldiers as
black as ebony, and that they can go through the infantry manual as handsomely and with as much ease
as perhaps any of their own troops, and that if they
have an opportunity of seeing them, they may see
them with bright blue uniforms, and if coming into
line, with muskets and bayonets glistening beautiful-
ly but terribly. Colonel Williams has given much
attention to carefully drilling his regiment. We hear
that the colored troops are quite anxious to come into an
engagement with the enemy, and that they think they
would prick his tender white skin with the points of
their bayonets. The few contests they have had in the
vicinity of Baxter Springs with the enemy, show that
they are not lacking in bravery.

While a detachment of rebel Indians who were on
their way to Hilter Brand's Mills in the northern part
of the Nation, stopped to plunder the house of a fam-

ily near Tahlaquah yesterday, one of the women of
the house mounted one of the enemy's horses, and
came on here and reported their movements to Colonel Phillips. Such heroic action on the part of
a loyal woman of this territory is surely highly commendable. Her name should be preserved in the gal-
lery of Heroic Women. With a little presence of
mind, the loyal families living in the country might
often do very much toward keeping us advised of the
movements of the enemy. It is also probable that
there is a good deal of reliable information brought
in to Colonel Phillips concerning the movements of
the enemy, by people living in the country, that we
never hear of.

Our prospects are beginning to look a little brighter.
Colonel Phillips has received a dispatch from General
Blunt, who is now at Forth Leavenworth, urging him
to hold this post, no matter at what cost, and that he
will immediately send him reinforcements. We don't
believe that Colonel Phillips has had any intention of
abandoning this post, so long as his supplies came
through safely. We can fight while we have anything
to eat. But if the commanding General of the Department had not decided to do something to assist us
in keeping the country in our rear free of the enemy,
so that our supplies can reach us, the thought of falling back from this section would no doubt have to be
seriously considered by Colonel Phillips in the course
of a month or so. But a month's time may change
the aspect of things, not only in this section, but

throughout the country. It is not, I suppose, so much the question of ability to hold this post, but the question of ability to hold a larger portion of this country that concerns Colonel Phillips most. We do not know the number of troops General Blunt will have in his new command, but I do know that he is an officer who will not be content to remain inactive in the rear and allow his sword to rust, while there is an enemy in front. He is, every inch, a fighting General.

A small party of our Indian soldiers had a skirmish with a detachment of Standwaitie's men near Park Hill, June 5th, and had two men killed, and two seriously wounded. The enemy are reported to have also had several men wounded. Ambulances were immediately sent over to Park Hill to bring in the killed and wounded. Our scouting parties have been in that section very little recently. It is reported, also, that the rebels shot one of their own men, because he endeavored to save the life of one of our Indians. It has been suggested, however, that this story be taken with a grain of allowance. Our loss in this instance is probably due to the fact that our Indians were not quite as vigilant as they might or should have been. Small detachments of our troops should know by this time that when they are out of sight of our camp they are, as far as their safety is concerned, in the enemy's country, and liable to surprise at any moment.

Several of our Indian soldiers, who have had permission to visit their homes in the northern part of

the Nation near Maysville, have just returned, and report that the enemy have a force of upwards of one
hundred men in that section, murdering the loyal Indians, and committing all kinds of depredations. This
force of the enemy crossed the Arkansas River near
Webber's Falls, and marched up through the Nation
near the Arkansas line. As complaints have been coming in for several days of their depredations, Colonel
Phillips has determined to send a force of two or
three hundred cavalry in pursuit of the rebels. That
will soon put an end to the little reign of terror. It
is desirable to afford all the protection possible to those
loyal families who are endeavoring to live upon their
homesteads. And since Colonel Phillips has had command of the Indian Territory, it can hardly be said
that the enemy has had even a transient possession of
any portion of it.

The enemy killed two of our pickets on the night of
the 7th, within less than three miles of this post, by
sneaking upon them in the dark. They seem to act
upon the assumption that anything is fair in war. It
is supposed that they intended to prepare the way for
making another raid upon our animals, as soon as they
should be sent out with the herders the next day. The
night and day picket stations should be at different
points. But if they had it in view to make another
raid for such a purpose, they must have given it up
for some reason, for a detachment of our cavalry sent
out to-day several miles beyond the picket station
where the men were killed, returned without having

found any signs of the enemy. As two of our men escaped from the outside picket station, and came in to the next most distant station on the road leading from the post, the rebels perhaps thought that what they had done would be reported to Colonel Phillips' headquarters before our animals should be driven out to graze. When it becomes necessary for the men of an outside picket station to leave it, they should fall back upon the next interior station and await the approach of the enemy; but in the meantime it is the duty of the non-commissioned officer in charge to send a messenger in to headquarters, post-haste, to report what had already taken place. If the enemy should continue to advance and attack this second station, the non-commissioned officer in charge of it should send another messenger as swiftly as possible to his commanding officer, with such information as he has been able to gain of the enemy's movements. The courier should also be instructed as he starts on his flying errand to cry out at each of the stations he passes, " Men! up and at your posts, the enemy are advanccing!" Each station should detain the enemy as long as it can with safety do so. But of course if the officer in charge of it discovers the enemy advancing in strong force, he should not deploy his men in such manner as to make their capture or destruction an easy matter. If it should be a light advance guard of the enemy approaching, a well directed fire of the pickets will, perhaps, in most instances, stop their progress until the main force comes up. In the presence of an enemy picket duty is full of danger to the soldier, and if he relaxes his vigilance while on such duty, it may be not only at his own great risk, but he may also endanger the safety of the entire command to which he belongs. He should, therefore, be impressed with the responsibility of his position. Colonel Phillips has such an arrangement of picket guards, that it would now be almost impossible for the enemy to approach nearer than three or four miles without alarming our camp.

CHAPTER XV.

An agreement in regard to the cessation of picket firing—Mostly young men in the army—They have no Alcestis to die for them—General Cooper's army moves back twenty miles, perhaps to find better grazing—A rebel reconnoitering force west of the Fort—General Cabell's force near Cincinnati— The Indians harvesting—The wheat crop good, what there is of it—Major Foreman after Standwaitie—Engagement on Green Leaf prairie—The enemy finally driven from the field —Federal and Rebel pickets in swimming together—The Federals exchange coffee for tobacco—Desertion of rebel soldiers—Rebel discipline believed to be more severe in some respects than the Federal—Remarks on flogging and severe discipline—Major Foreman with six hundred men sent to meet Federal supply train—The enemy preparing to attack it again—An Indian prophet and the superstitions of the Indians.

On June 9th some sort of an agreement was arrived at between General Cooper and Colonel Phillips, by which the pickets of the two opposing armies along both sides of the river shall cease firing at each other as much as possible. This to my mind is a very sensible arrangement, for very little is accomplished by banging away all day long at each other, as if the two armies were skirmishing preparatory to going into action. We can sometimes hear from this post the volleys of small arms at different points along the river, as if the two forces were actually approaching each other in line of battle. If either party should attempt to cross the river, then it would of course be perfectly proper for the other party to fire upon them. But I do not apprehend that the firing will entirely cease immediately, as it will be easy for those of restless dispositions on either side to find some pretext for firing an occasional shot. Picket duty is very monotonous, and the *young* men like to do something occasionally for excitement. Perhaps it is needless for me to specify and emphasize the *young* men, for among our white troops I believe that over one-half of the enlisted men are between the ages of twenty and thirty years. We have quite a number under the age of twenty, counting myself among them. It will therefore be seen that we have a good deal of the spirit of youth among us; so much indeed that there is always some one ready to undertake almost any adventure that it is possible to propose. It is well enough to have a good deal of such *esprit de corps* in an army, if it is properly guided by older and cooler heads. But there is a thought that comes into my mind in regard to the great number of young men who have enlisted into our armies. It is this: If the war continues a few years longer, and it is as destructive of young men and men under middle age as it has already been, will not this great loss of young men just growing into manhood, and men just commencing to assume the duties of citizens, be seriously felt throughout the country for the next few generations? No one I think can doubt but that most of the strong, healthy and vigorous young men who are full of patriotic pride and feel a deep interest in their country's welfare, if they have not already, are now enlisting into the army. What proportion of these young men will return to their homes sound and healthy as they left them? Perhaps only a small proportion. The blood that courses the veins of these men is the kind of blood that should flow through the veins of the children of the rising generation. The patriotic spirit which animates these young men, is the kind of patriotic spirit which should animate the children of the future of this great country. The nation is surely making a great sacrifice, but the principle involved is a great one, and when we take into account the benefits that must accrue to future generations if our arms are crowned with success, as they must be, I believe that it will be admitted that the prize is worth much of the best blood of the country But the noble sacrifice of the heroic dead or living should not be regarded lightly, nor soon forgotten by the rising generation. Many of us may wish that we could have been born a generation or so later; but as we are here we should not endeavor to escape the responsibility, if we are true to ourselves, of doing our best to leave a desirable form of government—an ideal form—to those who shall come after us. And moreover some of us may reasonably hope that we shall escape the enemy's arms and the sickness of the camp, and enjoy for a time, at least, that desirable existence which the war is being waged to secure. But each of us that attains to a ripe age, as the years pass by and his thoughts turn to the scenes of the war, will remember with sadness that his company left a comrade upon this field and another upon that. And those of us whose heads are now filled with youthful thoughts will be crowned with hoary hairs, and instead of bounding over the plain as now, a staff will be used to assist locomotion. What a mystery is life!

We come to the final remark, that our young soldiers who are cut off when life is sweetest, and going down to their graves by the thousand almost daily, have no Alcestis to die for them. But they have proved themselves as generous as Alcestis, for they have laid down their lives for the living and unborn millions of their race. If life on the average is desirable or worth living, what an immensely greater amount of happiness there might be if the aged, who have but a short term of years before them, could die for the young. But the gift of life scarcely anyone desires to part with, though he knows he can retain it only for a short period. The old will never be sacrificed in war that the young may live the natural periods of their lives. The strongest and best must always do the fighting.

Information was received at this post on the 10th, that General Cooper's command on the south side of the Arkansas river has moved back about fifteen miles. Two women who brought this information

claim to have been detained in the camp of the rebels
about a week ; but they do not complain of any dis-
courteous treatment.   They think that the enemy
were about to make some important movement, and
that their detention was to prevent them from advis-
ing us anything concerning it.   Even if the main
body has left, it is probable that a force deemed sufficient to guard the fords of the river and to watch our
movements, will remain.   As they have no particular
point to hold, we can see no forcible reason why they
should be content to stay in camp all summer within
sight of us.   But the movement they are reported to
have just made, does not seem to be an aggressive one,
though it may turn out to be such.   It is possible that
they have moved their camp to a place where they
will have better grazing facilities for their animals.
We need not suppose that their horses will stand hard
service on grass any better than ours.   If their animals have any advantage over ours, it is probably due
to the fact, that they were kept at places during the
winter where plenty of hay and corn were put up for
their use.   Their horses may have had some slight
advantage too, by having had good grazing several
weeks earlier than ours.   As the country in their rear
towards Texas, is not infested with union guerrillas,
as the country in our rear is with rebel guerrillas ;
and as their supply trains, if they have any, are not
annoyed by our troops, their cavalry horses have nothing like the current hard service to perform that ours
have.   But we hope that this state of things will be

all changed in a few weeks, that we shall have troops enough down here to take the offensive, and put the enemy to looking out for the safety of their trains, etc. We believe that they will find that we can and will act as vigorously on the offensive as on the defensive, and that their lease on the south bank of the river is almost at an end. If Colonel Phillips should get reinforcements soon, he would no doubt cross the river and attack General Cooper in his camp. If successful, this would be better than forcing him to detach a portion of his troops for the protection of his supply trains.

A rebel reconnoitering force of about two hundred men were on the opposite side of Grand river this morning, probably not more than three miles from this post. They have ascertained that we have no force on the west side at present, and that the river here is so high that we cannot use the two little flatboats to take over a cavalry force, and that they can sport around with impunity almost within sight of the guns of the fort. As the Arkansas and Verdigris Rivers are both fordable, they know it would not be difficult to escape, even if we should send a force in pursuit of them. They may have been making a kind of survey of the situation, with the view of seeing if their batteries could be used against us with much advantage from the west side. It is the impression of our officers that they could not. The opposite heights, we believe, are too distant even for the best long range rifled guns to be very effective against our

19

works on the bluff. And supposing that they should hammer away at our fortifications for several days, they would at the end of that time still have the river to cross, which we should warmly contest, whether they attempted to ford it, or should bring pontoons to throw across it. When the river is low enough for a few hundred yards above or below the fortifications, and the enemy should attempt to force either of these crossings, we could quickly throw up temporary breastworks to cover our battery, and with grape and canister inflict a heavy loss upon them before they got over. But I will not state farther what we could do in an event that is not likely to occur. It is barely possible, however, that Generals Cooper and Cabell have contemplated joining forces to reduce this place.

Several loyal Cherokee women, who have just arrived from near Cincinnati, a small place about sixty miles east of this post, on the State line, report that a large force of the enemy, perhaps upwards of a thousand strong, were encamped at that point a few days ago. These women state that the enemy were all white troops, and appeared to be moving northward. We think that this is a party of General Cabell's force, which has been operating in western Arkansas during the last month. Should General Cabell undertake to co-operate with General Cooper, Colonel Phillips will have his hands full. This movement to the east of us, and right on the line of the Nation, looks somewhat as if the enemy intended to be in readiness by the time our next supply train comes down in about two weeks. They have commenced to set their toils early. A cavalry force can march in a day and night from the Arkansas line to any point on the Grand River, and thus easily co-operate with any force General Cooper might send to the west of us. Instead of making a demonstration against the troops here, it seems to be the intention of the enemy to withdraw to a convenient distance, so that our supply train will attempt to come through without our reinforcing its escort. If they make another effort to capture it, as they doubtless will, we may count upon their coming better prepared than last month. We shall also probably be better prepared to defend the train.

The few small patches of wheat that were sown last fall, by a good many families, in different parts of the Nation, are now just beginning to be harvested by the Indians. The season has been favorable, and the yield fair to the acreage. Beyond fifteen or twenty miles from this post, it is regarded as very dangerous for the men to work in their fields without guards for protection. An Indian is in his natural element when he has an opportunity of sneaking upon his foe, and there are many rebel Indians who have returned for this purpose. They regard this as a good time to get even on old grudges, which may have existed between their grandfathers in Tennessee or Georgia. The way the harvesters arranged it, is, I believe, for four or five or a half dozen men to combine to assist each other. About half of the party works while the other half stands

guard. It is thought that there has been enough
wheat grown in the nation this season, which, if carefully harvested, will go far towards subsisting the Indian families, thus dispensing with the necessity of
their being refugees about our camp, and fed by the
Government. Colonel Phillips is disposed to afford
them all the protection he can, while they are engaged
in harvesting their wheat crop, by keeping the country
as free of the enemy as possible. A dispatch was received on the 14th instant, from Major Foreman, who
was sent out a few days ago, with a force of about
three hundred and twenty-five Indians and white men,
stating that he is in hot pursuit of Standwaitie's Indians, who for upwards of a week, have been committing numerous depredations in the country to the
northeast of us. While Standwaitie is permitted to
remain in the nation, most of his followers return to
their homes in the section in which he operates, and
coming in contact with some of our loyal Indians,
who have also returned to their homes, a kind of private war springs up between the belligerent parties,
generally resulting in bloody contests. The reputation Major Foreman has as a fighting officer, justifies
us in believing that he would either bring the rebel
Indians to an engagement, or drive them out of the
Nation. But from the information received, it does
not seem likely that they will make a stand north of
the Arkansas River. They have shown very little disposition to come into a square fight.

Colonel Wattles, of the First Indian regiment, who

was sent out on the morning of the 15th, with a force of about three hundred men, to make a reconnoissance for a distance of fifteen or twenty miles along the north side of the Arkansas to the east of us, met a force of the enemy the next morning, about equal to his own, near Green Leaf Prairie, some ten miles east. Through his scouts, Colonel Phillips had heard of this force of the enemy, and knew that it was not much, if any, superior to the force under Colonel Wattles. Well, the two forces having met, a fight or the flight of one party was of course inevitable. But the two opposing forces determined to test each other's strength and bravery. The enemy posted themselves in the woods, near the road leading to Webber's Falls, in a rather advantageous position, and seemed to wish our troops to commence the attack, which they did very soon. Colonel Wattles did not, however, commence the attack directly in front, as the enemy desired, but threw out skirmishers, and commenced a movement to turn the enemy's right flank. By this movement our troops had the shelter of the woods as well as the enemy. Our force now having gained as good a position as that held by the enemy, the skirmish line was advanced, followed by the other troops in line, about two hundred yards back. The enemy, after some firing at different points along the skirmish line, forced it back upon our main line. But he did not come dashing furiously along with drawn swords, with the determination of breaking through our ranks. Nor did our troops move forward like a hurricane, but rather steadily until the enemy commenced to fall back. There was very little dash displayed on either side.

The position of the enemy at this point, according to the account of an eye witness, was just such a one as Colonel Jewell would have delighted to have had, were he living and had been on the field: He would have said: "Men, are your carbines and revolvers in perfect order? Do you see the enemy there? Unsheath sabres, follow me." And in an instant he would have swept like a storm through the ranks of the enemy, and few of them would have escaped the edges of our swords. He could instantly seize the situation, and there was no dallying with the foe afterwards.

After the skirmishing and fighting, which lasted upwards of an hour, the enemy retreated in the direction of Webber's Falls, having had a number of men wounded.

Our casualties were: one man killed, seven wounded and five taken prisoners. The five men taken prisoners belonged to the battalion Sixth Kansas Cavalry, and were not captured in the engagement, but while on their way down to join Colonel Wattles. They expected to find our troops at a certain place, but instead found the enemy, and were right in his midst before discovering their mistake. Some of our impetuous white soldiers, when they hear of a prospective fight, get permission, and rush away to take a hand in it, instead of waiting to take their proper places in their companies. While we admire their bravery, we are sometimes called upon to condemn their rashness and indiscretion.

As soon as a messenger came in and reported that the force under Colonel Wattles had been fighting the enemy at Green Leaf, and were falling back, Colonel Phillips immediately sent out Lieutenant-Colonel F. W. Shaurtie with two hundred men—mostly Indians— to relieve Colonel Wattles. But the reinforcements had not marched more than half way to the place where the engagement occurred, when they were met by the force under Colonel Wattles returning to this post. The enemy and our troops had turned their heels on each other. Through his scouts Colonel Phillips knew very nearly the exact strength of the enemy, and he was not at all satisfied with the conduct of Colonel Wattles.

The enemy's pickets and ours were in swimming together in the Arkansas on the 19th instant. Though they agreed beforehand that they would not endeavor to take advantage of each other, yet they were cautious not to come nearer than a rod of each other, and the men of each party took care to keep nearest the water's edge of their own side of the river. The next day they were less distrustful of each other, and an equal number of men from each side had a friendly conference in the middle of the Arkansas. The two parties talked for sometime in a good-natured manner of the various contests in which each had participated, of some relative or friend who was taken prisoner in such an engagement; of the prospects of the war, and of the operations of the armies in the east. By an agreement of the first day's conference, the rebel soldiers were to-day to bring some tobacco, and our soldiers some coffee, for exchange with each other. Both parties kept their promises, and at the meeting on the 20th, exchanged their coffee and tobacco with each other in the middle of the river. As I was acquainted with our river patrol, I had the curiosity to witness the meeting. At this conference the rebel soldiers mentioned of having the five white prisoners captured by their forces at Green Leaf, on the 16th instant. They also in the course of the conversation said that there had recently been a good many desertions from their army, and that four men who were tried not long since for desertion, have been found guilty and sentenced to be shot, and that the sentence is expected to be carried into effect in a few days. From what we have frequently heard, I believe that the rebels are more rigid in their punishment of deserters than the military authorities in our armies, although with us the penalty is death for desertion in time of war. With us there is not much trouble taken to find deserters, and bring them to trial. I have been with our army on the border and in this territory now nearly two years, and there has not yet been a deserter from the troops with which I have been serving, caught, tried, condemned and executed to my knowledge. We have had a small number of desertions during this period. It is possible, however, that there have been some executions for desertion at Forts Scott and Leavenworth, as the courts-martial for the trial ot deserters have generally been convened at those posts. There is such a sentiment against inflicting the death penalty, even in cases where the charge is murder, that I have no doubt but that there are officers who would prefer, if the discharge of their duties permitted, to be relieved from the disagreeable duty of approving the findings of the court in case of desertion. It is highly gratifying to note the spreading of this more humane sentiment. There is a tendency of our Government not to punish its soldiers so rigorously as formerly for certain offenses. Flogging has been abolished in the army and navy since the war commenced, and no one will contend that the *morale* of our army has suffered in consequence. It was a barbarous practice, and originated in a less enlightened age than this. Indeed, I doubt whether there ever was an army that was composed of more true gentlemen than is our army at this moment. Supposing that the law had remained on the statutes permitting an upstart of an officer to have a soldier flogged for any petty offense, imaginary or real, and thousands of patriotic men throughout the country would not have so readily come forward and offered their services to the Government? A government that recognizes the manly spirit of its citizen soldiery, will lose nothing by treating them as men in the end. There must of course be discipline; for there has not yet probably been a single regiment organized for the war, into which there has not enlisted several regular *dead beats*. But men of this class who persist in violating law and order, as soon as their true characters are known, should be drummed out of the service in disgrace, or if their offenses demand a greater punishmens, confined in military prisons for definite periods. But even these hard characters the lash and buck and gagging, are not likely to make better. What their prison discipline should be I am not prepared to say, except that I believe it should be of such a nature as would have a tendency to reform them instead of hardening their perverse natures.

Colonel Phillips sent out Major Foreman on the 20th instant, with a force of about six hundred men and one twelve-pound howitzer, to meet our supply train, which has probably left Fort Scott, and is now on the way down. It it is not delayed by high water at the crossing of the Neosho River, he should meet it between that point and Cabin Creek. He will have time to march leisurely, and to send out scouting parties to the east and west of his column to ascertain if the enemy have as yet shown any signs of activity in the country above here, with the view of making another effort to capture our train.

From information received from the enemy's camp on the south side of the river, it is evident that they are making preparations to attack our train at some point above this post. There was great activity in their camp yesterday, and last night they sent out two strong columns of cavalry, one of which is to pass to the east of us and the other to the west of us. Our scouts are watching them closely, and Colonel Phillips is advised of every movement they make. The force that moves to the east of us, it is reported, intends to join General Cabell, who has about fifteen hundred men and several pieces of artillery at a point between the Arkansas line, near Cincinnati, and Grand River. Though we do not know their exact intentions, everything points to their intention of concentrating all their mounted forces in the neighborhood of Cabin Creek, and to await the arrival of the train and escort. Should our troops guarding the train find the enemy too strongly posted at this point on the west side to be able to dislodge them, and attempt to cross Grand River at Grand Saline and come down on the east side, General Cabell will be on hand to thwart the movement, or he may cross the river and join General Cooper's force on the west side. They, no doubt, think that they have us in a tight place, and that they will certainly succeed this time in taking our rations from us. But our officers are not asleep and ignorant of their movements and designs. They will have to fight harder and show greater deeds of valor than before if they come off victorious in the contest for the prize.

There is an old Indian prophet, fortune teller and medicine man at this post, who sometimes has crowds of silly clients around him, desiring him to forecast the future for them. Their faith in his nonsensical performance is remarkable. The belief that certain persons are gifted with prophecy, that they can raise the curtain and peer into the future, and read trifling

incidents in regard to love scrapes, fortunes, friends
lost, &c., is wide spread, and quite common among
every people whose history is known to us. The Indians here are no more superstitious in this respect
than the white people in the most intelligent portions
of the country, and even in the most intellectual cen-
tres. In nearly all the newspapers that come to us
from the great cities of the country, may be seen advertisements of " Fortune Tellers "—"your future told
by astrology," " clairvoyance," " or cards." These
people must have customers, or they could not afford
to pay for their advertisements. And their advertisements indicate that they get their living by fortune
telling, which we know is the case. Even here in the
far west, there is probably not a single family that
has been living in the country half a dozen years,
that has not been visited by wandering gypsies on fortune telling business.

But to return to my Indian prophet. He prepares
a poultice from different kinds of herbs, and applies it
to his head during the night. It is stated by those
who are somewhat familiar with him, that he takes
into his stomach a certain quantity of the juice of these
herbs. Any way, it is said that the herbs affect his
nervous system and mind in some mysterious manner so that he has very vivid dreams and a kind of
nervous exaltation. And even after he awakens he actually has, or feigns to have, a wild, wierd look. It
is in this state that he affects to read the future to those
around him, whose relaxed jaws and raised eyebrows

show their faith in him. To be fully equipped as a prophet, it has been suggested that he should have a witch's cauldron filled with frogs' feet, the beaks of birds and claws of wild animals, and stir them, muttering cabalistic words.

CHAPTER XVI.

The rebel pickets shout across the river that the Federal supply train is coming—Another rebel force gone to meet the Federal supply train—Movements of the Confederate armies in the East as reported by rebel pickets—Vicksburg closely invested by General Grant—Federal troops in southwest Missouri—Federal supply train detained by high water at Neosho River—Federal supplies running short at Fort Gibson—High water in Grand River—Indian women report heavy firing in the vicinity of Cabin Creek—General Cabell on the east side of Grand River, near Cabin Creek, with artillery—The suspense—A National Salute fired in honor of Independence Day—Beef and Beans for barbecue—The pinch of hunger—Horses and dead rebels floating in the river—Two days' fighting at Cabin Creek—Gallant charge of the Colored regiment—Total rout of the enemy—How the Federal troops crossed Cabin Creek under fire—General Cabell unable to join General Cooper's division on account of high water—Arrival of supply train at Fort Gibson.

The rebel pickets shouted across the river on the 24th instant, that our commissary train was on the way down, and that Colonel Dodd was commanding the escort to it, which is composed of two infantry regiments and four pieces of artillery. This is really news to our officers here, as we have not heard what troops and how strong a force would guard it down. Our hostile neighbors across the river seem to be better informed of the movements of our train and troops in the country above than we are. Livingston, the guerrilla chieftain, whom I have frequently mentioned as operating in the vicinity of Baxter Springs, it is thought sends couriers to General Cooper every three or four days, and that they must either travel at night or take a route not much frequented by our troops. If Colonel Phillips would have carefully posted at half a dozen points twenty-five or thirty miles above here, say three men at each station, well armed and mounted on good horses, I believe that the enemy's dispatch bearers could be captured.

A large part of the remaining force of the enemy on the south side of the Arkansas made a movement in some direction on the 25th. Their pickets intimate that this force has marched out to join the cavalry General Cooper sent out a few days ago to attack our train. That their pickets should venture to refer to the movements of this force in connection with our train looks as if they feel very confident of success, or else believe that we are perfectly advised of all their movements.

It is now reported by our scouts that most of the enemy's camp has been removed back to Elk Creek, some twenty miles south of this post. This explains the activity noticed in their camp on the 25th instant. Should we endeavor to cross the river and compel the flight of the detachments guarding the different fords, they would endeavor to warn their baggage trains at Elk Creek by signals, so that they could be moving

south, several hours before we could reach that point.
The troops of this division, however, are too busily
engaged elsewhere to make a dash on the enemy's
camp.

The rebel pickets on Sunday, 28th instant, stated that
they had just heard that the Confederate army in the
east, under General Lee, has recently gained a great
victory over the Federal army, and that our army has
fallen back to the immediate vicinity of Washington.
They also stated that General Lee is preparing for another invasion of Maryland, and intends entering
Pennsylvania with the army of Northern Virginia,
with the view of capturing Philadelphia and Balti-
more. Though, in our isolation here, news from the
East is a long time reaching us, yet that which comes
shows that both the Federal and Confederate armies
are displaying great activity, and that a great conflict
is imminent. The loss of a great battle now, or the
capture by the enemy of either of the large cities
above mentioned, would be extremely damaging to
our cause, and I know that thousands of loyal hearts
are trembling in regard to the impending result.
Our defeat would encourage the faint hearted, and
those in the North who have all along opposed the
war, to cry for peace at almost any price. Our forces,
under General Grant, are still besieging Vicksburg,
and our lines are tightening around the enemy there.
We may expect to hear of some definite action at that
place shortly, as the enemy have now run short of
supplies, with very little hope of being provisioned

again, as they are surrounded from all sides, and therefore completely isolated from other divisions of the
rebel army.   It seems that General Grant has not relaxed his grasp in the slightest degree since he commenced the siege.   He has perhaps nearly a hundred
thousand men, and has already made several furious
assaults on the enemy's works.   The capture of Vicksburg and opening of the Mississippi River to the Gulf,
will break the backbone of the Confederacy in the
West, if not indeed of the entire South.   When the
Confederacy shall thus be cut into two nearly equal
divisions, there can be very little co-operation between
the eastern and western Rebel armies.

And should reinforcements of a thousand or so men
come down with our train the enemy in our front will
not likely occupy their position on the south side
much longer.   What a grand idea it would be if our
forces, when the half year is up, could make an advance all along our lines, east and west, and overthrow
the enemy at every point.

Several Indian women who have just arrived from
near the Arkansas line a few miles south of Maysville,
state that it was currently reported when they left, that
General Brown, commanding the Missouri State troops
in southwest Missouri, recently had a fight with General Marmaduke's cavalry and defeated it with consid-
able loss.   We do not hear much about the movements
of our troops southwest of Springfield and around
Cassville, but hope that they have not been idle.   We
have expected however, that they would have moved
20

forward and re-occupied Fayetteville before this. Had they done so a month ago, it would have relieved us of the necessity of using so many of the troops of this command in watching the movements of the enemy along the Arkansas line to the east of us, and our isolation would not have been so complete as it is at pressent. Even at this moment it is probable that a force of the enemy is moving from Arkansas northeast of us, to attack our supply train. If there are as many volunteer troops in Southwest Missouri as there were nearly two months ago when I was at Cassville, it is surely strange that the Department Commander does not permit them to march into Arkansas and seek the enemy. At any rate a large infantry force is not required in Southwest Missouri.

A dispatch from Major Foreman states that our commissary train was detained on the north side of the Neosho river, on account of high water. He thought, however, that it would be able to cross in another day, provided no other recent heavy rains have fallen upon the region which that river drains. If it crossed that stream as he predicted, it is now within a day's march of Cabin Creek, where we anticipate it will be attacked by the enemy. All the detachments that Colonel Phillips has sent out to make reconnoissances within the past two days, report having discovered signs of trails through the prairie, which show that the enemy have marched in several strong divisions, to some point thirty or forty miles above this place. They have had a month to make preparations for this event, and no doubt will make a heroic effort to accomplish their purpose. Their cavalry horses are reported to be in better condition than ours, having had less hard service to perform during the spring than ours. And they have an advantage in being able to choose whatever position they wish.

We feel quite anxious here in regard to the result of the struggle, which will doubtless be decided in the course of the next two or three days. We are now, and have been for some ten days, issuing to the troops at this post less than half rations ; a thing that has not occurred before in that division of the army with which I have been connected. Our hard bread and flour, sugar, tea and coffee, are nearly exhausted, so that after two days more we shall have to subsist on beans, rice and fresh beef. Fortunately we have sufficient salt for seasoning purposes for perhaps ten days yet. Fresh beef without salt would likely undermine the health of our troops in a short time. A considerable quantity of wheat has been obtained recently, which under a stress can be cooked and used for food. But the soldiers, whites and Indians, appear very cheerful ; and we do not apprehend that we shall be obliged to kill the dogs, and mules and horses here, before our provisions reach us. The shortness of rations and the isolation of our position sometimes causes the soldier to jocularly refer to such a contingency. The Indian dogs would not be fit for anything except soup, as there is very little flesh on their bones ; besides they are generally quite small. Probably nearly every boy, soon after he begins to read, drifts into reading the histories of wars and sieges. Nothing can be more interesting to the young mind of the budding man, judging by my own experience. Well, as we are into the same kind of war as those we used to read about, we know that we are liable to be subjected to hardships and privations as severe as any of those mentioned in the histories we read. We do not absolutely know what a day may bring forth. But our stomachs would rebel against such food as the flesh of dogs, and mules and horses, in fact absolutely refuse it for some days yet. While a dog's flesh is perhaps equally as clean as that of a hog, our education through generations has been such that we refuse the former with disgust, almost amounting to nausea, and relish the latter as a delicacy. Horses and mules are clean-feeding animals, indeed as much so as sheep and cattle ; yet the thought of having to use their flesh for food, would almost derange the appetite of those who are not even getting their full rations. If our imaginations did not act so powerfully on our stomachs, I cannot see why the flesh of these animals, if slaughtered in good healthy condition, should not be as wholesome as beef and mutton. But there is an old saying, " That which is one man's food, is another man's poison."

. Grand River has risen considerably since June 29th, and we hear that there have been heavy rains in the direction of southern Kansas recently. The rise in the river that is just commencing here now, is proba-

bly from the same rains that caused the big rise in
the Neosho, and detained our train there several days.
How this rise in the Grand River will affect the operations of the two opposing forces above here, we will
know in a few days.

Two Indian women came into our camp July 1st
from a section about fifteen miles north of Tahlaquah,
and they report that a large force of the enemy, composed of cavalry and artillery, passed their places yesterday evening, moving westward in the direction of
Grand Saline. This, we are informed through our
scouts, is the force I mentioned about a week ago as
being encamped at Cincinnati, on the Arkansas line,
under command of Brigadier-General Cabell. If the
enemy arrive on the ground at the place they have
chosen to make the attack, as they doubtless have, before our troops and train come up, they will be able
to fortify themselves to some extent. They can also
make a thorough survey of the position they have
chosen, so that if they are driven from one point, they
will have another position equally as good for attack
or defense. It is not likely that they feel so sure of
success, that they will not leave a way open for retreat.

A deserter from the rebel command, now encamped
on Elk Creek, was brought in this morning, July 1st,
and he states that just before he left the enemy on
the 28th ultimo, General Cooper had sent out another
division of cavalry to join the force that had gone
out several days previous. He says that they are very

confident of success this time, as they have made
great preparations, and are well advised of the movements of the train and escort since they left Fort
Scott. It was the intention of the first division that
went out, he thinks, to examine all the positions between Flat Rock and Cabin Creek, and to select the
one which would be the most advantageous for making the attack. An experienced engineer officer accompanied them, so that nothing should be laking to
make the organization of the expedition complete.

Well, from all the information we have been able to
obtain, it is regarded as certain that the enemy's forces
have converged at a point about forty miles above here
in the neighborhood of Cabin Creek, yesterday evening (June 30th). Our train and escort, according to
our calculation, should arrive there July 1st, perhaps
in the afternoon. The contest for the prize will soon
have been settled. As it is now eleven days since
Major Foreman left here with his force of six hundred
men and one twelve-pound mountain howitzer, he has
had ample time to march as far north as Hudson's
Ford on the Neosho, or perhaps to Baxter Spring,
fifteen miles still further north. In either event he
will probably advise Colonel Williams, commanding
the First regiment Kansas colored volunteers at Baxter Spring, of the preparations that the enemy have been
making to capture the train. As Colonel Williams
has the reputation of being a gallant officer, and as he
will doubtless be anxious to give his colored troops an
opportunity of displaying their valor on the field, we

feel quite sure, from what we have heard of him, that, if his orders are not too positive to remain where he is, he will accompany the train with his regiment. At such a time as this he should not be hampered with orders that would keep his regiment inactive when it is needed, within the hearing of booming artillery. Though there is still some prejudice in regard to using colored soldiers in the field beside white soldiers, and though I think that this prejudice has been somewhat respected, yet, under the present pressure, I do not believe that any serious objection will be made to the colored regiment coming down to participate in the fight, for if it does, the proportion of white troops will be less than Indians and colored soldiers, unless there is a regiment of white troops along that we have not heard of. I hope that Colonel Williams will be permitted to bring his regiment along, and that his men will show a disposition to enter the lists in competition for bravery, if the enemy make the attack which we believe they have planned; so that our enemy neighbors across the river may become fully satisfied that colored soldiers are not myths.

We have been discussing the situation at Cabin Creek, and it was suggested that this night our officers may be in conference concerning the plan of attack or defense for the morrow. If such is the case, we hope that their deliberations will be full of wisdom, and that they may have strength and valor to carry out their plans.

Another day has dawned; the sun has climbed the

middle sky and is now descending low on the western heights; our rations are well nigh exhausted, and our soldiers are beginning to feel the pinch of hunger. I pause a moment in anxious suspense.

I have just been to the river, and I find that it has risen nearly two feet since this hour yesterday evening. Every one is anxious for news from our train and troops, for it is regarded as quite certain that an engagement has taken place or is in progress. Several Indian women who have just arrived from Grand Saline state that they heard artillery and musketry firing yesterday evening in the direction of Cabin Creek. They also state that they heard of a large force of the enemy being encamped near Grand Saline, who were unable to cross Grand River on account of its being so full, and that the river is unusually high at that point this season. They seem to have been much frightened when they started, and came as quickly as possible, that they might be under the protection of Colonel Phillips, and learn the result of the engagement, as they have near relatives in the Third Indian regiment. Colonel Phillips has watched over the Indians with such solicitude, that the men, women and children regard him almost, if not quite, with real affection. They show commendable zeal, too, in keeping him advised of the movements of the enemy. And from my own observations since I have been with this command, I believe it would have been impossible for any other officer to have won such affectionate regard from these Indians.

To-day (July 3rd) was very quiet along the Arkansas; the enemy's pickets were in suspense as well as our troops at this post. They do not even seem to have heard of the artillery and musketry firing of Wednesday evening. Or if they have, they do not care to say anything about it. If the commanding officer of the expedition has sent any dispatches back to General Cooper at Elk Creek, it is not likely that they show anything definite to have been accomplished when the courier left. The different scouting parties that Colonel Phillips has sent out in various directions the last three or four days, who have returned, report that the enemy are displaying very little activity around us at present. Their force south of us has no doubt been reduced quite low to furnish men for the expedition that has gone after our train. If we had means of crossing the Arkansas, and a regiment of cavalry to spare, it would be a good time to make a dash on their camp. The river has continued to rise since yesterday evening, and is now quite full at this point. It is not likely that it has been fordable at any point between this post and Grand Saline for the last four days.

To-day being the 4th, or Independence Day, a national salute of thirty-four guns was fired this morning at sunrise, by Hopkins' battery. The sunrise was unusually fine, and the mountains in the distance, just before the first rays of the sun fell on the plain below, seemed more charming than at any other time since we have been encamped here. Though we have not had a barbecue to-day with all the delicacies of the season, we have made the best of that which we had. Most of the messes have had either rice, or beans, or hominy, or wheat, with coffee and fresh beef. There is, perhaps, some slight difference in fare of the various messes throughout the camp, for some had accumulated a larger surplus of rations than others during the past month, when we commenced to issue a reduced ration about two weeks ago. Men are economical or wasteful in their army life, just as they are in their every day life around their homes. The food we get is quite nutritious, if we would only get accustomed to it. To make a very radical and sudden change in the diet of soldiers, may result very injuriously to them. We shall be fortunate if evil effects do not flow from the change of food which we have recently been subjected to.

Several horses and men were discovered floating in the river nearly opposite the fort to-day. As they were first noticed about a half mile above the fort, and nearest this side, and out of the strong current, they were sometime in passing, and a good many people gathered along the banks to see them. We have no boats fit for service in the river in its present condition, and I heard of no efforts being made to bring the men to shore. Their clothing showed that they were not Federal soldiers, for at one or two points they floated near enough to shore to see whether they had on blue blouses or sky-blue trousers. A good many conjectures were advanced as to whether they were recently friends or foes, and how they came to get drowned. The mystery of their deaths, however, will probably be cleared up in a few days, when we shall have been better informed of the operations of the two opposing forces on the river north of us.

The train and escort arrived at Fort Gibson, July 5th, just before twelve o'clock, although we heard, early in the morning, that they would get in during the day. I made a good many inquiries concerning the cause of delay since they crossed the Neosho River at Hudson's ford. But we may now go back ot the Neosho River to Fort Scott, and trace the progress of the train to Fort Blunt or Gibson. The train left Fort Scott with the following troops as an escort: One company of the Third Wisconsin cavalry, company C Ninth Kansas cavalry; six companies of the Second Colorado infantry; one section of Blair's battery, and one twelve-pound mountain howitzer. This force and the train reached Baxter Springs, on the 26th of June, where they were joined by Major Foreman of this division, with the six hundred men and one twelve-pound howitzer, which I have already mentioned as having left here on the 20th ultimo. This force and train moved fifteen miles south of Baxter to Hudson's Ford on Neosho River, where they were detained two days on account of high waters. While they were thus detained, Colonel J. M. Williams, commanding the colored regiment at Baxter Springs, received information which led him to believe that the escort and train would certainly be attacked on the way down, and perhaps within a day or two after they crossed the

Neosho River, by a large force of the enemy. He, therefore, determined to march his colored regiment to Neosho River, and offer its services to Lieut. Colonel Theo. R. Dodd, Second Colorado infantry, commanding the escort. Colonel Dodd accepted this reinforcement to his escort without interposing any objection on account of color; and the whole force moved forward as soon as the river was low enough to ford. I should almost be justified in dwelling a moment right here, for I think that this is the first time in our history that white and colored troops have co-operated—that is, have joined hands in a common cause against the enemy. It is a grand step in the direction of wiping out the idea that man's right to life, liberty and the pursuit of happiness, should depend upon the color of his skin. The first day's march south of the Neosho River, Major Foreman, with a force of cavalry, on the left flank discovered a fresh trail, and on following it some distance, came upon, and captured one and killed two of Standwaitie's pickets. The man the Major held was badly frightened, and was easily persuaded and even anxious to tell all he knew. Such information as he was able to give, however, was of little value, as our troops marched in such order that it would almost have been impossible for the enemy to surprise them. In the afternoon of Wednesday, July 1st, our train and escort arrived on the heights on the north side of Cabin Creek. The stream, where the old military road crosses it, runs nearly directly east, perhaps inclining a little to the southeast, and empties into the Grand River not more than three miles distant. The topography of that section is perfectly familiar to me, as we were encamped there one year ago, having moved there shortly after the capture of Colonel Clarkson, referred to in a previous chapter. We were in that immediate vicinity nearly two weeks. It was a good point for a camp, and our reconnoitering parties were daily sent out through the Nation to the south and southeast of our main camp.

But to return to the recent operations at Cabin Creek. A little skirmishing occurred a few miles north of the heights, near the crossing of the military road, but the resistance of the enemy was not sufficient to cause a halt of our troops and train. It is all prairie north of the heights for several miles, but descending the heights and getting into the bottom, there is a heavy growth of timber and thick woods. At this season, some places the woods are so thickly clothed with foliage, that foot or cavalrymen could not be seen twenty yards in front. As the advance of the escort came upon the heights overlooking the strip of timber along Cabin Creek, which is upwards of two miles wide at the military crossing, Colonel Dodd, the commanding officer, directed that a skirmish line be thrown out at once, and that the train be parked on the prairie as fast as the teams drove up. The train having been corraled without the slightest excitement or confusion, there was detailed to guard it the Second Colorado infantry, one company of the First Kansas colored infantry, and one company of the

Sixth Kansas cavalry. The other troops and artillery were to be held in readiness to operate against the enemy. The skirmish line now pushed forward to the right and left through the woods towards the stream. It had not proceeded far when considerable firing commenced on both sides, but not at very short range.

Our cavalry moved steadily forward, determined to develop the strength of the enemy on the north side of the stream if possible. As he did not have more than four or five hundred men on the north side, they could not stand much pressing, and soon broke. Some fled up the stream under cover of the timber, and some down it, and some made their horses attempt to swim it at the nearest accessible point, but are supposed, in plunging over the steep bank, to have been drowned, and washed down the stream. Our cavalry did not pursue them vigorously, but moved cautiously, as it was not known but that the enemy had a massed force on the north side, which would rise up at the proper moment and endeavor to throw our troops into confusion. But there was no massed force on the north side, and our cavalry soon reached the north bank of Cabin Creek, to discover the stream raging and foaming along furiously, and evidently too deep to be fordable in the shallowest place. The rains which caused the rise in Neosho river, also caused the high waters in Cabin Creek; besides a more recent heavy rain falling on the head waters of Cabin Creek, kept it up longer. When our cavalry arrived on the north bank they found that the enemy lined the woods on the op-

posite shore for nearly a mile up and down the stream.
They opened a brisk fire upon our troops at every point
when they approached the water's edge, particularly
in the neighborhood of the ford. This soon brought
down a portion of the colored infantry under Colonel
Williams. After his arrival, and the formation of his
line along the north bank, there was some sharp musketry firing over the stream for some time, from both
forces. At convenient distances apart, signal stations
were established by Colonels Dodd and Williams, to
watch the movements of the enemy, and to warn the
different bodies of our troops when they might be in
danger of being overwhelmed by a superior force of
the enemy. Several signal stations were high up in
the boughs of trees, where the men remained for hours.
Colonels Williams and Dodd being convinced that
there was not a sufficient force of the enemy on the
north side of the stream to make them any serious resistance, determined to take its soundings with the
view of forcing a crossing that evening. Major Foreman, with a force of cavalry, was to try the ford and
the colored infantry was to form in line on the banks
above and below the entrance to the stream, supported
by two howitzers. A few shells were thrown into the
woods on the opposite shore, to drive the enemy from
his concealed position, and the colored infantry stood
in line ready to deliver a volley into the ranks of the
enemy, should they come within range, and the cavalry started into the foaming, eddying stream. The
enemy immediately opened fire at rather long range,

and the cavalry having entered the stream only a few
yards, and finding it not fordable, returned. A consultation was then held between Colonels Dodd and
Williams, and Major Foreman, and it was decided that
further operations should cease until the next morning, when the stream would likely be fordable, as it
was already beginning to run down. Night was coming on, and orders were given to set the guards at all
necessary points, and to refresh the troops with food
and sleep. After the disposition of the troops had
been made for the night, and all had satisfied the demands of appetite, another consultation of officers was
held, at which were representatives from all the different detachments composing the escort. At this conference the plan of operations in regard to forcing a
crossing of the stream in the morning, was discussed
and agreed to. It was decided that the signal stations
should be established next morning, very nearly as
they had been during the evening, as already described.
It was arranged that the positions of the troops should
be about as follows: The section of Blair's battery and
the twelve pound mountain howitzers, were to take
positions on eminences above and below the ford, two
hundred yards or so apart, so that their fire would
converge to a point wherever desired on the opposite
shore. Our officers saw that the enemy could not cross
the apex of this inverted Λ without a dreadful loss of
life, while our four pieces were discharging grape and
canister in a continuous stream. Our troops were to
enter the base of the inverted Λ in the following or-

der: Major Foreman with the Indian cavalry, and some
detachments from the battalion of the Sixth Kansas
cavalry, were to take the advance. This force was to
be followed by Captain Stewart, with one company of
the Ninth Kansas cavalry, one company of the Third
Wisconsin cavalry, and the First Kansas colored infantry, under the immediate command of Colonel
Williams. The cavalry was to form in line as fast as
they crossed over, to be supported by the colored infantry as fast as they could get over. With these
plans for the morrow the officers separated, each going
to his proper station to partake of refreshing sleep.
Each left the council of war in good spirits, fully determined to do his duty, as soon as the present veil of
darkness should be removed, and Aurora should declare
that a new day had dawned. The Goddess of Liberty,
with contracted brow and storm-clad ægis, watched
over them. The videttes had no occasion to report to
the officer of the guard any hostile movements of the
enemy, to disturb the slumbering troops. Not a sol-
itary shot from the various picket and vidette stations,
fell upon the stillness of the night. No doubt but
that stern expressions, as if grappling in bloody conflict with the foe, played over the countenances
of many of the sleeping heroes during the night.
It was known that the enemy had nearly two
thousand men, a force superior to ours, besides
they were not hampered in their movements by
having to guard a large train. It was known too,
that he had chosen his own position, and that

21

we could not expect to pass the stream without a hard fight.

At daylight on the morning of the 2nd our troops were up making preparations for the struggle soon to commence. An officer who had made the rounds of the guards reported that the stream was probably fordable on the morning of the 2nd. He also reported that the enemy seemed to be displaying considerable activity, as if preparing for the coming storm. When our men and animals had satisfied the demands of hunger, the wagon masters were directed to have their mule teams harnessed and hitched to the wagons, in readiness to move at a moment's notice; ammunition was given to the soldiers to replenish their cartridge boxes, and their arms inspected to see that they should be in complete order. And everything was in readiness, and our toops moved out about eight o'clock in splendid order, as if going on parade or out to drill. Major Foreman marched at the head of the column of cavalry, and was followed by Colonel Williams at the head of his colored infantry regiment, which marched with a firm steady step, with their bright muskets glittering in the morning sunlight at a right shoulder shift. The section of Blair's battery and the howitzers marched in the rear; but when the head of the column had reached a point within two hundred yards of the ford, it halted a moment, and the field pieces and howitzers were ordered to take their positions on the elevations which had been selected for them. While these movements were being made the skirmish line advanced to

the bank of the stream, and the skirmishers were exchanging shots here and there with the enemy quite
lively. The stream running across the inverted Λ
nearer its base than its apex, the area of the apex on the
opposite shore, it was estimated, would be sufficiently
large for our troops to form in *echelon* as soon as they
crossed over. The bugler beside Major Foreman
sounded *forward*, and in a moment more the head of
the column entered the base of the inverted Λ and the
storm burst forth furiously. The artillery opened with
shell and shrapnel, and swept the woods on each side of
the apex of the inverted Λ, but did not entirely succeed in driving the enemy from their positions behind
logs and felled trees. Our cavalary, under Major Foreman, continued to move forward, and just as they were
about to enter the ford, a large force of the enemy advanced from under cover of the thick woods to within
a few yards of the opposite bank, and delivered a volley into the ranks of our advancing column, wounding
several men. The field pieces and howitzers immediately after this poured a stream of grape and canister
into the ranks of the enemy, and they quickly disappeared behind their temporary defences. Major Foreman continued to move steadily forward until he
reached about the middle of the stream, which was
well up the flanks of the horses, when the enemy discharged another volley of musketry into the ranks of
our advancing troops, wounding Major Foreman and
several men seriously, so seriously that they were obliged to be taken to the rear. This casualty caused a

momentary halt in the stream, but not a retreat. The enemy were not allowed to gain any advantage by it, for a steady stream of grape and canister was poured into them by our batteries, and the colored infantry, which had not yet entered the stream, were formed along the bank, and also discharged volley after volley into their ranks, whenever they attempted to move towards the opposite ford. A few moments after Major Foreman was wounded and taken to the rear, Captain Stewart of the Ninth Kansas cavalry marched to the front with his company, with drawn sabers, and when his horses had passed the deepest water, dashed forward and reached the south bank. The Indian cavalry, detachments of the battalion of the Sixth Kansas cavalry, and the colored regiment followed in close order, and quickly reached the south bank, and formed in line, in *echelon*. The battery stationed at the left base of the inverted Λ was directed now to play upon the enemy, directly in front and to the left, and the battery stationed at the right base was directed to play upon the enemy directly in front, and to the right, instead of the two lines of fire converging to a point some distance south of the south ford. The troops formed in line, the bugle sounded *forward*, and Captain Stewart led the cavalry, and Colonel Williams the colored infantry, with fixed bayonets. No angry stream now separated the contending forces, and when the enemy saw our troops approaching them in double quick time with glittering bayonets and flashing sabres, they made a few feeble efforts to stand, but soon broke and could not be rallied. Immediately after our troops reached the south bank of the stream and formed in line, they commenced a brisk fire upon the enemy at short range, and drove them from their improvised defences in less than ten minutes. But they retreated only about three hundred yards, and commenced to form again. Our troops followed them steadily with lines formed as perfectly as on drill, and poured volley after volley into their ranks, as rapidly as the men could load and fire, and move forward. When the enemy attempted to form his last line, our troops were perhaps less than one hundred and fifty yards from him. Then it was that the bugles sounded the charge, and our troops rushed forward impetuously, and swept the field like a storm.

When the colored soldiers discharged their last volley, and then started forward on the double quick, the long line of bristling bayonets they displayed were not allowed to approach nearer than fifty yards of the enemy, when he turned and fled in great disorder. Captain Stewart, who had led the cavalry in the charge at another point, dashed into the ranks of the enemy, and many felt the eager points or edges of the swords of his men. The route of the enemy was complete. Captain Stewart, with all the cavalry pursued them for five miles south, cutting and shooting them down in great numbers. It is the almost universal opinion of officers and soldiers, that had not our troops been hampered with the care of the large train, they could have captured or destroyed the entire force of the enemy; and Captain Stewart thinks that had it not been inadvisable to leave the train too far, he could with the cavalry which he had, have captured most of the enemy in the course of a few hours. But our officers learned on the same evening that the train and escort arrived on the heights of Cabin Creek, that General Cabell, with fifteen hundred cavalry and four pieces of artillery, had arrived at Grand Saline, three miles east of Cabin Creek, on the east bank of Grand River, the day before, and was unable to cross and join General Cooper's divisions on account of high water. It is likely that General Cabell was to have had command of the entire rebel force, as there was no General officer with the rebel force that our troops fought. Colonels Standwaitie and McIntosh's Indian regiments, and the 27th and 29th Texas mounted regiments, were the rebel troops with whom we had to contend. We heard that General Cooper's assistant adjutant general, did more than any other officers to hold the rebel forces together. Standwaitie, with three men, is reported to have left the field very soon after our troops crossed Cabin Creek, and to have swam Grand River, some seven or eight miles to the southeast. Several other detachments attempted to swim the river at other points. If the enemy could have detained our troops and train at Cabin Creek another day, General Cabell would probably have been able to cross Grand River with his force, and to have joined in the engagement.

After the rout of the enemy, it is not believed that

they made a halt north of the Arkansas river, so much were they demoralized.

We may now glance a moment over the field at the casualties. I have already mentioned the wounding of Major Foreman; and of the cavalry under him, there were four enlisted men killed, ten wounded and eight missing. Captain Stewart's company "C," Ninth Kansas cavalry, had one man killed, three wounded slightly, and one seriously. Colonel Williams' colored regiment had one officer and twelve enlisted men wounded. Three of the colored soldiers were mortally wounded and died on the field. It is supposed that the loss of the enemy in killed and wounded must be upwards of a hundred, as they were exposed to grape and canister and shrapnel for some time before they could open fire upon our troops with any effect; and also while our forces were crossing the stream, and forming in the apex on the south bank. They must also have suffered severely from the galling fire of the colored soldiers, after they passed the stream, formed, and moved forward in line. In crossing the stream, the colored infantry were obliged to unfasten their belts, so as to hold their cartridge boxes above the water, which came up to their armpits. The whole plan of dislodging the enemy, and driving him from his strong position, was skillfully conceived and magnificently and boldly executed. A military genius would not have conceived a better and more successful plan. To whom we are mostly indebted for the success of our arms, it would be difficult to say, where

every one performed his duty so nobly. The enemy
against whom we have been operating this spring and
summer, are now doubtless satisfied that "niggers"
can fight, and fight bravely under "yankee" officers.
The Texas soldiers, if they had felt inclined to wait a
few moments when Colonel Williams was leading the
charge of his colored regiment, might have had an opportunity of seeing the fire in the eyes of the colored
soldiers. But men who once delighted to ply the lash to
the backs of colored men were now extremely anxious
to get out of sight of these same colored men as quickly
as possible. A beautiful thought to my mind comes
up in connection with this first regular engagement,
participated in by the colored troops. They in effect
say, "we are willing to meet on the field, man for man,
in defence of our freedom and our rights."

Our killed having been buried, and the wounded
taken up and provided for as well as possible, the
train, guard and artillery moved out and crossed Cabin
Creek after twelve o'clock. The escort continued to
move with great caution, as it was not known but that
the enemy might receive reinforcements and attempt
to make another stand, as there are two rather strong
positions between Cabin Creek and Fort Gibson. But
our cavalry on the flanks noticed that the trails of the
enemy through the high prairie grass did not point to
either of the positions from which an attack would
most likely be made if intended. It was ascertained
that the enemy, after the engagement, broke up into
detachments; and that a good many attempted to

swim Grand River with their horses for fear of being cut off by our troops if they endeavored to reach the Arkansas. The men and horses seen floating in the river opposite the fort yesterday are supposed to have belonged to the enemy, and were doubtless drowned in attempting to cross Grand River on the last day of the engagement at Cabin Creek.

CHAPTER XVII.

The Federal supply train returns to Fort Scott—The Battalion of
the Sixth Kansas Cavalry and the author accompany it—Colonel Phillips commended for his successful military operations
—Federal troops with which author has acted for two years
have been uniformly successful—The colored soldiers anxious
to meet the enemy—Their physical endurance—Well adapted
to campaigning in warm climate—Colonel Phillips will be
able to cross the Arkansas river and attack General Cooper—
Large quantities of hay should be put up at Fort Gibson—
Salt works at Grand Saline—Families of English blood cling
to their homesteads—On the march up the beautiful Grand
River country—Looking out for General Cabell's force—The
escort meets General Blunt at Cabin Creek—Examination of
the battle-field—Active operations to be commenced against
General Cooper immediately—The train and escort pass the
section of Livingston's operations—Arrival at Fort Scott.

THE supply train started back to Fort Scott July
7th, and as the battalion of the Sixth Kansas cavalry,
which has been with Colonel Phillips' division of this
command since the first of last January, was ordered
to accompany the train as a part of its escort, my
chronicles of the operations of the Federal troops in
the Indian Territory will not hereafter be so full as
usual. As my duties may take me to some other field,
or so far away that I will not be conscious of all that

is going on here, a little review of the past six months
may be of some interest. In looking back over this
period, the first thought that comes into my mind is,
that Colonel Phillips has shown remarkable executive
ability in the management of the troops of his division.
And we feel quite sure that no graduate of West Point
could have been found who would have displayed
greater military sagacity than our commander, Colonel Phillips, in the handling of troops, in seizing
advantageous positions, and in meeting all the contin-
gencies liable to arise in administering the affairs of a
large district like his. From the time that this division
left the Army of the Frontier at Elm Springs, he has
gained in popularity with his troops and the people
within his military jurisdiction. With every possible
shade of humanity flocking to his camp, he maintained a tone of moral order that would be creditable to
the best organized army unencumbered with such
difficulties. His lines of march have nowhere been
marked by the smoking ruins of destroyed towns. I
do not believe that half a dozen houses have been
burned during the last six months by his troops in
southwest Missouri, northwest Arkansas, and in the
Indian nation. When his troops left northwest Arkansas the latter part of winter, I will venture the belief
that many rebel families even regretted it, for he
respected their persons, and such property as they
possessed, as was not needed for army use. I have
already stated that they exchanged their chickens,
eggs, milk, butter, &c., with our soldiers for certain of

their surplus rations. By great care and diligence he prevented the small-pox from spreading among our troops early last March. He has kindled among the Indians such a strong feeling of friendship for the Government, that their women ride sixty miles to inform him of the movements of rebel troops. And this spring and summer he has displayed conspicuous bravery at Webber's Falls, the Rapid Ford, and in the engagement with the enemy on the morning of the 25th May, when they attacked our train four miles northwest of Fort Gibson. His marching here and seizing this post in the face of a large force of the enemy, was a master movement which the military critic would be especially happy to dwell upon, had he been commanding troops in a section where military operations are conducted on a larger scale. And his holding this place against the forces of two Generals of the enemy, during the most trying season of the year, would afford thought for further words of commendation. If the Government intends that promotions shall be earned by meritorious services, his promotion should not now be long delayed. I doubt whether another officer of his rank can be found in the service who has been entrusted with a command of equal importance, and who has accomplished so much. When we hear that the Generals around Washington, without commands, are almost numerous enough to make a battalion, we feel the injustice of the Government, in neglecting to properly reward him for his meritorious services, more keenly than we might otherwise do.

It is a rather pleasant reflection that the troops. with which I have acted for two years, less one month, have never met with a single reverse, though we have repeatedly marched up and down the border from the Missouri River to the Arkansas River, and had numerous contests with the enemy. When we came into this country early in the spring, we did not feel sure that Colonel Phillips would be able to hold it with the force which he then had under him. And when Colonel Harrison, without sufficient cause, withdrew his troops from Fayetteville, and retreated to Cassville, Missouri, we felt sure that the pressure of the enemy would be still greater to force us from this position. We have not only held our position, but we have defeated the enemy in every engagement; even where he had the choosing of time and position in several instances. In fact, the military operations in this Territory under Colonel Phillips, since we came here in the spring, have been as brilliant and successful as our campaign under General Blunt, in northwestern Arkansas, last fall.

Assistant Adjutant General Gallaher, an officer who has honored me with his friendship, has kindly answered questions that I have sometimes put to him, in regard to points upon which I was not fully advised. I have not, however, drawn on him very often for information.

It is likely now that active operations will be commenced against the enemy on the south side of the Arkansas shortly. We have a sufficient number of troops, and artillery enough to march out and attack them in their camp; and unless they stand firmer than they have done in all the recent contests in this section, we shall rout them completely. I have talked with some of the colored soldiers, and they seem anxious to meet the enemy on an open field. They said that the other day, at Cabin Creek, they expected to have an opportunity of letting their bayonets drink a little rebel blood, but that the enemy were not inclined to grant them this privilege. These colored soldiers say that they have heard that the enemy are furious for the blood of those negroes who have gone into the " Yankee " service, and that they have come down here to give the rebels an opportunity of satiating themselves with their blood. But they are convinced that there will be as much rebel as negro blood spilt, when the time comes for the enemy to slake his thirst for blood. With their slave clothes they have thrown off the slave caste of expressi n. They are armed with one of the most recently improved patterns of musket, and they have been drilled until they can handle them, in going through the manual, as gracefully and with as much ease as almost any of our white troops. Had there not been a prejudice against them going into the field with the white troops, they would probably have been to the front long ere this. Though they had not acted with the white troops until they left Baxter Springs ten days ago, they have, nevertheless, seen considerable service at different stations along the border. Most of them were brougnt up in Missouri and are quite intelligent—far more intelligent than plantation hands. They are strong built, and in size are fully up to the average of our white soldiers, and in regard to endurance, particularly in a warm climate, I doubt whether our white soldiers, or even those of the enemy, can compete with them.   Indeed it is their capacity for endurance that has contributed in keeping them in slavery so long.   Perhaps their masters never once thought that this capacity for endurance would be turned to advantage in gaining their freedom, as it is likely to be from now on until the close of the war. There are sections of the south where the climate will be very unfavorable for our northern troops during a summer campaign.   But colored troops who are acclimated, can occupy such regions without detriment to their health, and without increasing the percentage of mortality by sickness.   All this the rebel leaders failed to take into account when they made war on the Government and attempted te secede.

In view of the prospective active operations soon to be commenced, it would be more agreeable to my feelings to remain with this command a while longer. As Colonel Phillips has shown his ability to hold all the country north of the Arkansas, except as to cavalry raids of the enemy, with his three Indian regiments, and one battery, and one battalion of white troops, we do not doubt but that, with the additional troops now here, he will be able to carry our arms beyond the Canadian River, and sweep around and cap-

ture Fort Smith. This would be the natural plan of
operations, whether it is carried out or not. Whoever
may command our troops in this section will hardly
be satisfied to remain inactive north of the Arkansas
during the balance of the summer and autumn. Unless some disposition has been made of the troops in
southwest Missouri, of which we have not heard, a
force almost equal to ours here, we believe might
easily be concentrated at Cassville in a short time,
and marched down the western border counties of
Arkansas to Van Buren, and form a junction with the
forces under Colonel Phillips at Fort Smith.

The principal object of the battalion of the Sixth
Kansas cavalry accompanying the train through to
Fort Scott, is to have the dismounted men furnished
with remounts at as early a day as practicable. A
good many men of the four companies of this battalion
lost their horses on the 20th of May, when the enemy
made a raid on our herds near this post. Others have
lost their horses for want of forage, and by being worn
out in the service by constant scouting and marching.
Detachments from this battalion have accompanied
nearly all the reconnoissances sent out since we have
been with this division. We have not been able to
act in a body, for the reason that we have been called
upon to furnish detachments for reconnoissances going in this direction and in that, and for guards at
the fords along the Arkansas. There are no horses
in this country suitable for cavalry service; and we
are really deficient in that arm of the service. The

commanding officer here will probably have large
quantities of good prairie hay put up this fall at this
post, so that there will be no necessity for our animals
running down so much in flesh another season, even
if the service shall be as arduous as it has been this
season. When the enemy shall have been driven
south towards Red River, as they doubtless will be
before autumn, unless part of our force is ordered to
some other field, if the government would send down
here, from Fort Scott, half a dozen mowing machines
and hands to work them, all the hay required for animals at this post could be put up in a month or so.
There should be no unnecessary delay in attending to
the matter, as the season is near at hand for putting
up hay. Excellent prairie grass can be found within
ten miles of this post on the west side of Grand
River. With most of our troops south of the Arkansas, a very strong guard would not be required to protect the workmen; and government trains could be
used to haul the hay in, to be put up in large ricks.
The corn and oat rations, however, will have to be
transported here from the north. The Indians raised
some wheat this season, but have in cultivation but
very little corn; not more than enough for their own
consumption. The season has been favorable for corn
crops, and the yield would have been heavy had a
large acreage been planted and given proper attention.
Though the Indians have a fine country, and were
considered to be in good circumstances before the war,
this wealth consisted mostly of stock, lands and

22

money. They have never raised a surplus of cereals, and some seasons not sufficient for their own use; for traders among them in *ante-bellum* times brought large quantities of salt, as well as cattle, ponies and peltries, into Missouri to exchange for corn, flour, etc. Their teams, also, frequently came without being loaded with commodities for exchange, but brought gold to make their purchases. Whilst occupying this rich country our troops will be able to get but little out of it to contribute to their support, with the exception of hay and fresh beef. The salt works, however, might be re-opened at Grand Saline, but the expense of working and protecting the workmen operating them would, perhaps, be more than the cost of transportation on salt from the east. Now in the States the white families, consisting of the old men, women and children, both union and rebel, have generally stuck to their homesteads, when they have not been burned, and endeavored to raise the same kinds of products that were raised on their farms in former times; but, of course, in smaller quantities and numbers. From what I have seen, I believe that the nomadic and pastoral tendencies are almost entirely extinguished in the English race. Wherever I have seen a family whose faces showed their English blood, I have seen this strong attachment for the homestead. If the calamities of war have destroyed their dwellings, they have, in many instances, moved into the smoke-house, or barn with such effects as they were able to preserve. To those brought up with the usual

notions of country life, there are many hallowed asso-
ciations that generally cling around the homestead.
Fathers and mothers, for instance, recall the earlier periods of their lives, when they struggled against adver-
sity, and when their children, some of whom may be
away in the army, played upon the green sward around
them, or climbed the peach, apple and cherry trees to
assist in gathering these fruits. Or to take one case
out of many similar ones, it may be that the parents
now getting advanced in years, have lost a child, a
bright little fellow, whose memory is still cherished.
A child buried in a sacred spot upon the homestead or
in the little cemetery near by, increases the attachment for the old home where they have passed the
greater part of their lives. With us the affections for
our departed relatives and friends are not so transi-
tory as among the Indians. They display emotions of
grief when a near relative is sticken down by death,
the same as we do, but I am told that such grief is
generally more evanescent than with us. I believe,
therefore, that it is less difficult for an army to occupy
a region inhabited by a people whose home attach-
ments are very strong, than a country like this in
which the people have less settled habits of life.

No one could have easily believed, if he had seen
our Indian soldiers a year ago, that they could have
been brought under such discipline, as to make them
such efficient soldiers as they have recently shown
themselves to be under Colonel Phillips. When I
saw hundreds of men, women and children, bathing

perfectly nude in the Neosho River a little over a year ago, the thought never entered my mind that the men could be used as soldiers to fight an enemy, except Indians of the same character. But under Colonel Phillips, these same Indians, during the spring and summer, have contended successfully, and in point of numbers, less than man for man, mainly with white troops of the enemy. Were it not for the white troops of the enemy, there would now be no armed resistance to the authority of the Government in this whole region, so skillfully has Colonel Phillips managed the Indian affairs of this Territory.

The commissary train finished unloading on the 6th, and was all ferried over Grand River during the night, to be in readiness to start north early on the morning of the 7th. The crossing was slow and tedious, as the trains were obliged to be taken over on flat boats attached to ropes stretched across the river. It would be a great convenience if we had a steam ferry at this post, when the river is high. It is not likely, however, that one will get here until the Arkansas River is opened to navigation to its mouth.

In a few days I shall have quite different surroundings, though, in a military point of view, I cannot say more pleasant ones. It has been some pleasure to chronicle the steady progress of our arms, under such great disadvantages as we have had to contend with, and to feel conscious that our commander has not made a single mistake, during the six months that we have had our eyes upon him. The importance of this position is now recognized by higher authorities, and there is no thought of abandoning it. Nor is this all. It will be a point from which expeditions will be fitted out to operate in that section south of the Arkansas, lying in the direction of the Red River. From this time on the enemy will probably cease to play around us, as they have been doing during the past summer and spring.

I shall miss the continual picket firing, that has sounded in our ears during the spring and summer, with the exception of a few days' intermission, from along the banks of the Arkansas. As I have been with that portion of our troops occupying the most advanced positions in the enemy's country, over a year without a break, I shall hardly feel at home for a while, removed from the field of active operations. If I am to keep up my Chronicles of the Rebellion on the Border, it would be better that I should remain with the most active division of the army.

A few days more will take us to Kansas, where we shall see a larger sprinkling of white faces than we have been accustomed to see here, provided that the enemy has not decided to make an effort to capture our empty train, since he failed to take it loaded. One section of Hopkins' battery and detachments from the Second Colorado, and the Indian regiments, will also accompany the train forty or fifty miles, and even further north if deemed necessary.

The train and escort left the west side of Grand River, opposite Fort Blunt, on the morning of the

7th, and marched to Flat Rock Creek, twenty miles.

Strong flanking parties were kept out during the day, and the most recent signs of the enemy we saw were his trails going south, probably from the field of his defeat at Cabin Creek, on the 2nd instant. It was deemed advisable, however, to move cautiously until we passed Cabin Creek, as it was not known but that General Cabell might have crossed Grand River at Grand Saline, with his force, with the view of attacking the train on its return. Flat Rock is familiar to most of us, as we were encamped here two weeks in the latter part of July, last year. It was from this point that the "Indian Expedition," returned to Southern Kansas, from whence we marched to Lone Jack *via* Fort Scott, a distance of over two hundred miles.

We met General Blunt, July 9th, with a force of about four hundred men, under command of Colonel Judson, of the Sixth Kansas cavalry. He also had two twelve pounder mountain howitzers attached to the sixth, and two six pound field pieces, under Captain E. A. Smith. He left Fort Scott only three days ago, and has marched in this time one hundred and twenty miles. As soon as the report that the enemy had attacked our escort to the train on the 1st instant reached him, he started out on a forced march. He will have to tone himself down a little very shortly in regard to rapid marches, over long .distances, or his cavalry horses will be run down, and unfit for active service, before his soldiers have an opportunity of meeting the enemy on the field. He will have when he arrives at

Fort Blunt (Gibson), eight field pieces and four howitzers, and between three and four thousand cavalry and infantry—quite an effective little army. If properly handled, this little army will be able to drive the enemy from his present position and to capture Fort Smith, unless it has recently been strengthened by increasing the garrison, or building new fortifications. It is General Blunt's intention to move against General Cooper immediately on his arrival at Gibson. Those who know General Blunt, do not doubt his fighting qualities. It is safe, therefore, to predict that the enemy will be obliged to fight very shortly, or retreat from their camp on Elk Creek. General Cooper would not likely be able to hold his present position undisturbed many days longer, even if General Blunt were not on the way to Gibson, for, as I have already stated, we had reasons for believing that it was the intention of Colonel Phillips, as soon as the force which he has sent to this point, or perhaps to Horse Creek, twenty miles further north, with the train, returns, to cross the Arkansas, and attack General Cooper in his camp. Those who have been with Colonel Phillips will believe that he should have control of whatever movement is made against the enemy, and that to him should belong the praise or blame of its success or failure. But that he would be able to rout the enemy, there can be scarcely a shadow of doubt. If General Blunt goes on now to Gibson, and takes the troops there, and attacks and routs the enemy, his friends will no doubt claim for him

all the glory, though he will not be justly entitled
to it.

I spent a little time in looking over the field of the
engagements of 1st and 2nd instant, during the few
hours the train stopped there. The position of the enemy was even stronger than I had supposed, and it is
a little surprising that they should have given it up
without a harder struggle than they made.

From reports that have reached us since we left
Gibson, we have expected that we should be obliged to
fight General Cabell's force in this vicinity. We heard
that his command was encamped not more than ten or
fifteen miles from Cabin Creek, on the east side of
Grand River.

We went into camp, on the Neosho River, on the
10th. The escort under Lieutenant Colonel Dole returned to Fort Gibson on the evening of the 9th,
having accompanied us fifteen miles north of Cabin
Creek. The crossing of the Neosho River is just
about half way between Forts Scott and Gibson. The
only trouble north of this point to be apprehended is
from guerrillas. Livingston operates through this
section, and is now reported to have about two hundred effective men. He was at Sherwood, Missouri,
about ten miles northeast of Baxter Springs, a few
days ago, and is perhaps watching for our train. The
train and escort left Neosho River on the morning of
the 11th, and, after marching leisurely, passed Baxter
Springs about three o'clock. We went into camp
early on Brush Creek, about six miles north of Baxter

Springs. We were at that point not more than seven or eight miles from Livingston's old headquarters.

When we crossed the State line, and passed into Kansas, about a mile south of Baxter Springs, I saluted with reverence the State that has to me always represented a principle, a principle, too, involving the very essence of progress.

We have been out of the State nearly eleven months, and I am sure that others felt as I did, when they first stepped upon her soil. This, the southeast portion of the State, is a fine section, and will be densely settled within a few years, after the hostile forces on both sides of the line shall have sheathed their swords, and peace shall reign over the land.

CHAPTER XVIII.

The battalion of the Sixth Kansas Cavalry to remain at Fort Scott a few weeks—News of the battle of Gettysburg and surrender of Vicksburg and Port Hudson — Remarks on the progress of the Federal arms—Backbone of the Confederacy broken—Frequent contests between the State Militia and guerrilas in Southwest Missouri—Guerrilla warfare leads to retaliation and personal grudges—Major Livingston, the guerrilla leader, killed by the Missouri Militia—Remarks on the nature of his operations—Colonel Crittenden, commanding the Militia in Southwest Missouri, after the enemy—Colonel Cloud on the march to Fayetteville—General Blunt attacks General Cooper's army at Honey Springs—Preparations for the battle—Furious charge of the Federal troops—Complete rout of the enemy and capture of one piece of artillery, colors and prisoners—General Cabell came up after the battle was over.

The train and escort, composed of the battalion of the Sixth Kansas cavalry, arrived at Fort Scott July 14th. We shall remain here a few weeks, subject to the orders of Major Blair, the Post Commander. In the meantime, the dismounted men of the battalion will be remounted upon fresh animals, and those who have brought their horses through will draw full rations of forage for them for a few weeks, which will greatly improve their condition. There is a strong contrast between our sun-faded and badly worn uniforms and the bright new uniforms of most of the soldiers around this post. The fields of growing corn and harvested grain, and herds upon a thousand hills, make us feel that we have come into a land of peace and plenty. It would be difficult to find four companies that have seen harder service than this battalion during the last year.

Coming here is almost like entering a new world. News reaches us of the operations of our armies in the east, in Tennessee and along the Mississippi River, of not more than two days old. We have just heard of the great battle of Gettysburg, in Pennsylvania, on the 1st, 2d and 3d instant, and the defeat of the rebel army under General Lee; and of the capture of Vicksburg, Mississippi, by General Grant, on the 4th instant, with 27,000 prisoners, 128 pieces of artillery, eighty siege guns, and arms and ammunition for 60,000 men. We also hear that Port Hudson, below Vicksburg, on the Mississippi, has surrendered to General Banks since the fall of Vicksburg, with between eight or ten thousand prisoners, fifty to sixty pieces of artillery, small arms for fifteen thousand men, and large quantities of quartermaster's, commissary and ordnance stores. The Mississippi River is now open to navigation from St. Paul to the Gulf of Mexico. The fall of Vicksburg and Port Hudson cuts the Confederacy nearly through the middle, and the leaders of the rebellion must now see that their cause is utterly hopeless. We have broken the enemy's lines from Gettysburg to Cabin Creek this month, and unless some of our military commanders make a series of great blunders, the destruction of all the rebel armies cannot be delayed longer than a year or so. Those who have predicted that the war for the Union would be a failure, should now begin to see their mistake if they do not desire it to be a failure. There will no doubt be as hard fighting yet as we have already had; for since the enemy holds no strong position in the west, he can use all his forces in the field, and act on the offensive instead of on the defensive. He can send flying columns of his troops here and there, and cause a great deal of annoyance to such divisions of our armies as are occupying advanced positions. And he may also be able to make cavalry raids far into the rear of our armies. To keep our lines of communication open from the Ohio River to the southern line of Tennessee and central Mississippi, is no small task for our troops. While the enemy in Georgia, Alabama and Mississippi, are not hampered in their movements by defending important points, our troops are occupying so much of their territory that they will, very likely, soon find it difficult to draw supplies for their large armies. The first two years of the war the negroes produced most of their supplies, and performed a good deal of the drudgery for their troops. This season, however, the negroes are not only not raising crops for the enemy and assisting him in various ways, but they are actually fighting their old masters with muskets in their hands. With the exception of portions of the Carolinas and Georgia and Alabama, the male negroes have probably already mostly escaped from their masters, and are rapidly enlisting into the Union army, and singing songs of deliverance from their cruel bondage. The rebel leaders have not probably calculated the extent they would be weakened by the slaveholders losing their slaves. Indeed, they do not seem to have set up their men on the military chess-board at all before commencing hostilities, but have plunged blindly into the conflict. If they thought that the slaves would not strike for their freedom the first opportunity, they were surely very short-sighted. The institution for which the Southern States have attempted to secede and keep alive, is now practically dead. But the death-throes of a monster may deceive those who only look at the surface of things. Very few people of the South, in their sober minds, care but little about independence without the institution of slavery is kept alive. It is really painful to think that there are so many good people who are incompetent to examine introspectively what a great moral wrong slavery is. It can be accounted for by self-interest and education through generations. We are fighting to wipe out this great moral wrong, and the South is fighting to perpetuate it. We gradually gain strength the more this question is discussed and talked about. The South gradually loses by the same means. A moral principle will bear discussion and a thorough examination; but an immoral one will not. Evil doers wish to keep their evil actions in the dark.

While still keeping my eye on the army under General Blunt and Colonel Phillips, I shall, during my stay at this place, give more attention than I have hitherto done to the operations of our troops along the border counties of Missouri, Kansas and Arkansas.

A small party of our soldiers who have just arrived from Neosho and Carthage in southwest Missouri, report that the militia are actively engaged in that section in fighting and chasing bushwhackers and guerrillas.   Scarcely a day passes that a contest does not take place between the belligerent parties. On the 13th instant a man was killed near Granby. It was at first supposed that he was murdered by some of the Missouri militia stationed at Newtonia or Neosho.   He had been out harvesting, and shortly after returning home in the evening, two men, supposed to have been bushwhackers, rode up, and claiming to belong to the Seventh Missouri militia, called him out, shot him down, and then quickly left.   This is a fair sample of the manner in which the war is carried on in Missouri by the enemy.   It sometimes leads to bloody retaliation, for we occasionally hear of a rebel civilian who has been mysteriously murdered. All acts of private war should be discountenanced as much as possible, for if it were extensively carried on in those States where the people are nearly equally divided in their sentiments for and against the Union, the bitterness, hatred and feelings of revenge which it now engenders. would continue between families of different neighborhoods, long after peace shall have been concluded between the Government and the rebellious sections. Where men have entered either army, and are willing that the cause which they have espoused shall be submitted to the arbitrament of battle, they have no personal feelings against individuals, or private grudges against their neighbors calling for revenge. No high-minded soldier ever wounds the feelings of prisoners whom he has helped to capture in battle, by applying to them reproachful epithets. But if we take two neighbors, one of whom enters the Union army and remains away from his home during the war, and the other a rebel, who stays around his home during the war and depredates upon the property of his Union neighbor, and they both return to their respective homes after the war, we cannot reasonably expect that very friendly relations will ever exist between them. The rebels have too often acted as if they expected to have everything their own way in the future; as if the Union people had no rights which they were bound to respect, and as if their property would be confiscated in a few years. Now that the downfall of the Confederacy cannot be delayed to a very distant day, unless almost a miracle should intervene in its behalf, those rebels who were counting upon the confiscation of the property of Union prisoners with so much self-satisfaction, are perhaps beginning to regret their hasty actions. They perhaps also regret that they have frequently been so forward in pointing out the property of Union citizens for seizure by the rebel armies.

Information reached this post the 16th, which is regarded as reliable, that Livingston was killed about two days ago at Stockton, sixty miles southeast of here, by the Missouri State militia. It seems that Livingston was leading a charge of about two hundred and fifty men against a small force of the militia posted in a brick house, and that when the enemy came within range of their carbines, they delivered a volley into them, killing Livingston and three or four of his men, besides wounding several. The rebels, after the loss of their leader, retreated, and will not likely be so troublesome in that section very soon. It is the hardest blow the guerrillas of that section have received during the war. Major Tom Livingston, as he has generally been called, has operated in Newton, Jasper and Barton counties, Missouri, since early in the war. Our troops have had a great many contests with him, with varying results. Small detachments of Federal troops have found it difficult to pass through the section in which he operated, so thoroughly has he guarded all the passes and roads. And during the past two years he has killed and captured quite a number of our soldiers. But, as stated in another place, he has not been accused of murdering any of our soldiers that he has taken as prisoners, with the exception of one or two colored soldiers that he captured last spring in the vicinity of Spring River. Colonel Williams retaliated by shooting an equal number of rebel prisoners which he had captured and held, and then informed Livingston what he had done. Sometime after this occurrence Livingston's

force captured several other colored soldiers, but did
not order them shot. They were exchanged man for
man for rebel prisoners. Only by severe measures can
most rebel officers be brought to listen to the appeals of
justice. But that which has made Livingston's name
so familiar to every one along the border, is the success with which he has so often eluded our forces when
sent in search of him. Time and again expeditions
of cavalry have been sent into Jasper county for the
purpose of capturing or driving him out of that section. Some of the expeditions have scouted the Spring
River country thoroughly for several days without finding any of his men. Others have had skirmishes with
some of his men, who have generally quickly disappeared, not to be found again. The country along Spring
River is thickly clothed with young timber, or woods,
and affords many excellent hiding places for guerrillas
and outlaws. While he has not captured or destroyed
much Government property, he has kept the enemy in
our front well advised of our movements in this section. Before the recent battle at Cabin Creek, General
Cooper's troops seemed to be as well informed of the
movements of our train and escort as we were. Last
year detachments of the Sixth Kansas cavalry chased
and skirmished with him a good deal, and it was
reported and believed that he wore a steel breast plate
or something that was bullet-proof. I have heard not
less than three men of our regiment say that they took
deliberate aim at him with their carbines at short range,
and were satisfied that they struck him: but that the

23

carbine balls were turned aside by something impenetrable which he wore. In Homeric times, the soldiers would have said that some goddess turned aside the death-dealing missiles. Rebel citizens say that Colonel Coffey is expected in southwest Missouri soon, to take command of Livingston's force. But he will not make such a successful leader as Livingston has been.

On the 17th inst. Colonel Crittenden, commanding at Newtonia, sent out two hundred mounted militia in the direction of Carthage and Spring River, with the determination of driving Livingston's old band out of that section. This force had a skirmish with the enemy in which four rebels were killed and one of the militia wounded. The next day a trail some distance south of the place where the skirmish occurred was discovered, and it is believed that the larger portion of the guerrilla force of that section have gone south. Major Burch, commanding a battalion of the Eighth Missouri militia cavalry at Neosho, has been displaying great activity lately in scouting the country for a distance of twenty-five miles north, west and south of his station. He is regarded as a brave and very efficient officer, and the guerrillas will doubtless prefer to keep a safe distance from his troops. His soldiers are well mounted and armed, and know the country as well as the enemy.

Colonel Cloud, with most of his regiment, the Second Kansas cavalry, and two or three Arkansas regiments, were at Cassville on the 18th instant, and are expected to move south towards Fayetteville and Van Buren in a few days, with the view of co-operating with General Blunt, who recently went down to take command of the troops at Fort Gibson.   Since General Herron's division was ordered to join General Grant, in the seige of Vicksburg, several months ago, there are not so many of our troops along the southern line of Missouri as there were during the lattter part of the winter; but I still think that there have been enough to spare a force sufficient to re-occupy and hold Fayetteville, Arkansas.   After the withdrawal of our troops from northwestern Arkansas several months ago, our position at Fort Blunt has been much more difficult to hold than it was before Colonel Harrison left Fayetteville, for, as I have already stated, the enemy have been able to direct all his forces in western Arkansas and the Indian country against the division of Colonel Phillips.

Colonel Blair, the Post Commander, has just received a despatch from General Blunt, stating that he attacked and routed the forces of General Cooper at Honey Springs, on Elk Creek, twenty-five miles south of Fort Gibson, last Friday morning, July 17th.   A detachment of about twenty men came through from Fort Blunt with despatches and the mail.   Nearly all these men were in the engagement at Honey Springs. I have therefore talked with several of them, to get the particulars of the battle.   General Blunt reached Fort Gibson on the 11th, two days after we met him at Cabin Creek.   He rested the cavalry and artillery that he took down with him for four days, as the Arkansas

River was still too full to be fordable. In the meantime he collected all the flat boats that could be found, for the purpose of crossing his artillery and troops over the Arkansas at the mouth of Grand River. On the evening of the 15th he directed that a given number of men from each regiment, battalion and battery, be supplied with four days' rations in haversacks, and forty rounds of ammunition in their cartridge boxes, and to be in readiness to march at a moment's notice.' His troops, artillery and ambulances, being in readiness to move, the General took four hundred cavalry and four pieces of light artillery, and at midnight of the 15th crossed Grand River near the Fort and the Verdigris River, seven or eight miles to the southwest, and then marched up the Arkansas to a point about eighteen miles southwest of Fort Gibson, and forded the river. It was quite deep, coming up to the flanks of the horses. The caissons were detached from the artillery wagons and carried across the river on horses, to keep the ammunition dry. After he had crossed his forces over the river and replaced the caissons, he marched rapidly down the south bank to a point opposite the mouth of Grand River, with the intention of cutting off and capturing the enemy's pickets, stationed along the river guarding the fords, etc. But they had by some means got wind of his movement, and being mounted upon good horses, only two or three were captured. He arrived opposite the mouth of Grand River before twelve o'clock the 16th, and immediately set the boats in motion and got his troops

and artillery all ferried over before night, and at once
set out on the march for Elk Creek, where, according
to information he had received through his scouts,
General Cooper was encamped with six thousand men,
Texans and Indians. His own force was less than
three thousand five hundred effective men. General
Blunt's scouts reported to him that General Cabell,
with three thousand men and some artillery, was on
his way to join General Cooper, that Generals Cooper
and Cabell were making preparations for a combined
attack on Fort Blunt in a few days. General Blunt
was therefore determined to hasten forward and attack
General Cooper before General Cabell could form a
junction with him. He made a night's march from
the South bank of the Arkansas to Elk Creek, reaching
there at sunrise. Four companies of the Sixth Kansas
cavalry under Captain H. S. Greeno, with their two
mountain howitzers, took the advance and drove in
the enemy's outposts at daybreak. Captain Greeno
followed them up closely until they fell back upon the
main force, posted in the timber on the south side of
Elk Creek. The enemy commenced to flank him and
he fell back upon the infantry and artillery, which had
not made such rapid progress, and were some distance
in the rear coming up. General Blunt marched his
entire force up to within half mile of the enemy's line,
and halted a short time to enable his men to take lunch
from their haversacks. Soldiers should always, as far
as practicable, be allowed to replenish their stores of
force before going into battle. The weather was quite

warm, and a night march had much fatigued the infantry, so that they required food and rest before engaging the enemy. After his troops had lunched, and rested a short time, General Blunt formed them into two columns for making the attack. The right, under Colonel W. R. Judson, of the Sixth Kansas cavalry, was to move forward to the right of the Texas road, and the left, under Colonel W. A. Phillips, was to move forward to the left of the road. The whole force, cavalry, infantry, and artillery, marched in columns of companies up to within a quarter of a mile of the enemy's position in the woods, and then came into line on the right and left of the road, and halted for a moment. While General Blunt with his staff and escort were examining the position of the enemy, one of their sharp shooters wounded one of the General's escorts. The cavalry in the meantime had been skirmishing with the enemy, and was forcing him to show his exact position. The line moved forward a hundred yards or so, and halted again. General Blunt then directed Captain Smith to bring his battery into position, and to open with shell and shrapnel upon a wood where it was believed that the enemy had a battery and a large force massed. Captain Henry Hopkins was next directed to bring his battery into position a few hundred yards distant from Captain Smith's, and to open upon the enemy in another place. It was now soon discovered that the line of battle of the enemy was nearly a mile and a half in length. The cavalry on the right and left were now warmly engaged, and the enemy commenced to reply with his artillery. General Blunt went to Colonel Williams and said, ".Colonel, I think that we have got the location of one of the enemy's batteries. I wish you would keep your eye upon it, and if you see an opportunity, I should like to have you take it at the point of the bayonet with your colored regiment." Colonel Williams remarked that his men were eager to charge the enemy, and if it were possible he would take the battery. He then addressed his men briefly; he told them to pay strict attention to orders; to reserve their fire until the order to fire was given, and then to take deliberate aim at the waists of the enemy; that they would now in a few moments have an opportunity of displaying their valor on an open field; and that the eyes of the country were upon them. He then took his proper position and gave the order, *fix bayonets, forward, march.* He then moved up within short range of the enemy's line and halted a moment, and gave the order *ready, aim, fire,* and instantly a long line of muskets were leveled upon the enemy, and the smoke and roar of the volley told that the swift messengers of death and destruction had sped forth on their bloody mission. The enemy at the same time were keeping up a brisk fire all along the line. The colored regiment had perhaps fired less than half a dozen rounds when Colonel Williams was wounded in the breast, and was borne to the rear. Lieut.-Colonel J. Bowles then took command of the regiment, and after continuing the firing for a short time, and observing carefully where the smoke arose from the rebel battery, and seeing that it was not very far off, he pointed to it with his sword, and telling his men that he wanted them to take it, gave the order *charge bayonets*. The regiment moved forward, increasing its speed until within a few yards of the rebel line, and then with a shout rushed like an avalanche, upon it, bayoneting a great many rebels and capturing one piece of artilery. The enemy seeing what was coming, limbered up, and quickly removed the other pieces out of reach. Seeing now that the centre and strongest point of the enemy's line was broken and in disorder, General Blunt ordered his entire line to charge them, and in a short time they were routed completely at all points. He pursued them about three miles, but as his troops were much fatigued from having marched all the previous night, he bivouacked on the field. Our cavalry, which continued to watch the movements of the enemy, discovered General Cabell coming in sight with a large force of about three thousand men, about four o'clock in the afternoon. The enemy whom we had fought in the morning, having received large reinforcements, General Blunt expected that they would return and attack him that evening or the next morning. But they did not. Nor did they retreat further South after General Cabell came up.

General Blunt called the engagement the battle of "Honey Spring," as that was the name of General Cooper's camp on Elk Creek. The First Kansas colored infantry and the Sixth Kansas cavalry suffered

most in killed and wounded on our side; though all
our troops that participated, behaved with the utmost
coolness during the entire battle. The Sixth Kansas
cavalry suffered more than the rest of our cavalry on
account of having been assigned to the task of turning the enemy's left flank, which they did handsomely
by sweeping down upon them in a saber charge.
General Blunt is familiar with the fighting qualities of
the Sixth, as he was only a few rods from Colonel
Jewell when he fell leading his regiment at the battle
of Cane Hill, the 29th of last November. But I will
not endeavor to bestow undue praise upon the Sixth
regiment because I happen to belong to it, for I know
that every regiment of Kansas troops in the division
with which I have served, have acted with conspicuous
bravery upon every field.

Our loss in this engagement was seventeen killed
and sixty wounded. The loss of the enemy was 150
left dead upon the field, and 400 wounded and seventy-
seven prisoners. And we captured from him one
piece of artillery, two hundred stands of arms, one
stand of colors, and fifteen wagons. The stand of
colors belonged to the 20th Texas regiment, and there
seems to be some controversy as to whom it now belongs as a trophy. Colonel F. W. Schaurtie, in command of a portion of the Indian cavalry, picked up
the rebel colors on the field in front of the First Kansas colored infantry, after the enemy's line had been
broken. Lieut. Colonel Bowles, of the First Kansas
colored infantry, asserts his men shot down three rebel

color bearers, including the last one holding this stand of colors, and that he forbade any of his men to leave ranks to pick it up, until our line should advance on the right and left. After hearing several statements in regard to the matter, I am induced to think that the captured colors rightfully belong as a trophy to the First Kansas colored infantry. Colonel Schaurtie is a brilliant young officer, and if his men did not really kill the rebel color bearer, he will hardly contest the right to hold the colors as a trophy for his men.

General Blunt, after having buried the dead of both armies, and gathered up our wounded in ambulances, returned to Fort Blunt on the 19th instant. The rebel forces were too much demoralized to take the offensive, and General Blunt was not prepared to pursue them further south.

CHAPTER XIX.

The enemy burn the Court House and Academy at Carthage—County records carried away in Missouri—Rebel guerillas near Fort Scott—Rebel women carry information to the enemy—Cholera and Small-pox at Fort Gibson—Probable cause of Cholera breaking out—A soldier killed by Captain Tough—A little too much drunkenness—Major Blair closes the whisky shops—Resisting the draft—Great riot in New York City—Remarks on neutrality—Arrival of Colonel Phillips from the front—The supply train starts to Fort Gibson—Recruiting of the Fourteenth Kansas Cavalry—Large bounties paid by the government for recruits—State bounties in some of the States—Skirmish between several squadrons of Federal troops through mistake—Skirmish with guerillas near Balltown—Appeal of the rebel government for more troops—Description of the country around Fort Scott—Recruiting colored troops.

A small detachment of our soldiers who have just come up from Carthage, sixty miles southeast of this place, state that rebel bands are collecting in considerable force in Jasper County, under Colonel Craven, who formerly lived in that section; and that there is a fair prospect of a fight between them and the militia in a few days. They have recently burned the court house, and a fine brick academy at Carthage, to keep our troops from using them as a means of defense, as they used the brick building at Stockton not long since, when the rebel Chieftain Livingston was killed. The guerillas of Missouri know that court houses and strong buildings can be of very little benefit to them in the way of defenses, and that our troops are always delighted to get them in such places. They would not likely make much of an effort to dislodge them with small arms, but would probably try to hold them, until a section of a battery could be brought from the nearest post to play upon them. A few shells thrown into a building, should they take refuge in one, would soon start them out. From what I have seen on several occasions, I think they would prefer to run the gauntlet of small arms, than to have shells bursting around their heads in a court house hall. But burning such buildings in the towns, as would answer the purpose of quartering a company of troops, may be of some advantage to the enemy, while he is determined to keep up a guerilla warfare. In the burning of county property, which has been done in a good many instances, the enemy have not often destroyed county records, for most of such records were carried away or concealed by the rebels when General Price's forces were driven out of Missouri in February, 1862. As a general thing, perhaps, both parties feel an interest in preventing the destruction of county records. Unless the county records can be restored after the war, a good deal of confusion is likely to arise in regard to the titles to property. Those owning real estate in Missouri, cannot but feel some anxiety in regard to tne matter. Though it may be that the General Land Officer will show to whom any given piece of property was conveyed by the government, it will *not* show the title of the present owner to such property if it has been sold by the original purchaser from the government.

The enemy are getting quite bold in this vicinity of late. A party of guerrillas, under Captain Taylor, crossed the line on the night of the 24th, and came within about two miles of this post, and robbed several families. Major Blair, who is kept quite busy in fitting out trains to carry supplies to our troops in the Indian country, is also obliged to be constantly on the alert in looking after the guerrillas in this section. If our troops become a little inactive along the border, the enemy soon finds it out and commences committing depredations. The commanding officer at the post should have a sufficient cavalry force at his disposal to send out two detachments every day, to the east, the southeast and the northeast of this place, say twenty-five or thirty miles. But even such a measure would not absolutely stop their depredations and raids into Kansas, for they generally stop during the day at some isolated and lonely spot where our troops are not likely to find them. If they return to their retreats by separate paths and byways, they need not make a trail that could be easily followed by our troops. Rebel families from Vernon county, Missouri, come in here every day to trade with our merchants, and, no doubt, easily get such information in regard to our

movements as to keep the enemy well advised. I
made some inquiries for my own satisfaction in relation to this matter, and I found that almost every day
there are women of questionable loyalty, coming in
here from Vernon and Barton counties, Missouri—
sometimes, too, from a distance of twenty-five or thirty
miles. They generally claimed to have passes, and I
presume they did, having got some one to vouch for
them, so that they come and go undisturbed. They may
purchase not only articles for domestic use, but also
ammunition for the enemy. My own idea is that we
should be more vigilant in such things. Loyal men,
no doubt, often thoughtlessly vouch for parties whom
they should not. It would not be pleasant to know
that we have been furnishing the enemy with the
means for our own destruction. Yet there is reason
to believe that we have sometimes done it.

A detachment of cavalry just up from Fort Gibson,
report that the cholera has broken out among the
troops at that post, and that quite a number have already died from that dreadful disease. General Blunt
is also on the sick list. It can hardly be what is
known as the Asiatic cholera, for that type of cholera
generally appears in the east and travels westward.
When we were on short rations at Fort Gibson last
month, I suggested that there was some danger of
constitutional disturbances following our radical
change of food. Of course, I had not the slightest
idea what form the constitutional disturbance would
likely take. By inquiry I ascertained that the men

did not relish their food; and I felt sure, too, that it was not making good healthy blood, without which no one can display prolonged activity, nor long retain good health. From the 22d of June to the 4th of July, nearly all the white men belonging to the garrison force at Fort Gibson, lost from one to several pounds of flesh. Nor is this all. At the end of our fast, nearly everyone had sustained a loss of energy and bouyancy. Even after we commenced to issue full rations, the loss of power was not immediately restored to the men. It may be that the digestive and assimilative organs became enfeebled with the rest of the system. This, however, is a question which the medical profession should be most competent to decide. After the system becomes deteriorated by poor food, it must, of necessity, take some time to build up good healthy tissues, even when nutritious food has been supplied to the stomach and alimentary system.

The small-pox, also, when we recently left Fort Gibson, was still afflicting our troops there—particularly the Indians. Since I referred to this disease last March, we have lost a good many Indian soldiers by it. But the greatest mortality caused by it has been among refugee Indian families. Though my bump of curiosity has taken me around to notice everything I could think of, it never took me to the small-pox hospital. Considering the heterogeneous mass of humanity we had together last winter, we are, perhaps, fortunate that we were no worse afflicted during the spring and summer, and no doubt would have been, were it not for the vigilant eye of Colonel Phillips.

On the 28th, W. S. Tough, Captain and Chief of Scouts, shot and killed a soldier on the street. It seems that the soldier was drunk and making some demonstration which led Tough to believe that he was endeavoring to draw his pistol. From what I can find out about the matter, however, I think it would have been much more creditable to Captain Tough to have turned his pistol against the enemy. Why a Captain of civilian scouts should be one hundred and fifty miles from the front is unaccountable to me anyway. Nor have I heard of him being with us any time during the spring or summer. We have noticed more drunkenness among the soldiers since we came here two weeks ago, than during the six months in Colonel Phillips' division. In fact, a drunken soldier, white or Indian, was a rare sight. Major Blair, the Post commander, is going to issue an order shortly, closing up those whisky shops that sell intoxicating liquors to soldiers. It would be a great blessing, not only to many families, but to many inebriates themselves, if some effective measures could be adopted to check the evil. The evils likely to arise from the use of intoxicating liquors, should be pointed out in the moral teaching of the head of every family as clearly and forcibly as possible. But there will be legislative tinkering on the subject of prohihition for generations yet.

The enforcing of the draft is beginning to cause a good deal of excitement in the eastern cities, and has already resulted in a great riot in New York city, where hundreds of men have been either killed, beaten or bruised. To my mind, men who will risk their lives in resisting the draft rather than enlist in the service of the Government at this time, cannot be counted on much for their loyalty. That there should be so many traitors to the Government in the North, is really surprising. Every leader who advises resisting the draft, should be either hung or banished beyond our lines. The Government must either act firmly or surrender to the enemy. It cannot afford to trifle with the foe at home any more than at the front. Everybody now is either friend or foe of the Government. There is no half-way ground; and anyone pretending to be neutral is endeavoring to hide his disloyalty behind that term. It would be much more honorable for them to come out and avow their disloyalty. These very men, too, who wish to be neutral, if they are assaulted or robbed, are as quick to appeal to the Government for protection or relief, as the staunchest supporter of the Union cause. But if they are really neutral what right have they to ask the Government for protection of life or property? In the first place, the Government cannot recognize the right of any one to remain neutral in a life or death struggle like the present. Those who believe that the Government is worth preserving, should willingly risk their lines in its defense; that is, if they are not too cowardly to shoulder the musket. It would doubtless be safe to predict that many of those now claim-

24

ing to be neutral, and who have had, or may yet have
supplies taken from them by our army, will ask the
Government to pay for such supplies after the war. As
there is not the remotest probability of the Government paying the enemy for supplies taken from them I
don't see how it can pay the neutrals for supplies taken
from them, since by their own choosing they have not
classed themselves among its friends. These riotous demonstrations in the North, I have no doubt, give great
encouragement to the enemy, and will have a tendency to prolong the war. Since the recent great victories of our armies from the East to the far West, the
enemy, like a drowning man, are willing to catch at a
straw. Though the rioters may greatly assist the enemy by keeping many of our troops at home who
should be at the front, yet the riots will prove a weak
straw for the enemy to cling to.

Colonels Phillips and Wattles came in on the 30th
from Fort Gibson, with a smaller escort and a number
of the wounded from the battle of Honey Springs.
They do not furnish any additional information in regard to that battle. From conversations with several
other parties, I am satisfied that the account which I
have written out is substantially correct. Had I gone
more into details, I should have given greater prominence to the part which Colonel Phillips' brigade took
in the engagement. I should like to see not only Fort
Scott, but every town in Kansas through which Colonel Phillips passes, give him a warm welcome. No
citizen of this State has so honorably earned the grati-

tude of his fellow-citizens as he has, for in his various contests with the enemy during the last six months, he has saved this State from invasion, and the homes of our citizens from desolation. The small politicians may receive ovations in the same places where he passes unnoticed, but the small politician will long have been forgotten, when he will live in the memory of our people as one of the real heroes of the Great Rebellion. This war, in which the great principle of human freedom is involved, marks an epoch in history that will live long after the history of wars waged for political power will have dwindled into nothingness. There are many now living, who will, in less than twenty years from this, doubtless regret that they did not take a hand in this great struggle for justice and right.

The large commissary train is now nearly ready to start for Fort Blunt. It is encamped on Dry Wood Creek, twelve miles south of here. The escort will be under command of Colonel Thomas Bowen, of the 13th Kansas infantry, and will, perhaps, be in readiness to march by August 2d. It is not known yet whether the enemy will make another effort to capture it or not. The latest information from Fort Gibson indicates that General Cooper has been reinforced by General Steele, from Texas, with three or four thousand men and some artillery. Unless General Blunt receives reinforcements soon, the enemy may assume the offensive and attack him, or send a force north of him to attack the train. It is likely, however, that

the escort will be strengthened by troops from Fort
Blunt by the time it reaches the Neosho River.

The *Fourteenth* Kansas cavalry is being recruited
very rapidly, and in a few weeks will be ready to elect
field officers.   Major Blair, commanding this post, will
probably be made Lieutenant-Colonel of the regiment.
Two or three companies raised in Southern Kansas
for this regiment have already been doing escort duty
for several weeks.   The Government is now offering
three times as much bounty for each enlistment as it
was under the first and second calls of the President
for volunteers two years ago.   Some time in the
future I have no doubt but that there will be a demand made for equalization of bounties.   Those who
enlisted early in the war, should surely fare as well as
those who enlisted several years later.   Several of the
States that have not yet filled their quotas of troops
under the several calls of the President, are offering
larger bounties for enlistments than the Government
allows.   Kansas at present is unable to offer any State
bounty.   In the east there are men known as " bounty
jumpers."   They enlist into the service, receive the
Government and State bounties, and then desert and
go to some other place and enlist again under another
name.   From accounts that I have seen, it seems that
there are men who have made quite large sums of
money by such dishonorable transactions.   I regret
that my duty as a conscientious observer of the actions
of men in connection with the war, compels me to remark. that even here there are many whose chief in-

terest in the Government is to get fat jobs out of it, and to fleece the soldiers of their hard earnings by charging them and their families exorbitant prices for everything they get. Their loyalty is not of that kind that leads men to brave the dangers and hardships of the field and the camp. The less loyalty we have of this kind the better off we shall be.

Information has just reached here from Kansas City that the Government sent out from that place, on the 2nd instant, a large train for new Mexico; and as it was thought that Quantrell, with his guerrilla force, would attack it about the time it would cross over into Kansas, Captain Harvey, of the Sixth Kansas cavalry, with a detachment of forty men, was ordered in the direction from which it was believed that the enemy would approach the train. He had not marched many miles, however, when he came in contact with Captain Coleman of the Ninth Kansas cavalry, and a lively fight ensued before the mistake was discovered. As Captain Coleman had a much larger force than Captain Harvey, the latter retreated, and perhaps got the worst of the affair. He had several men wounded, and was himself run over and trampled under the horses' feet and seriously injured. As Quantrell's men don the Federal uniform whenever it suits their purpose, our troops in Jackson and Cass counties, Missouri, do not always know when they are meeting the enemy until he has delivered his fire. With all the activity that our troops have displayed in those counties during the last six months, the guerrillas there are still as trouble-

some as at any time since the commencement of the
war. Though the country through which they range
and carry on their predatory war is not mountainous,
a portion of it is so thickly wooded that it is easy for
them to find retreats miles from any human habita-
tion. When they make a successful raid on a small
body of our troops, or a train, or a town, and capture
certain supplies that they require, it is stated that such
supplies are conveyed to their retreats and kept for
future use. Our troops have on several occasions
found out their retreats, and captured or destroyed the
property which they had stored.

Two bushwhackers were killed on the 7th by our
troops near Balltown, twenty-two miles east of this
post, in Vernon county, Missouri. They are believed
to have been in the party that killed Whitesides, the
enlisted scout, a few weeks ago, only a few miles east
of Fort Scott, near the State line. One of the bushwhackers had a pass through the Federal lines in his
pocket. It is doubtful whether the enemy keep ahead
of us in the killing business; and if they do not, we
can stand it longest. Even without the aid of the
colored soldiers, the northern and middle States can
furnish many more able-bodied men than the rebellious states. One would have thought that the leaders
of the rebellion would have carefully consulted the cen-
sus returns, and studied the resources of the North,
before plunging the country into a war in which they
could not reasonably hope to be successful, unless they
went into it on the hypothesis that one southern man

could whip five "Yankees," as I heard a man say in
Texas, about the time of the election of Mr. Lincoln.
By reason of their own narrowness, the southern people have not allowed themselves to become acquainted
with the strength and resources of the North. A news-
paper like the New York Tribune, that discusses the
affairs of the whole country freely, was not allowed to
circulate in the South before the war. To have it found
upon his person in some of the Southern States was
almost worth a man's life. They could tolerate almost
any of the shortcomings to which human nature is
prone, but to say that "Slavery is wrong" was an unpardonable offense. No criminal was so damnable in
their eyes as an abolitionist.

Dispatches from the East of recent date show that
the rebel leaders are bewailing their misfortunes pit-
eously in their appeals to their followers. They are
beginning to feel the weight of the strong arm of the
Government, and it seems to me that nothing but blind
stupidity could induce them to continue a struggle that
is utterly hopeless, unless they wish to make a show
of dying in the last ditch. It is now more difficult
for the so-called Confederate Government to raise
additional troops than it is for the United States.
They commenced conscripting before we commenced
drafting; and I think that the rebel armies east and
west have lost a great many more men by desertions
than our armies have.

It is now generally thought that Kansas will not be
obliged to draft any men, under any former calls of

the President, as she has already furnished very nearly
her quota.   Her citizens have responded to the several
calls of President Lincoln with a patriotic promptness
that challenges the admiration of the country.   But
to fill her quota under the present call for four hundred and fifty thousand men, may possibly require the
enforcement of the draft before many months shall
have elapsed.   Nearly all the young men full of patriotic pride, and who were willing to risk their lives for
the Government, have already enlisted.   There are
many that will be subject to the draft who have a
great dread of being made targets for rebel bullets.
It is said that they shudder, and that their teeth almost
chatter when they read of the great battles in which
the men fall in heaps upon each other, and have their
limbs torn from their bodies by shot and bursting
shells.   To those of timid natures, and who almost
faint at the sight of human blood, it is not likely the
battle field, with the wounded and dying, is a very fascinating picture.   At any rate they have a horror of
contemplating themselves as going to make up such a
picture.

   The 10th of August is the second anniversary of my
enlistment.   Many comrades whose faces were familiar
at the morning roll call, on drill and on the march,
have dropped out of the ranks and lie buried upon
distant fields.   The forms and features of fallen comrades, when my thoughts turn back upon the past two
years, rise up before me and arouse feelings of
real sadness.   But ere our work shall have been

accomplished, our ranks will doubtless be thinned still more by death.

Fort Scott has recently been made the Headquarters District of the Frontier, commanded by General Blunt. Captain J. G. Haskell, his Chief Quartermaster, and Major H. Z. Curtis, his Assistant Adjutant-General, will remain here for the present. Since August, 1861, this has been the principal place on the border for organizing and equipping our troops for the field. Though only four miles west of the State line, it has not yet been captured by the enemy. They have, however, at different times, captured and killed our pickets, and made several raids on the Government stock grazing on the prairie near town. The place has increased in importance, as a business center, since it has been made a regular depot of supplies. The merchants have a trade extending to a distance of sixty to seventy-five miles around, besides a large trade in outfitting sutlers who accompany the army. It is not likely that the town will diminish in importance even after the war, for it is located in a rich agricultural region, besides the rich deposits of bituminous coal in this vicinity will probably be extensively worked in a few years, which will cause capital and immigration to flow into this section. The prairies around us, now clothed with tons of wild grass per acre, will teem with fields of golden grain. But hundreds of tons of this wild grass can now be used to good purpose by the Government as forage for its animals. Captain M. H. Insley, the Depot Quartermaster, has commenced letting contracts for forage and fuel, and in a few months we shall see long hay ricks rising on the Government lots, and great quantities of corn and oats filling the Government cribs, and the estimated number of cords of wood and tons of coal stored in their proper places. Farmers and teamsters will have no trouble in finding active employment from this time until late in the season. Everybody has an opportunity of making money but the soldier. The farmer gets a good price for everything that he raises; and the mechanic good wages for his labor. A civilian who can barely make a living now would probably be in poverty in ordinary times. When the war closes those who have remained at home will have had opportunities to become almost rich, while the soldiers will have grown poor. It will require unusual energy and economy for the ex-soldier to ever get even with his civilian neighbor in regard to social standing and ease. And no one ever estimates the sacrifice the volunteer soldier makes when he offers his services to his Government.

There has been quite an excitement among the colored men about town for several days in regard to drafting them. The farce of drafting a considerable number was gone through with, but as the officers had no legal authority to draft them, they have been released and returned to their business, or enlisted voluntarily. Enlistments for the Second Kansas colored regiment have been going on at a lively rate for several days; and it is quite likely that the recruiting officers have endeavored to impress the able-bodied colored men with the idea that they may be drafted shortly, and that it will be better for them to enlist now and secure the generous bounty offered by the Government. Indeed it has been suggested that the recruiting officer got up the excitement for the purpose of increasing the number of enlistments per diem. There is a strong incentive to resort to such a trick, for the sooner the officers get their company organizations complete, the sooner they will get mustered into the service. I think, however, that a straightforward course is best in such matters, then there can be no excuse for complaint on the part of the soldier after enlistment. Our enthusiasm for a good cause should never make us dishonest towards those whom we wish to act with us. I see no objection, however, to the recruiting officers making pretty little speeches to those whom they wish to become candidates for enlistment, by appealing to their sense of patriotism, and by telling them "what a grand and heroic thing it is to die for one's country." There are a good many men whose patriotism is quite latent, and who need some stimulant to arouse them from their state of indifference. They do not always see the connection between the peace and happiness of their quiet homes and the stability of a Government founded on just laws. It therefore becomes proper to point out to them, in as forcible language as possible, that there come times in the history of Governments when they find it necessary to call on their citizens to assist in enforcing the laws, and in defending the life of the nation against foreign or domestic foes.   Pictures might be drawn bringing vividly before their minds the fact that, were it not for the strong arm of the Government, their families might very shortly be weeping over their slaughtered bodies in the midst of the ruins of their desolated homes.   The fife and drum corps often performs excellent service in stirring up the martial pride of those just in from the country.   Every soldier who enlisted early in the war will remember the stirring air of "The Girl I left behind me."

CHAPTER XX.

A Post established at Baxter Springs, with a Detachment of Cavalry—Bombardment of Charleston and probable fall of Forts Sumter and Wagner—Guerrillas along the Border displaying unusual Activity—Large quantities of Hay being put up for the Government at Fort Scott—Burning and Sacking of Lawrence by Quantrell—Murder of one hundred and fifty of her Citizens—Escape of the Desperadoes into Missouri—Federal troops in pursuit—The Guerillas break up into small Detachments—Kansas needs a State Militia—Looking around for some one to blame—General Ewing and Schofield Denounced—Some favor the wild notion of a Grand Army of Invasion, to destroy everything in Missouri for a distance of forty miles from Kansas—Folly of the Scheme—Generals Cooper and Cabell threatening General Blunt—Paola Mass Meeting—Plan of removal of Rebel Families considered.

A detachment of the Third Wisconsin cavalry was ordered by Colonel Blair to Baxter Springs, on the morning of the 17th, for the purpose of occupying that place as a regular station. Several months ago, in looking over the route of our trains from Fort Scott to Gibson, I remarked, that there was great need of a detachment of cavalry at Baxter. There is no point between this place and Gibson, where a small force of cavalry can be stationed to better advantage. And had not all his cavalry that could be spared been employed on escort duty, Colonel Blair would have ordered several companies there months ago. Some sort of fortifications have already been constructed, and one or two companies of colored infantry and a piece of light artillery are stationed there to defend the place. With this detachment of cavalry also stationed there, to scout the surrounding country, guerrilla depredations should shortly almost cease. At any rate the guerrillas in that section can be watched more closely, and perhaps prevented from concentrating in sufficient force to attack our trains.

Reports from the East state that General Gilmore's forces, besieging Charleston, are gradually battering down the enemy's works. From accounts, the bombardment of the city and of Forts Sumter and Wagner, recently, must have been terrific. It is thought that Sumter will certainly fall in a few days, as great breaches have already been made in some portions of the defences. Our siege-gun batteries keep pouring in such a steady stream of shot and shell, that the enemy do not get time to repair the openings. The fall of Charleston will be a great humiliation to the rebels, since it was at that place they seized the first Government property, and made the first attack upon the United States troops. They are not having such a jolly time as when they were besieging Major Anderson's little command, in April, 1861. They will, unquestionably, be in a bad way when the hot-bed in which their secession ideas have been nurtured since the days of Calhoun, shall have been captured by our forces.

Information recieved here from several points along the border towards Kansas City, indicates that the guerrilla bands in the counties of Jackson, Cass and Johnson, are displaying unusual activity. It is just a year ago since they concentrated in Jackson County, and attacked Lone Jack, and captured two pieces of artillery from our troops. This present great activity portends some mischief. It is not thought now that they can get together more than three or four hundred men in that section. But considering that every man is almost loaded down with repeating rifles and revolvers, this force is equal to about a thousand of our best troops. Our officers operating along the border know approximately the number of men each guerrilla chieftain can muster. With that number of men they are not likely to attack any of our stations along the border, for they have never to my knowledge attacked a superior force of our troops. They have, however, fought like tigers to get out of a tight place. For fifty miles south of Kansas City, we have, I should think, not less than fifteen hundred troops. They know, or should know, the character of the enemy with whom they have to deal. And of course they understand perfectly that they cannot with safety relax their vigilance for a single day. Quantrell's band is known to be composed of the worst men in the country, and would no doubt like an opportunity to cross the line and invade Kansas. The people of this State know that they have repeatedly threatened to make a raid into it, to recapture the stook, etc.,

alleged to have been taken from Missouri by our
troops. From what we know of his men, we have
reason to believe that they will not only commit such
depredations as robbery and plunder, but that their
trail will be stained by the blood of our citizens, and
the torch they may also apply almost indiscriminately.
But they are closely looked after by the troops under
General Thomas Ewing, commanding District of the
Border.

Nothing further has been heard of the gathering of
the guerrilla bands under Quantrell north of us, and
everything has been unusually quiet at this post, and
in this section for several days. Our scouting parties
into Missouri return without having heard anything
of the guerrillas, who have for the last year infested
Vernon and Barton Counties. Indeed for several days
past, each day is a repetition of the day before. The
sentinels guarding public property at different points,
walk leisurely to and fro upon their beats, with their
bright muskets on their shoulders, as in times of profound peace. Captain M. H. Insley, the Depot Quartermaster, is beginning to receive the new hay recently contracted for, and a number of large ricks have
commenced going up. The dust has been flying all
day, on all the roads leading into town, caused by the
numerous civilian teams hauling hay and coal, for delivery on contract. While the work of laying in the
winter supply of fuel and forage is going on, there is
also great activity at all the Commissary, Quartermaster and Ordinance store houses. Trains from Fort

Leavenworth are unloading at one place, and trains for Fort Gibson are loading at another place. The depot and staff quartermasters, commissiaries and ordinance officers, are kept busy in supplying the troops in the Indian country with stores furnished by their respective departments. Considering the amount of Government property stored at this post, some of our officers feel apprehensions for its safety, for if the enemy should capture or kill our pickets, and make a dash upon the place in the night, we are not sure that Colonel Blair has a sufficient number of troops at his disposal to successfully defend the town, or public property. He is vigilant, however, and may not permit the enemy to approach very near unobserved.

Information reached this post, on the evening of the 22d, that the city of Lawrence in this State was sacked, burned and nearly two hundred of her citizens killed, by about three hundred men under Quantrell, at day-break on the morning of the 21st instant. It seems that Quantrell crossed the State line on Thursday evening, 20th instant, with his force, and marched all night, and reached Lawrence Friday morning at four o'clock, and immediately commenced their fiendish work of robbing, burning property, and shooting down the male citizens who were unarmed and defenseless. A gentleman who escaped from the scene of the slaughter and desolation, described to me this evening, quite vividly, what he saw, and I have obtained particulars from other sources, all tending to show that it would be impossible to exaggerate the fiendish-

25

ness of the ruffians. The ruffians, when they approached the city, threw a guard around it to prevent any of
the men from escaping. They then marched into the
principal part of the city and commenced their work.
Everything in the way of money and jewelry was tak-
en, the houses set on fire, and the men shot down in
the presence of their families. Many instances are
reported, in which men were shot down while their
wives, daughters and mothers were clinging to them,
and begging that they might be spared. But the en-
treaties of the women, that the lives of those so dear
to them might be spared, had no effect on the harden-
ed hearts of the monsters in human form. If
there were no women to remove the lifeless bodies of
the men, they were left to be consumed by the devour-
ing flames. The loss of life by this worse than fiendish
act, cannot be accurately known until the ruins of the
desolated city have been carefully examined. I have
also heard that the enemy threw a good many bodies
into wells and cisterns. In less than half an hour after
the enemy entered the city, it was in a sheet of flame.
All the best portion of it has been burned, and hundreds of families have not only lost all their male
members but their houses and effects also. For cruelty and heartlessness, I doubt whether this outrage has
a parallel in modern warfare. And were it not already committed, it would be difficult to believe that
three hundred fiends could be got together in this
country for the purpose of committing it. They surprised and captured twenty-five colored recruits, who

were shot dead on the spot. A few men escaped through corn fields adjacent to the city. Someone carried the news of the enemy being in the city to Senator Lane, and he escaped on horseback. He had left but a moment when they surrounded his house with the full confidence that they had caught him. After they had satiated themselves by robbing, burning and murdering for several hours, they withdrew and marched towards Missouri. They remounted themselves on fresh horses, obtained from the public and private stables in Lawrence, and each man led back the horse which he rode into the city, or obtained a better one in its place. With fine fresh animals, our best cavalry companies on the border, on account of the hard service their horses have performed this summer, could not have kept up with the enemy many hours. If Quantrell is hotly pursued by our troops, he can leave his led horses and the goods with which some of them are known to have been packed. But as it is only about thirty-five miles from Lawrence to the State line, it was soon apparent that he would get back into Missouri unmolested, or, at any rate, with a trifling loss of men and property.

An interval of two days brought additional particulars. General Lane, a few hours after his flight from his home, collected together about twenty men, and followed and overtook, and skirmished with the rear of the enemy about twelve miles from Lawrence. He also dispatched couriers to various points where we had troops stationed, with the view of having them intercept the enemy. Anyway, our troops between Kansas City and Paola got word of the destruction of Lawrence, and the massacre of her citizens, and made an effort to intercept Quantrell on his return. A few miles north of Paola our troops and citizens attacked him, but as he was not disposed to fight he managed to evade them, and get into Missouri with the loss of two or three men, and some of the animals that were being led. As it is mostly a prairie country between Lawrence and the State line, and as our officers were informed, a few hours after he passed into Kansas, of the fact, I am yet unable to understand why more effective measures were not taken to pursue him the moment he invaded the State, and to intercept him on his return. The section that he passed over between the State line and Lawrence is rather thickly settled, and some of the citizens on his line of march are surely chargeable with gross negligence in failing to inform the people of Lawrence, and our officers, of the enemy's movements. It is reported that Captain Coleman sent a messenger to warn Lawrence that Quantrell had passed into Kansas, and might be moving in that direction. But the messenger was either intercepted by the enemy, or the enemy reached Lawrence before him.

Our troops are still continuing the pursuit, but as the enemy have reached the heavily wooded country of Cass county, they will probably break up into small bands, and return to their isolated retreats, where it will be difficult to find them. Colonel

Saysear, of the First Missouri State Militia cavalry, commenced a vigorous pursuit of Quantrell soon after he crossed into Missouri, and overtook him on Big Creek near Harrisonville, and killed six of his men. Majors Plumb and Thatcher, of the Eleventh Kansas cavalry, have also overtaken several detachments of the enemy, and killed a number of his men.

As Quantrell's men have so often threatened the destruction of Lawrence during the last eighteen months, and as the place is second in size and importance in the State, and the home of Senator Lane, it is unaccountable why several companies of troops have not been stationed there. Having always been opposed to the border ruffians, it has since the war been an object of especial hatred by them. If a battalion from the regularly organized forces could not have been spared from active service on the border, then a militia force should have been organized for the protection of the city, somewhat on the plan of the Missouri State troops. Kansas needs a State militia organization just as much as Missouri, for our towns, as distant from the State line as the second tier of counties, are liable to attack and destruction by detachments of guerrillas from Missouri at almost any time. It is possible for a small detachment of men mounted on good animals to penetrate the State, unobserved, for a distance of thirty-five or forty miles, during a single night's march. Even if their horses should get much fatigued, they would have very little trouble in getting fresh ones. There are a great many men who do not wish to enter the volunteer service, yet who could be easily induced to enter the militia service of the State for their immediate protection. With a well organized militia, there would be no need for any portion of the volunteer forces to occupy a place as distant from the scene of active operations as Lawrence.

Now that Quantrell has committed his fiendish act and escaped deserved punishment, our people, political leaders particularly, are looking around for some one upon whom to cast the blame. A good deal of excitement seems likely to grow out of the barbarous act of the enemy, for it is a shock to not only the people of this State, but to the entire North, and to loyal hearts everywhere. It is, however, in perfect keeping with the principle for which the South is fighting. Our people could never be led to commit such atrocious acts, except by way of retaliation; and even then, I think few men could be found mean enough to take gold rings from the fingers of ladies, as Quantrell's men did. But there is a phase of the discussion of this great crime that I regret to hear. Some are loud in their denunciation of Generals Ewing and Schofield, and there are others who not only denounce these officers for permitting the enemy to invade the State, but insist that it is the duty of the citizens of Kansas to assemble at some point and march into Missouri and down her border counties, and burn and destroy everything for a distance of forty miles from the State line, regardless of the political status of the owners of property. I have heard some men who were boiling over with indignation, and apparently ready to join the Grand Army of Invasion, declare that there are no loyal men in Missouri, and that the torch should be applied, and not a house left standing within a hundred miles of Kansas. This remark was suggested: "Gentlemen, if you are really so full of loyalty and martial enthusiasm, why don't you enlist into the Fourteenth and Fifteenth regiments now organizing and needing recruits?" Though every loyal person regrets the calamity at Lawrence, it is no time for reckless talk. Nor should men on this side of the line think of holding the Union people of Missouri responsible for the acts of the enemy. It is an absurd and extravagant notion, and savors more of political buncomb than true devotion to the Government. Our people should remember that Missouri has sent to the field, including her State troops, nearly a hundred thousand loyal men, upwards of Six times the number of men this State has furnished for the war. Union people in Missouri are every day being murdered and robbed by guerrillas and bushwhackers, though the State militia are furnishing all the protection in their power. Are the loyal people there entitled to no sympathy? As I have already described the scenes of desolated homes in Missouri, I will only add the remark, that life, and liberty to enjoy it, is as sweet on that side of the line as on this. The Missouri troops now at the front, and who have participated in the capture of Fort Donelson and Vicksburg, and the great battles in Tennessee, have enough to torture their minds, in contemplating guerrillas burning their homes and leaving their families houseless and defenceless, without our troops or people committing unjustifiable acts to increase their anxiety. And moreover, those whose loyalty to the Goverument consists in extravagant expressions, should also remember that a considerable portion of the soldiers of most of the Kansas regiments were citizens of Missouri up to the time of their enlistments. And if reports be true, and I have endeavored to get at the exact truth, the Missouri State troops have followed Quantrell more persistently, and killed more of his men, than have our Kansas troops that are stationed along the border.

A man named Morgan was killed on the 28th, a few miles east of Dry Wood, Missouri. From such facts as I have been able to obtain, it appears that this man has been in the habit, for some time, of coming to this post and getting such information in regard to our operations, along the border and in the Indian country, as he could pick up, and of carrying it across the line to bushwhackers, and thus keeping them perfectly advised of our movements. If there are any persons who come here for the purpose of getting information to betray us into the hands of the enemy, and lose their lives in the operation, it will perhaps have a wholesome effect on the minds of others engaged in similar service. The permission granted to people of questionable loyalty, to trade with the merchants of this place unrestricted, has perhaps cost us the lives of quite a number of our soldiers.

Several special messengers with the mail and despatches, who arrived on the morning of the 30th,
from Fort Gibson, report that the enemy, under Generals Cooper and Cabell, are no longer assuming such
a threatening attitude as they were a few weeks ago.
They have fallen back from their old position on the
south bank of the Arkansas River, near Fort Gibson,
to the north fork of Canadian River, about fifty miles
further south. General Cabell has gone to Fort Smith
with his division, as we have a column of troops under General John McNeil, ready to march down the
line *via* Fayetteville to Van Buren. It is thought that
General Blunt will be ready to move forward and attack General Cooper in a few days. After beating
General Cooper he intends to swing to the left, and
attack Fort Smith, and take it by storm if the enemy
defends it. Our troops are getting full rations, and
are well supplied with ammunition. The cholera and
small-pox have almost disappeared, and the soldiers
are in good spirits, and ready to open a vigorous fall
campaign against the enemy. General Cooper has
been beaten so often the last year, I doubt whether
he can keep his troops together to make a hard fight.

A mass meeting of the citizens of Kansas is to take
place at Paola in a few days, for the purpose of considering the plan and setting the day when they shall
invade Missouri *en masse*, and march down the border
with fire and sword, and thunder and lightning, and
make it impossible for bushwhackers to invade this
State again. If the citizens of the State nearly all

turn out, and their martial ardor keeps up at a white
heat, I think that the recruiting officers of the Fourteenth and Fifteenth regiments should be on the
ground. They should be able to get recruits enough
to fill their respective regiments in a single day. But
the noisiest are not always most eager to make personal sacrifices for the cause which they pretend to
champion. Stirring speeches are to be made by General James H. Lane, United States Senator from this
State, Colonel C. R. Jennison, and a number of
other orators. As an unprejudiced observer of current events, I must express my belief that the politicians of Kansas are inclined to make political capital
out of the Lawrence calamity, which I do not think is
at all creditable to them. If the citizens of the State,
when they assemble at Paola, would express their horror, in a suitable manner, of the enormity of the
crime committed by the enemy at Lawrence, so that
the civilized world might see the barbarous method of
warfare the Confederacy is fostering, and then adjourn
sine die, I think that they will have acted more sensibly than if they issue flaming manifestoes of devasta-
tion of the country of our neighbors across the line.

A rebel force of about one hundred men passed
Balltown on the morning of September 1st, moving
south. The men are believed to be a portion of Quantrell's command who participated in the Lawrence
massacre. If they can find any other unguarded
point, or a small detachment of our troops, we may
expect to hear from them again shortly. They will

not likely have any opposition to their movements. down the border unless they come in contact with the Missouri militia stationed at Neosho, or some detachment of our troops on a scout. In fact, if they keep near the State line, the country is open to the Arkansas River. The State militia have not made regular stations at Carthage and Lamar, for the reason that those towns have been destroyed, and the country around them desolated, leaving scarcely anything in that region to protect. This devastated territory the enemy can march over and occupy for weeks without our knowing it, if they are not aggressive; and then, at their leisure, can make raids into Kansas, or into the counties east of the border counties of Missouri. In the interior of Missouri such raids are impossible, or at any rate, quite rare, for the reason that no considerable body of guerrillas can collect together, or come into a neighborhood without the Union families knowing it.

Since Quantrell's raid on Lawrence, and the agitations of irregular organizations from this State going into Missouri for the purpose of burning and destroying everything, a good many rebel families who have been living in the border counties of Missouri, have commenced moving south. In those sections infested with guerrillas, I think that the rebel families who give them aid and comfort should be sent south of our lines. Such action would probably do more to stop bushwhacking and the guerrilla warfare, than burning or destroying the property of rebel families, and leaving them in the country. Let rebel families understand that they can remain on their homesteads, provided no guerrillas infest the section, and I believe that they would generally discourage guerrilla warfare. A regular invasion by the organized forces of the Confederacy I would not consider as sufficient grounds for their removal. By removing them south the rebel authorities would be obliged to provide for them, and the inducement for husbands and male relations to return to the State would no longer exist. As soon as our troops occupied Missouri, an order of this kind should, in my judgment, have been published by the commanding General. Then, if the enemy persisted in their illegitimate warfare, we could stand it as well as they. If the officers and soldiers operating with the regular forces of the Confederacy, wish their families to remain at their homes in Missouri until the present contest shall have been decided, let them prevail on the rebel authorities to stop the guerrilla warfare in those States occupied by our troops. We are able to stop it quite effectually, and without resorting to any barbarous methods. The question arises, shall we do it? I think that we should, for it is no time for sentimental considerations to turn us aside from our duty. Union families within the rebel lines would perhaps regard themselves fortunate if they could be sent within our lines if they could take with them their personal effects. To compel the removal of thousands of families would no doubt entail great hardships on many of them.

But such hardships would be borne by them to save our people from the cruelties of their relatives and friends, whom they have been in the habit of harboring and encouraging.

CHAPTER XXI.

General Schofield coldly received by the people of Leavenworth
City—Colonels Jennison and Hoyt speak in Fort Scott—The
crowd sing "John Brown's body lies mouldering in the
grave," &c.—More of General Lane's Grand Army of Invasion
—Few trophies to bring back—General Schofield issues an
order against invasion—The Missouri State troops would
resist it—Battle of Perryville and defeat of General Cooper—
General Blunt captures Fort Smith—Generals Steele and Davidson capture Little Rock—Colonel Blair sends out a reconnoissance—A new department wanted—General Gillmore
captures Forts Wagner and Gregg in Charlestown Harbor—
Sympathizers of the rebellion receive anonymous notices to
leave the city—Supposed to be the action of the Union League
—Arrival of General Blunt and Staff and Colonel Judson—
The Bourbon County Fair—Activity of the enemy along the
border again.

GENERAL SCHOFIELD, the commanding General of
this department, visited Leavenworth City a few days
ago, and was coldly received by the citizens. At a
recent mass meeting held there to take action in regard
to the Lawrence massacre, resolutions denouncing him
as a sympathizer with the enemy, and demanding his
removal, were adopted. Throughout the State the feeling against him is quite bitter, for nearly every one
holds that he is exceedingly stupid or careless of his

duty, to permit such a large force as Quantrell had to organize in the center of his Department, and march forty miles into Kansas without being pursued by our troops. Unless he can completely destroy Quantrell's force immediately, which is now perhaps an impossibilty, the people of this State will petition President Lincoln to remove him from the command of this department. When the present excitement wears off a different feeling may prevail.

Colonels Jennison and Hoyt made rousing speeches in town on the evening of the 7th, for the purpose of arousing the martial enthusiasm of our citizens to a point that will induce them to enlist into their regiment, the Fifteenth. Their efforts in this direction are very commendable; but when they endeavor to excite passions that need restraining, I cannot go with them. The lawless spirit is always rampant enough, without receiving a *quasi* public sanction. They talked freely about burning everything in the two border tiers of counties in Missouri, and received a few feeble cheers from the crowd. Colonel Hoyt was one of the attorneys who defended John Brown, when he was tried for treason by the Virginia authorities, and therefore drew a large crowd, as our people were curious to see him and hear him speak. He is a young man of considerable talent, and should he conduct himself properly, perhaps has a brilliant future before him. In the course of the evening, before the crowd dispersed, the popular war song, "John Brown's body," &c., was sung with a good deal of feeling and earnest-

ness. There are many here who condemn John Brown's
seizure of Harper's Ferry, and think that he deserved
hanging for the invasion of Virginia. But for my
own part, I have regarded him as the first martyr of
the war, and I believe that he will live as long in the
memory of the nation, as any of our great military
heroes. Historians of the future, who write even con-
densed histories of this great contest, will not likely
omit the name of John Brown from their introductory
chapters. The name of this plain, simple man, in its
present connection, will live in the hearts of liberty-
loving people as long as our national history lives.
When the slave-holders hung him, they doubtless
little thought that they were raising a storm that
would shortly sweep away their cherished, and to
them divinely ordained, institution.

Colonels Jennison and Hoyt left on the 8th for
Paola, where they will join General Lane, who has
perhaps nearly five thousand citizens assembled for the
purpose of taking into consideration the plan of invading Missouri. It has been published that those in favor
of joining this Grand Army of Invasion, should bring
with them fifteen days' rations, blankets and complete
equipments for the field. Though General Lane is a
great man in Kansas, and has great influence over her
citizens, and could probably by his eloquence persuade
many of them to follow him right up to the cannon's
mouth, yet there are reasons for thinking that his citizen army will prove a failure; for it is not likely that
his victorious torchbearers, even if they should start

out as gallant knights on such a glorious crusade, would bring back with them many valuable trophies and guerrilla chieftains bound in golden chains. The cream has been taken from the milk repeatedly, and those who took it have consumed it or left the country. The fine milch cow that once furnished the rich milk has been terribly beaten, and turned out to graze on thorns and thistles.

It is now known to the people of this State that General Schofield has issued an order forbidding General Lane's Grand Army of citizens invading Missouri without authority from General Ewing, the District Commander. This order, unless revoked, will probably put a quietus on General Lane's contemplated invasion. Had he crossed the line and commenced to carry out his generally understood programme, it is now thought that he would have soon come in contact with the Missouri State troops. It is reported that they say with a good deal of emphasis, that they would shoot a Kansas invader, caught in the act of applying the torch to a Union man's property, just as quick as they would a bushwhacker caught in a similar act. It would be strange if they would stand idly by and see their homes destroyed by a mob. The idea of a mob of citizens from this State invading Missouri for the purpose of avenging the crime of Quantrell at Lawrence, has seemed to me wild from the beginning. I may remark, however, that there is an opportunity for those who have been clamoring for invasion to satisfy their martial ardor by enlisting into the service of the

26

United States immediately. They may have an opportunity yet of satiating their thirst for war.

Dispatches have just been received here from General Blunt announcing his capture of Fort Smith, and the defeat of General Cooper's army at Perryville, a small town in the Creek nation, about seventy-five miles south of Fort Gibson. At Perryville, General Cooper's army was completely routed and dispersed, and a large number of animals and nearly all his commissary stores captured. The enemy lost about twenty men killed and perhaps forty wounded and sixty prisoners in the engagement. They made a very feeble stand, and when they broke they could not be rallied again. Our troops pursued their flying columns far towards Red River. General Blunt moved on Fort Smith with preparations for a hard fight; but the enemy under General Cabell, after a little skirmishing west of the Potoe River, withdrew, and General Blunt marched in and took possession of the Fort and City. The latest dispatches via St. Louis state Generals Steele and Davidson have captured Little Rock, the capital of Arkansas. The city was taken without any hard fighting, but the enemy contested the advance of our troops while marching across the country. If the forces of Generals Blunt and Davidson form a junction now, the Arkansas River can be opened to navigation above Little Rock. It may be, however, that it has not a sufficient volume of water at this season to float even light draft steamers. But if Little Rock can be made a depot of supplies by direct shipment from

St. Louis, it will be more convenient for our troops at Fort Smith to transport their supplies from there than from this point. Fort Gibson, however, will probably still receive supplies from this place, until the Arkansas River is opened to navigation. A month or more may be required to perfect arrangements for bringing supplies through from Little Rock to the Army of the Frontier at Fort Smith, so that, in the meantime, supply trains will be sent out from here as usual. The large supply train that leaves this post on the 13th, will go to Fort Smith *via* Fort Gibson. Since the Lawrence massacre has given Quantrell the reputation of possessing a bold and daring spirit, it is thought that he may venture to attack this train. If he cannot get together a force larger than the escort, he is not likely to make an attack. Colonel Blair has sent out a detachment of cavalry to the east and southeast of this place, for the purpose of ascertaining if there are any recent indications of an enemy having passed down the border, or coming in from the south. The commanding officer of the escort will, however, understand the necessity of being extremely vigilant.

The politicians of this State are clamoring for a new department, to embrace Kansas and the Indian country. Senator Lane will probably prevail upon President Lincoln, to direct the Secretary of War to issue the necessary orders at an early day. As soon as its limits shall have been defined, it is proposed to have General Blunt put in command. Senator Lane ought then to be happy. General Blunt has been very successful in all his military operations, and has the reputation of being a good fighter, so that he may wish a more active field than the new department will afford. Now that he has captured Fort Smith, western Arkansas should be attached to his new department; then he will have a section in which there is an organized enemy to contend with. In the Indian country, since the defeat of General Cooper at Perryville, there is no foe worthy his attention. The bitterness of the people of this State against General Schofield is, perhaps, in a large measure, unjustifiable. He is in a position where it is almost impossible to satisfy all factions and parties. He has received direct instructions from President Lincoln to favor no one faction of the Missouri Unionists more than the other. Mr. Lincoln has not only recognized the loyal element in Missouri, but he has done it to the extent of selecting one of his Cabinet officers from that State. He seems to have watched over the State from the beginning of the war with special interest, for which her loyal people will ever feel grateful.

It is now officially announced that, after upwards of a month's bombardment, General Gillmore has captured Forts Wagner and Gregg, in Charleston Harbor, and that the city of Charleston is entirely under his guns. The vigorous bombardment of the city itself will now soon be commenced. The rebel strongholds are gradually crumbling before our victorious arms, and their territory is contracting day by day

One must be stupidly blind not to see that we are rapidly approaching the end of the struggle. The faint-hearted, and those who have all along doubted the ability of the government to crush the rebellion, should now fall into line, so that they may in the future have the pleasure of knowing, that towards the last of this important struggle they were on the side of justice and right, and did something towards maintaining our national life.

Captain Coleman, Ninth Kansas Cavalry, had a lively skirmish with a party of Quantrell's men on the 17th instant, killing three of the guerrillas and wounding several others. He also captured from them a considerable amount of the property which they took from Lawrence, such as horses, mules, goods, etc. Two of our soldiers were wounded in the affair, but not mortally.

Captain N. B. Lucas, of the Sixth Kansas cavalry, who has just came up from Fort Gibson with his company as an escort for General DuBoice, Inspector General, will continue his escort duty to Kansas City, and then remain in that section for a while to operate against the guerrillas of Jackson and Cass counties. He served with us in the Indian division under Colonel Phillips until General Blunt came down, and I know that he is an efficient officer, and that the enemy will feel his presence, now that he is detailed for duty on the border. When I recall our service together in the Indian country, I almost regret that Colonel Blair has requested of General Blunt my temporary detail

for special duty at this post, for it is much more satisfactory to be able to chronicle important events on the
spot, than to chronicle them after sifting the statements of half a dozen persons. This, however, is a
central position, from which I can follow the movements of our troops to the north of us along the border, or to the south, down the border as far as Fort
Smith and Fort Gibson in the Indian Territory.

On the 21st, quite a number of citizens of this
place, who are believed to be in sympathy with the
rebellion, received anonymous notices that they must
leave the city within ten days, if they regard their
personal safety as a matter of serious consideration. It
is generally thought that these notices have been sent
out by direction of the Union League of Fort Scott.
I am inclined to believe that this opinion is correct,
for, in a conversation with several members of the
League, with which I am somewhat in sympathy, they
tacitly admitted that such was the case. In war times
those who naturally dislike secret political organizations, feel compelled to adopt extraordinary measures
for their own safety. A great deal of leniency has
been shown certain rebel sympathizers here. The
soldiers and loyal citizens feel that those who sympathize with the rebellion, on account of the danger of
their betraying us, if possible, into the hands of a foe
that has unfurled the black flag, should not be permitted to remain in our midst. The great crime of
the Lawrence massacre, that has sent a thrill of horror
through the hearts of the loyal community, has pro-

duced in the rebel sympathizers a feeling of self-satisfaction, unless the expressions of their countenances
belie them. We cannot afford to tolerate among us
men who would betray us, and then have us cruelly
murdered. Though some of those who received the
notices alluded to above, have been quite bitter in
their denunciations of the government, recently they
have been more cautious and discreet, and have rarely
let slip any strong language. From inquiries, it appears that quite a number of those who received
warnings will leave this place temporarily, any way.
They ought to be able to see that, to the loyal mind,
they are regarded almost in the light of spies. A
number of officers also received these anonymous
notices. In several instances the thing was carried
too far.

General Blunt and staff and Colonel William
R. Judson, and a number of other officers belonging to the Army of the Frontier, arrived at this
post Wednesday, the 23d, from Fort Smith. A
brilliant reception was given the General and his
party. Colonel C. W. Blair, commanding the troops
here, ordered them out as a compliment to the hero
of many battles. He also directed Captain Smith's
battery to fire a Major General's salute, and the bands
to take their proper place in the line.

Colonel Blair, who is one of the finest orators in the
State, if not indeed in the West, made the reception
speech, in charming and elegant language. The an-
nouncement that Colonel Blair is to speak on any oc-

casion, is always sufficient to draw an immense crowd in this section. But aside from this fact, the citizens and soldiers of Fort Scott felt like honoring General Blunt for his brilliant campaign in northwestern Arkansas last fall, and for his scarcely less brilliant campaign in the Indian country the last two months, ending in the capture of Fort Smith. I must remark, however, that most of the glory claimed for him in his recent campaign justly belongs to Colonel William A. Phillips, whose heroic action through six months of extraordinary trials, made possible the recent achievements of our arms in the Indian country.

A detachment of soldiers which has just come from Southwest Missouri, state that Colonel M. La Rue Harrison, of the First Kansas cavalry, had a fight on the 21st with the rebel forces of Colonels Coffey and Brown, near the mouth of Buffalo Creek, Newton County, Missouri, and killed five of the enemy and wounded several others. This recent action indicates that Colonel Harrison is improving in fighting qualities. His precipitate retreat from Fayetteville last spring, when he was expected to co-operate with Colonel Phillips, was not by any means very creditable to him, and if what has been reported in regard to the matter be true, should have subjected him to censure by court martial. Perhaps he has determined to wipe out that little stain from his record

A great battle was fought on the 19th and 20th instant, near Chattanooga, Tennessee, between the forces of General Rosecrans, about sixty thousand strong, and the combined rebel forces of Generals Bragg, Longstreet and Hill, estimated at upwards of a hundred thousand men. It is reported that the losses in killed and wounded on both sides, will foot up twenty-five thousand men. Our troops have suffered a temporary check in their forward movement. It is the intention, however, to renew the contest as soon as reinforcements come up.

Our scouts brought in a report on Sunday, the 27th, that a band of guerrillas near Nevada, Vernon County, Missouri, have had under consideration a scheme to kill or capture our pickets between Fort Scott and the State line, and then make a raid on this place. Colonel Blair, however, had found out their intentions from his scouts, and has thwarted their contemplated movement by sending a detachment of cavalry to look after them. He has had the picket guards very skillfully posted between this post and Missouri, so that if the enemy should kill or capture the men on the outer station, they would not be able to pass the inner stations without causing alarm.

General Blunt who has been here since the 23d instant, is making preparations to return to Fort Smith, in about a week, to take command of the Army of the Frontier. The headquarters of his district will be removed from here, and his assistant adjutant general, Major H. Z. Curtis, who has been here attending to the regular business of the district, will accompany him, taking along all the records of the office.

The Bourbon County Fair commenced at this place

on the 30th, with a large attendance from all parts of the county. This is the first fair ever held in this section of the State, and the exhibitions of stock, agricultural productions, handy works of the ladies, &c., will compare favorably with the county fairs of the older States. To see the great throng of people from the country deeply interested in exhibiting their various productions, and discussing the merits of this or that animal, or this or that agricultural product, almost makes the soldier forget that he is a soldier. Many of those dressed in blue, who were in attendance to-day, will perhaps dream to-night of the peaceful times when their minds were filled with thoughts pertaining to the duties of domestic and social life. They will be wholly unconscious that they are sleeping in the habilaments of war, and that the storm may break forth upon them at any moment. Those who have been in service on the border since the beginning of the war, know that they may be aroused any night by the beating of the *long roll*, or the distant firing of the enemy, driving in our outposts. No town on the border has been subjected to so much excitement of this kind as this place.

Dispatches received from Fort Smith state that Colonel Cloud's brigade has been ordered back from that section to the southern line of Missouri, in consequence of the threatened invasion by a portion of General Price's army, recently driven from Little Rock by our troops under Generals Steele and Davidson. Colonel Bowen, commanding the

Second Brigade, stationed at Webber's Falls above Fort Smith, has probably marched to the latter place by this time, to relieve Colonel Cloud. Unless Generals Steele and Davidson continue the pursuit of Price's army from Little Rock, it will likely either march to Fort Smith, and attack our forces there, or turn north and invade Missouri. From such information as I can obtain, it looks as if the cavalry divisions of Marmaduke and Shelby were preparing for an immediate invasion of Missouri. The country north of the Arkansas River, above Little Rock, is open to the northern line of the State, and they would meet with little or no opposition until they passed into Missouri. But as soon as they enter that State, they are not likely to find much time for rest until they leave it, for the State troops and volunteers stationed at the different points, can soon concentrate in sufficient force to keep them moving. Since Vicksburg has fallen, and Little Rock abandoned, Price's army has really nothing else to do but to send its cavalry on this contemplated raid. The cavalry divisions above mentioned are composed of Missourians, and the officers and men in them will anxiously join an expedition that will give them an opportunity of briefly visiting their families and homes. I have seen enough to convince me that men apparently destitute of sympathetic and tender feelings, will subject themselves without a murmur to extraordinary dangers and hardships, if there is a prospect that they will be able to see only for a few moments, their families and those very dear to them.

While the enemy perhaps have no thought of permanent occupation, they doubtless think that a successful
raid to the interior of the State will give them numerous recruits, strengthen their cause, and show to
the country that the confederacy is not dead yet.
Should they be successful in accomplishing only a part
of their probable plan, it will stimulate the Copperheads of the north to continue their opposition to the
Government, and to renew the cry that "the war is a
failure." The Government has shown them great leniency, for under other governments less moderate than
ours in their treatment of criminals, many of them
would have been hung for their traitorous speeches
and actions. The patience of the loyal people has
been tried almost to the last extremity.

CHAPTER XXII.

General Blunt, Staff and Escort start to Fort Smith—Two Soldiers killed near Fort Scott by the enemy—Signs of an approaching storm—The enemy endeavor to capture or kill the Federal pickets, and to make a dash on Fort Scott—General Blunt's escort attacked by Quantrell near Baxter Springs, and nearly all killed—Colonel Blair with a cavalry force to the rescue—Members of the Band burned in the Band wagon—The enemy defeated by Lieutenant Pond at Baxter Springs—The invasion of Missouri by General Shelby, with two thousand cavalry and three pieces of artillery—The Missouri State militia in pursuit of him—The Militia capture his artillery and disperse his force—General Ewing's force joins in the pursuit of the enemy—The enemy driven from the State—General John McNeil to take command of the Federal troops at Fort Smith—General Lane speaks in Fort Scott—General Blunt starts to Fort Smith again.

General Blunt and Staff, his fine band, and everything pertaining to the Headquarters *District of the Frontier*, left this post the evening of the 4th inst., for Fort Smith *via* Fort Gibson. His escort is made up of detachments from the Fourteenth Kansas cavalry and one Company Third Wisconsin cavalry, and his band all belongs to the latter regiment. The soldiers belonging to the escort, the members of the band, and the officers of his Staff, altogether number about one hundred and fifty men. The papers and records pertaining to Headquarters, were mostly carefully packed in boxes a few days ago, under the eye of Major H. Z. Curtis, Assistant Adjutant General. Major Curtis' wife, a beautiful and accomplished lady, who has been here with her husband several months, also left the same day for her home in Iowa. The Band for half an hour before the General took leave of his friends, played some very fine selections while sitting in their seats in the Band wagon in front of Colonel Blair's residence, on the north side of the plazza. To me the music seemed unusually sweet. I think that each member must have taken special pains to perform his part well. A band wagon has been fitted up for their special purpose, and is drawn by four fine horses. The horses looked as if they were proud of the service required of them. At five o'clock General Blunt and some of his Staff got into his carriage, the bugle sounded the march and the escort filed out, with its silken guidon gayly flying at the head of the column. He intended to march fifteen to twenty miles that night, and then stop a few hours to refresh his men and animals with food and rest. At the rate he usually travels, he will reach Baxter Springs on the evening of the 5th, and Fort Gibson two days later.

Two soldiers of the Fourteenth Kansas cavalry, who were permitted to return home in Vernon County, Missouri, to see their families before starting south with their regiment shortly, were killed on the night of the 4th inst. It is reported that there were upwards of a hundred of the enemy in the party who killed these men. The young lady, a daughter or relative of one of the murdered men, who brought in the information, did not, in the excitement caused by the shooting, ascertain the name of the commanding officer under whom the rebels were acting. No loyal man in the Border Counties of Missouri can stop at his home a single night without great danger. It is folly to attempt it. From such facts as I have collected, however, I am satisfied that they have very recently entered the State, and are perhaps an advance detachment from the invading force mentioned several days ago. Though I can get no definite information as to whether the enemy are about to invade Missouri in force, I think that I have learned enough to justify me in saying that the rumbling sound of the distant thunder may be heard, and that the storm is beyond doubt coming, and may be upon us in a few days.

Colonel Blair for several days has been busy in putting everything in fighting order, in the event of the enemy making an attack on this post. There was an alarm in town on the night of the 4th, and the troops were under arms in a few moments. A considerable force of the enemy endeavored to make a dash on this place, or to capture or kill our pickets near the State line. Our picket guard at the outer station, as soon as they discovered the movements of the enemy, fired a signal, and then rode into this post as swiftly as possible, so that everything might be in readiness to receive the rebels should they have decided to make an

attack. Immediatery after the troops were aroused
and under arms, Colonel Blair sent out detachments of cavalry on all the roads leading in here from
Missouri, to discover, if practicable, the intentions of
the enemy. The cavalry, however, returned the next
morning, and the officers reported that they found no
signs of the enemy having appeared nearer here than
the outer picket station, and that their trail indicated
that they then marched off in a northeast direction.
It is supposed that when they found their scheme was
discovered by our pickets and the alarm given, that
they gave up the idea of making an attack on the post.
Had they attempted to come in, we would really have
had the advantage, for we could have ambushed them
at half a dozen points, Information brought in by
our scouts on the 5th, and information from other
sources, made it almost certain that the several detachments of the enemy which have passed so near us the
last two days, are a part of the invading force of General Shelby.

The 7th was a day of great excitement at this post.
Colonel Blair received a dispatch about one o'clock in
the morning from Baxter Springs, stating that General Blunt's escort had been attacked near that place
by a force under Quantrell, about five hundred strong,
and that nearly all his men and most of his staff were
killed and captured. The alarm was again sounded,
and all the troops called out under arms. Colonel
Blair immediately took most of the cavalry and started
to the relief of General Blunt. He left instructions,

however, looking to the safety of this post. Later in the day, two men who were with General Blunt in the engagement of Monday evening, and three men who were with Lieutenant Pond, commanding the station at Baxter Spings, arrived here and furnished additional particulars.

Between four and five o'clock Monday, 5th instant, Quantrell with three hundred men, and an officer belonging to Shelby's command, with about two hundred men, attacked the station at Baxter Springs. But as the companies there under Lieutenant Pond have rifle pits thrown up around a block house furnished with port-holes for small arms, the enemy, after repeated charges, could not dislodge them. While they continued the attack they soon saw that the casualties were likely to be all on their side. Lieutenant Pond had also one howitzer, which was effectually used, for when the enemy came near enough he poured grape and canister into their ranks with good effect. But they took the precaution to put a guard out on the military road leading from Fort Scott, about a mile north of Baxter Springs. Along towards five o'clock the guard discovered General Blunt's escort coming in sight, perhaps nearly two miles distant on the prairie. Quantrell was quickly informed, and immediately abandoned the attack on Baxter, and marched to meet General Blunt. The General's escort had just emerged from the strip of timber on Brush Creek, when the advance saw coming over a ridge in the prairie from towards Baxter, about

27

two hundred yards off, a large force dressed in Federal uniform.

The officer in command of the escort supposed that they were the troops from Baxter Springs. As soon as Quantrell was informed of the approach of General Blunt's escort, he posted several men in a position to observe it pass over a ridge in the prairie on the north side of Brush Creek, a mile or so distant, and to estimate the approximate number of men by the length of the column. With a good spy-glass the number of men in the escort could easily have been counted while passing over the ridge. Quantrell therefore knew that there was less than two companies in the escort, and marched forward to attack it without stopping to halt. The commanding officer of the escort made no effort to form his men in line until the enemy had come within fifty yards and opened fire. General Blunt, and several of his staff, quickly got out of his carriage and commenced to direct the movements of his men. But as the enemy had approached nearer, and were keeping up a steady fire, the escort fell back in some disorder. General Blunt endeavored to rally his men, but as the enemy were closing around him on all sides, it was impossible to keep them firm under the galling fire. In less than half an hour the entire escort and wagons were surrounded by the enemy. General Blunt and fifteen to twenty men cut their way through and escaped, but not without bullet holes through their clothing. All the rest of the escort, members of the band, and teamsters, were killed or wounded, and lay on the field within the radius of half a mile. The wounded who escaped death were supposed to have been killed, for every wounded man the enemy saw showing signs of life, they shot through the head or heart. A few of our soldiers fell into the hands of Shelby's men, who participated in the engagement, and were protected and treated as prisoners of war, but not without expressions of dissatisfaction on the part of Quantrell's men. Our loss in the affair already foots up eighty-five killed and about twenty wounded. Some of the wounded will die, and perhaps a few more of those who were wounded and died on the prairie in the vicinity of the field of the disaster, will be found, so that our total loss is not likely to fall short of ninety-five men. General Blunt had about a dozen wagons with him, and had he ordered them corraled immediately after the enemy opened fire, he could probably have resisted the attack. He may, however, have been pressed too closely to have had time to corral his wagons. Nearly all the members of the band were shot through the head, the band wagon set on fire, and their bodies burned in it. Their scorched and charred remains presented a horrible sight. Nearly all the band were Germans, and several of the ruffians are reported to have exclaimed : " This shall be the fate of the lopped-eared Dutch of Lincoln's hirelings!" Major Curtis' horse was shot under him, and he was shot and killed after having become dismounted. The bodies of Major Curtis, Lieutenant Farr, General Blunt's Judge Advocate, and two soldiers, will arrive here on the 8th, to be sent north.

The losses of the enemy in the engagements with Lieutenant Pond and General Blunt, are estimated at about thirteen killed. About a dozen of their men have been found on the field, and they are known to have carried away some of their killed and wounded. Their heaviest loss, however, was in the attack on the block-house, and they could not have taken it without artillery. General Blunt thought that they had captured Lieutenant Pond's force, or he would have made an effort to fight his way to it. Or had Lieutenant Pond known of the approach of General Blunt, and that the enemy had marched away to attack him, he could and it would have been his duty to have attacked him in the rear.

Quantrell took General Blunt's carriage with him, and marched south in the direction of Fort Gibson, and Shelby's men marched northward, and were, perhaps, the force that fired into our pickets again on the night of the 7th.

General Blunt and Colonel Blair arrived on the morning of the 12th, from Baxter Springs. As General Blunt now has definite information that Shelby, Gordon and Hunter have invaded Missouri, with a force of about two thousand men and three pieces of light artillery, and are marching northward, he will probably remain here a week or so, to make such disposition of his troops as will best protect the border counties of Kansas. This being a large depot of army supplies, and only a few miles from the State line, it is thought that Shelby may turn aside and attack us here in a few days. But we have one battery, beside four twenty-four pound siege guns, and troops enough to hold the place several days against an enemy of two thousand men. The heights to the east of us, should the enemy get possession of them, would give him positions from which he could throw shells into the town.

General Blunt has sent orders for the troops stationed at Webber's Falls and Skullyville to move into Fort Smith, and all the Indian troops stationed at different points in the Nation to concentrate at Fort Gibson. If Colonel Phillips has returned to take command of the Indian division, we need have no fears of the enemy capturing Fort Gibson. It is reported that General Shelby, with the assistance of his artillery, has been able to capture one or two posts in southwest Missouri. The militia, not being aware that the enemy had artillery with them, undertook to defend their stations, and were surrounded and attacked with it at short range, and compelled to surrender. Their losses, however, by capture have been quite light. Shelby has moved through Missouri very rapidly, having met with no serious opposition at first. But he had marched only a few days through the State when he ran into a hornet's nest. General Brown, commanding the State militia in Central Missouri, attacked him at Marshall a small town in Saline county, on the 13th instant, and after two hours' hard fighting, captured all his artillery, and dispersed his men in every direction. The enemy lost twenty men killed and a large number wounded, and a few prisoners. Nearly all the militia in southwest Missouri have joined the chase. General Ewing, commanding District of the Border, including border counties of Missouri, has taken the field in person, and is determined to press the enemy vigorously until they are driven from the State.

Lieutenant R. J. Lewis, of the Sixth Kansas cavalry, and Judge Advocate on the Staff of General Ewing, arrived here the night of the 16th, direct from the troops in the field, for the purpose of having requisitions for ammunition, quartermaster and commissary supplies, filled and sent forward at the earliest practicable moment. After the engagement at Marshall, most of Shelby's force retreated in a westward direction, and soon came in contact with General Ewing's forces. The State troops under General Brown did not stop the pursuit after the fight at Marshall, but are co-operating with General Ewing with hope of capturing Shelby's entire force. While our troops will not likely capture a very large proportion of the raiding force, they will prevent it from taking much property from the State. From the turn affairs have taken, it is thought that Shelby will be disappointed in regard to increasing his army of invasion. He is losing by desertions, and by those who have had enough of the rebellion and are surrendering to our authorities, fully as many men as he is gaining by rebel sympathizers joining him from the localities through which he passes. We shall not complain if he takes from the State every bushwhacker and rebel sympathizer in it. Several couriers who have just arrived from Fort Gibson state that Quantrell's force crossed the Arkansas River about a week ago, a few miles above that post. They surprised and killed six Indian soldiers and two or three negroes near the mouth of the Verdigris River. One of the negroes which they captured they intended to take with them to Texas. He escaped one night, however, and reached Fort Gibson after several day's wandering in the Nation. He states that he heard them say that they were on their way to Texas, and would not return to Missouri until towards spring. They regarded General Blunt's carriage as quite a trophy, and intend to exhibit it to their friends and admirers in Texas.

A messenger came in from the Osage Mission, October 20th, and reported that there was a small rebel force in the vicinity of that place on the night of the 18th, under Cy Gordon. They committed some petty depredations and then left.

On the 18th instant General Ewing's forces overtook and had a skirmish with Shelby's rear guard at Carthage, Jasper county, Missouri, and captured thirty prisoners, including one Major. No better officer could be sent against the enemy in the field than General Ewing. Some stragglers are also being daily picked up. The rebels are said to be much exhausted from constant marching and fighting since they invaded the State. It is difficult to capture a cavalry force

or compel it to fight, when its commanding officer does
not wish to risk an engagement with his adversary,
In his dispatches General Ewing states that he will
continue the pursuit of the enemy to the southern
line of Missouri.   And if they do not keep dwindling
in numbers until there is only a corporal's guard to
pursue, he will perhaps continue to follow them far
into Arkansas.

There is some talk now that General John McNeil,
who has for several months been in command of the dist-
trict of Southwest Missouri, will soon relieve General
Blunt of the command of the troops at Fort Smith.   It
is not thought by a good many that General Blunt
should be relieved just at this time. The Baxter Springs
disaster, should not, his friends say, be deemed a sufficient cause for his removal. It was more of an accident
than a blunder. He is a brave officer, and has never before met with defeat. He is popular with the Army of
the Frontier, and it is not generally thought that the
recent disaster would lessen the confidence of the soldiers in him.   He will go down with the supply train
in a few days at any rate, though it may be for the
purpose of turning over his command. If, however, he
desires to keep his command, Senator Lane will doubtless use his influence in his behalf.

General Thomas Ewing has been assigned to the command of the District of Kansas, with headquarters at
this post.   The border tier of counties of Missouri,
as far south as Barton county, will be included in his
district,   He is expected to assume command of his

new district in a few days, or just as soon as he returns
from the expedition in pursuit of Shelby's raiders.

Major W. C. Ransom, of the Sixth Kansas Cavalry,
arrived here on the 23d, with about four hundred men,
direct from General Ewing's command, which he left
at Neosho, Missouri. He has come up for ammunition and other supplies for the troops with General
Ewing. He reports our men short of almost everything, and much worn from constant marching and
skirmishing with the enemy for the last two weeks.
He is one of the most experienced and efficient officers
on duty along the border, and no better one could have
been selected to perform an important service like that
which has been intrusted to him. In recognition of
his well-known abilities, General Lyon, in July, 1861,
authorized him to raise the regiment to which he belongs. He worked more industriously and persistently in organizing and drilling his regiment than any
other officer in it. Kansas may well be proud of him.

Senator Lane made a big speech from the balcony
of the Wilder House on the evening of the 24th, to a
large audience. He discussed the political issues of
the day, the prospect of the early collapse of the Confederacy, and was particularly severe, and in my opinion justly, on the Copperheads of the North, or those
who are opposing and embarrassing the Government
in its efforts to crush the rebellion. He has apparently abandoned, and I think very sensibly, the
scheme of his crusade into Missouri, as he did not
refer to it directly. It would be difficult to see how

he could advocate it in the light of recent events—that is, in the face of the heroic bravery displayed by the Missouri State troops in capturing the enemy's artillery, and dispersing his forces. General Blunt was also called out, and made a short and neat little speech. He is not much of a speaker, and it is not likely that he is in the proper frame of mind to display his eloquence, even if he were an orator. There is little doubt but that he is still very sensitive in regard to the Baxter Springs misfortune, and probably feels that the eyes of the public are severely upon him. He knows that an officer whom the Government trusts with the lives of thousands of men, is expected to see to it that their lives shall not be wantonly or stupidly sacrificed by placing them in positions where they must contend with the foe under extraordinary disadvantages.

General Ewing and Staff and Escort arrived here October 27th, from Neosho, Missouri, having chased Shelby's flying columns beyond Cassville, and within a few miles of the Arkansas line. The enemy kept breaking up into so many small detachments, that there was not much of a force to pursue towards the last. The troops are all returning, and will go to their regular stations, since the storm that has swept over southwest and central Missouri has now nearly subsided. A retrospect of the recent military operations in Missouri shows that the enemy have lost more by the invasion than they gained.

The supply train started on the 28th instant for

Fort Smith; General Blunt accompanies it. The escort is composed of the Second Kansas colored infantry, two companies of the Fourteenth Kansas cavalry, Captain Smith's battery of light artillery of four rifled guns, one battalion of the Twelfth Kansas infantry, and General Blunt's escort. General McNeil and Colonel Cloud left Springfield about three days ago, for Fort Smith, and will not likely leave undisturbed any considerable force of the enemy that might be in northwestern Arkansas. On account of the rain and snow-storm which has prevailed in this section for several days past, the roads are heavy, and the progress of the train will be slower than usual. And the infantry, too, will find it disagreeable marching. A few days' march, however, will bring them into a region where the roads are firmer. Some of the troops going down now will have seen their first service in the field. But they have had sufficient instruction to become acquainted with their duties, and no doubt will make good soldiers.

It appears from dispatches received from Fort Smith that the scattered forces of Generals Cooper, Marmaduke and Shelby are reorganizing, and making preparations to march against that place with about nine thousand men and eighteen pieces of field artillery. But when we take into account the badly demoralized condition of Cooper's and Shelby's forces, we may conclude that such an army cannot be called into existence in a few days, nor even in a few weeks. While the rebel Generals in Arkansas and the Indian Terri-

tory may be able shortly to collect together a sufficient number of troops to make a demonstration
against Fort Smith, it is not at all probable that they
can organize an army very soon of such strength as
will enable them to make a successful assault, assuming of course that all our troops in the vicinity of that
place have been concentrated there, and would be
handled to the best possible advantage. We have got
a firm footing at Fort Smith, and will be able to hold
western Arkansas and the Indian country, unless our
officers make some unpardonable blunder. It is not
likely that General Marmaduke will be permitted to
occupy the country north of the Arkansas River much
longer. Should he endeavor to confine his operations
to the central or eastern portion of the State, north of
the river, General Steele, commanding an army at
Little Rock, should be able to send a force against him
and compel him to leave that section. Or if he
should move into northwestern Arkansas, Generals
Blunt and McNiel will look after him very closely,
and it is not thought that he or General Shelby will
attempt to make another raid through Missouri at
present.

CHAPTER XXIII.

All quiet along the Border—Lovely Indian Summer—Theory accounting for the Smoky condition of the Atmosphere— Reprehensible conduct of a Detachment on scouting service —Discussion over the question, "Who shall be the Commanding General of the District?"—Rebel guerrillas in the vicinity of Humboldt—Colonel Moonlight takes command of the Fourteenth Kansas Cavalry—Lieutenant Josling on a scout to Osage Mission—A Cold Wave—Distressing condition of Refugees—General Blunt authorized to raise another Colored Regiment—Citizens of Fort Scott opposed to Colonel Jennison taking command of the post—The supply train starts South—A Military Telegraph to be constructed to Fort Scott—Twelfth Kansas Infantry *en route* to Fort Smith—Federal expedition towards Texas—"Mountain Federals" in Arkansas—They annoy the enemy.

We are able to welcome the first day of November with the expression, "All is quiet along the Border." There have been very few days during the last three months that one would think of making such a remark. It is almost unnecessary to state here that we need not congratulate ourselves with the thought that this peaceful state will continue very long. Not many weeks are likely to elapse before we shall hear of guerrilla depredations in some of the border counties, causing at least a ripple of disturbance in the public mind. But the present peaceful condition is in admirable harmony with our lovely "Indian Summer," that has just set in. The whole visible horizon is tinged with smoke, as if we were in the neighborhood of a great conflagration. But the southwest breeze is soft and balmy, and altogether one could hardly wish for a more delightful season. As this section is all prairie, except strips of timber along the streams, we are without the great variety of autumnal tints, presented by extensive woodlands. To look out over our broad prairies is often compared to looking out over the ocean. The undulations or ridges of our prairies take the place of waves on the ocean.

In regard to the smoky condition of the atmosphere during "Indian Summer," it is generally thought, in this section, to be caused by the burning of the grass from the extensive prairie regions of the northwest. Though the breeze is from the southwest to-day, the smoke came with a chilly northwest wind. And the belief that it is caused by prairie fires, is strengthened by the fact, that when it first overspreads the country, particularly if there is a little more than the usual amount of moisture in the atmosphere, the smell of burning grass is distinctly noticeable by those having sensitive olfactory organs. I cannot champion this theory, however, for the smell of burnt grass might be due to prairie fires in the neighborhood. I am not sure that the number of square miles of prairie in the northwest denuded of grass every year by fire, would produce smoke enough to overspread such a wide region as we have to account for.

Captain Willets, of the Fourteenth Kansas cavalry, who was sent out several days ago by Colonel Blair, on scouting service in the direction of Lamar, Missouri, returned with his company on the 3rd, *via* Osage Mission, Kansas. He found no enemy, but, from accounts that have reached here, he permitted his men to engage in disreputable depredations, robbery and murder. If the statements made in regard to the matter are true, he deserves severe censure, if not indeed summary dismissal from the service. Gold hunting is not the business of our officers and soldiers, and when they undertake to engage in it they are no longer fit to wear the blue uniform of the United States Army. There are too many officers who do not appreciate the responsibility resting upon them in regard to controlling the actions of their men. Every officer of the army should be a gentleman, and have proper regard for his position. Several scouts who have just come from the supply train which General Blunt accompanied *en route* to Fort Smith a week ago, report that near the Arkansas line four of our soldiers were captured by the enemy. There was no prospect, however, of the rebel force under Colonel Brooks, which was at Huntsville recently, attacking the train.

There is some discussion just now as to whether General Blunt shall retain command of this district or not. His friends claim for him, also, that he is really the ranking Major General in the Department, as the appointment of Schofield as a Major General has not yet been confirmed by the United States Senate. But this continual wrangling of politicians, contractors, and sutlers, over the question as to who shall command the department and each of the different districts into which it is divided, does not tend to advance the interests of the public service. What do hangers-on of the army care for the efficiency and honesty of a commanding officer, if they can get permits from him to steal cotton and ship it north? At such times as we are now passing through, complaints are just about as likely to be made against an honest and efficient as against a dishonest and inefficient commanding General. Our officers holding important positions, if they wish to leave the service with clean records, cannot be too guarded in their dealings with those who are able to present credentials from men of high social and political standing. Money-making adventurers who are profiting by the misfortunes of the country, are, every loyal man knows, entitled to very little consideration from those who are conscientiously endeavoring to assist the Government in suppressing the rebellion.

Information was received on the 7th instant, that rebel guerrillas are getting troublesome again in the vicinity of Humboldt, forty miles west of this post. It seems that they have burned some property along the Neosho River below there, besides committing some petty depredations on the property of the loyal citizens of Allen County. Fears are entertained that they may sack and burn Humboldt, as we have no

troops stationed there at present. The rebels engaged
in these depredations are supposed to be a part of Livingston's old band, and to have crossed the State line
near Baxter Springs, and marched up the Neosho valley. That they should be able to remain in the State
and in the same neighborhood a week or so, is a little
surprising. General Lane's plan of burning everything in that section would perhaps be the most effec-
tual way of getting rid of them. But the people
would probably protest that such heroic treatment for
the cure of the disease would be worse than the disease itself.

Colonel Thomas Moonlight arrived here on the 8th
from Leavenworth to take command of his regiment,
the Fourteenth Kansas cavalry. He is determined to
have it thoroughly armed and equipped at once, and
every spare moment is to be devoted to drilling it, so
that it will be ready to go south with the next train.
He is a brilliant officer, and has served with distinction, as Chief of General Blunt's Staff, in all the campaigns south of this post. No better officer could be
found to thoroughly prepare a cavalry regiment for
the field.

Considerable interest has been manifested by the
people of this State in regard to the election for State
officers in Missouri, which took place on the 3rd instant. The election returns have nearly all been received by the Secretary of State, and they show that
the Radical or Repulican ticket has swept the State by
an overwhelming majority. As far as returns have

28

been received from the soldiers in the field, they show
from their vote that it is very largely republican. It
is certainly gratifying to contemplate such a grand
victory for great principles, in view of the disadvantages with which the loyal people of that State have
had to contend.

Lieutenant B. F. Josling, Fourteenth Kansas cavalry, returned to this post on the evening of the 11th,
with a detachment of his company from Osage Mission, where he was sent several days ago to check the
depredations of a band of guerrillas that recently visited that section. He marched over the country almost to the southern line of the State in search of the
rebels without finding them, and is satisfied from such
information as he could get, that after plundering the
Mission, they went south.

The season has arrived when wintry looking clouds
are seen scudding across the sky. When these lower-
ing clouds obscure the sun now and then, there is a
kind of fascination in watching the dark shadows chase
each other over the prairies in rapid succession.

A cold wave right from the arctic regions struck
southern Kansas on the morning of the 12th, and already there are reports of great suffering among the
refugee families encamped about the outskirts of the
post. The Marmaton River is frozen over solid, which
is unusual so early in the season. There is a larger
number of refugee families in this vicinity than I had
supposed; and in many cases their condition is distressing. Many of them are living in rude tents made

of bed clothing, or material of a very unsubstantial nature. Others during the latter part of summer and early autumn, purchased condemned army tents, and are making the best of them. But there are not many supplied with tents, as there have been no large sales of this kind of condemned public property at this post during the autumn. Last winter I thought that I saw a good deal of suffering among the refugees around Colonel Phillips' camp, but it did not equal the suffering in our midst at the present time. Insufficient fuel for heating purposes, and scanty clothing and covering are the principal causes of suffering among these people. We were encamped last winter in a wooded region, and the refugees could build great log fires to keep themselves warm during intensely cold weather. I have frequently seen them standing around their blazing fires, with wood generously piled on, on cold nights, with expressions of real happiness playing over their countenances. And I also saw rollicking children in some of those groups, who seemed wholly unconscious of the hardships to which they were exposed. But here the camp of the refugee is not protected from the chilling effects of the bleak northwest winds by heavy forests and bluffs, as it was in northwestern Kansas. Nor can the refugees here make great wood fires, like the fires farmers make in heavily wooded sections where they clear tracts of land for cultivation. All the families that I have visited recently, burn coal in cooking stoves, even for heating purposes. And as most of the stoves I saw

seem adapted to burning wood instead of coal, these
people have much trouble in getting their coal to burn.
At any rate they get only a small quantity of the
heat from it which it is capable of producing if
burned to the best advantage. Even those who have
stoves in which it burns freely, do not use it generously on account of their straightened circumstances.
It is a very cheerless sight, one that I shall not soon
forget, to see a mother and half a dozen children shiv-
ering around a stove in which the fuel half refuses to
burn, or is used in stinted quantities. The hardships
and privations of our soldiers in the field are often
very great, but the hardships and suffering of many
of their families are also entitled to consideration, and
should not be passed over lightly. It will be surprising to me if there is not a great mortality during the
winter among these people, who have recently exchanged plain comfortable homes for the cheerless tent, in a
region where howling winds and chilly blasts increase
their despondency.

General Blunt has received authority from the
War Department to raise another colored regiment of
infantry from this State, and recruiting officers will go
to work at once. The two colored regiments already
raised from Kansas, have taken but a small proportion
of the able-bodied colored men who have come here
the last two years. Many of them will, no doubt,
promptly respond to the present call, and show to the
country that they feel a sufficient interest in the war
to take up arms in defense of the Government as well

as in defense of their permanent freedom. This State, on account of the early struggles in behalf of the abolition cause, has been an asylum for the colored people since the beginning of the war. And they have shown that they are not insensible of the generous welcome extended to them by our people, by manifesting a patriotic pride in furnishing their proportion of soldiers for the field, as soon as they were permitted to enlist in the United States service.

There have been some recent intimations that Colonel Jennison, of the 15th Kansas cavalry, will take command of this post shortly, and that Colonel Blair will be relieved and ordered South with his regiment. Colonel Jennison is not popular in this section of the State, and should he be assigned to the command of this post, it is likely that a protest will be sent up by the citizens to the commanding General of the Department. His name has been connected on several occasions with certain transactions that are not sanctioned by a high code of morals and strict military discipline. It is painful to make these remarks in regard to a man whose whole heart has been in our cause. But when he comes forward to occupy an important and conspicuous position, his personal character should be carefully and dispassionately examined and held up to the public. We must not forget that the characters of our public men will have an immense influence in molding the character of the men of the rising generation. Nor should we, because he belongs to our party, and is working zealously for the success of the same principles that we are, neglect to criticise, in a good tempered spirit, his short-comings. I am satisfied that Colonel Jennison's services would be more valuable to the Government in some other field. Should he make a perfectly honorable record from now to the end of the war, it would almost wipe out the past.

The supply train started south on the 20th for Fort Gibson and Forth Smith, but will encamp on Dry Wood a few days to wait for the paymaster to come down and pay off the escort before they leave. Most of the escort belongs to the Fourteenth Regiment Kansas cavalry, recently organized, and as a large number of the men have not been paid since enlistment, the amounts due them will be of great assistance in providing for the wants of many of their families during the coming winter. The need that I mentioned last summer, of some method by which the soldiers can send their salaries to their families with perfect safety, is again felt. In some of the companies nearly all of the men are from Missouri, and their families are still living in that State, or scattered in this and adjacent counties of Kansas. The money they send home will therefore have to be trusted in the hands of friends, whom they cannot hold responsible for its loss by accident. Some of the officers and soldiers, however, will doubtless avail themselves of the Exchange Office here, and send their money to their families in cheques.

On the 25th of November, United States officials commenced making arrangements to construct a mili-

tary telegraph line between Kansas City and Fort
Scott immediately. The contract for telegraph poles
will probably be let in a few days, and their delivery
along the route commence in a week or so. This line
is much needed in directing the military operations of
this department. Though the rebels may endeavor to
destroy portions of it occasionally, it is thought that a
small cavalry patrol can protect it quite effectually.
It is sure to prove a great assistance to commanding officers along the border, in operating against
guerrilla forces when they become troublesome again.
Had this line been in operation when Quantrell made
his raid on Lawrence last August, troops and citizens
might have been collected, and directed to take up such
positions as would have made his escape almost impossible. In the next place, had the line been in
operation, he probably never would have made the
raid. Even if the Government had not taken the matter up, it would have been a good investment for the
citizens of Kansas to have taken hold of and completed at an early day. The business which the people
of this section will wish to transact over the line, will,
perhaps, fully pay the expense of operating it.

A battalion of the Twelfth Kansas infantry came
down from Kansas City on the 27th instant. After
remaining here a few weeks it will march to Fort
Smith to join the *Army of the Frontier.* This regiment, since its organization, has been on duty along
the border. Colonel Adams, its commanding officer,
is General Lane's son-in-law, and has perhaps been able

to keep it from going to the front until now. It is a fine regiment; the men are well drilled, and do not wish to be regarded as vain "carpet knights." It seems that Lieutenant Colonel Hayes has attended to drilling it and maintaining its high order of discipline.

Official dispatches received at this post on the 28th from Fort Smith state that General McNeil, who recently took command of our troops in that section, is getting them in readiness to start on an expedition towards Texas. Our forces already occupy and hold the country to the Wichita Mountains, a distance of about seventy-five miles south of the Arkansas river. The activity of our cavalry over the mountainous regions of the Choctaw and Chickasaw nations and southwestern Arkansas, has broken down and worn out a good many of our horses. Since our troops have occupied the country south of the Arkansas river, many of the Choctaw and Chickasaw Indians have shown a disposition to return to their allegiance to the Government. There is not, however, among them, such a strong sentiment of loyalty and real affection for the Government, as among the Cherokees and Creeks. These latter people have, from the beginning of the war, shown their devotion to the United States, even under the most adverse circumstances. The battles of Pothloholo, chief of the Creeks, with rebel white and Indian troops, during the winter 1861–2, before our forces marched into the Indian country, showed a chivalrous devotion to the Union cause. When the enemy finally became too strong for him, rather than submit to rebel rule, he withdrew his forces towards southern Kansas, and nearly all his people followed him and became voluntary exiles.

Now that our forces occupy the central and western portions of Arkansas, the War Department has authorized the raising of two or three more regiments from that State. The numerous desertions from the demoralized armies of Generals Cooper and Shelby, and the large numbers of "Mountain Federals" in different sections of the State, will enable the recruiting officers to get the complement of men for these regiments at an early day. "Mountain Feds" is a name given to local organizations of Union men who occupy mountain fastnesses and annoy the enemy, somewhat after the same manner that rebel guerrillas annoy our troops. There is this difference, however: Rebel guerrilla chiefs generally hold commissions from the rebel authorities, while the chiefs of "Mountain Federal" organizations are endeavoring to hold on to their lives as loyal citizens of the United States, until our forces can occupy the country and afford them adequate protection. We do not know that they have ever been charged with murdering their prisoners, like some of the guerrilla bands along the border.

Martin Hart, a prominent Union man from Hunt County, in Northern Texas, crossed Red River several months ago, with nearly two hundred loyal Texans, and joined our forces in the vicinity of Fort Smith. He has for more than a year past, kept alive the Union cause in Northern Texas and Southwestern Arkansas. He was finally captured south of Fort Smith, and hung by the rebel authorities.

CHAPTER XXIV.

General Grant defeats the enemy under General Bragg near Chattanooga—Arrival of a large quantity of Cotton from Fort Smith—Supposed crookedness in regard to it—Guerilla bands in Southwestern Missouri—How the people manage to keep good Animals in some instances—Temporary suspension in the Exchange of Prisoners—General Marmaduke, with two thousand men, near the Southern line of Missouri—Perhaps the last supply train to Fort Smith—General Ewing orders the seizure of the Cotton from Fort Smith—Snow Storm—Removal of General Schofield probable—Quantrell's forces cross the Arkansas River near Fort Gibson, on the way North—Were defeated by Colonel Phillips' troops—General Price threatens Fort Smith—Attempt of the enemy to spike the seige guns at Fort Scott—The Missouri militia defeat Quantrell—A large Rebel force in Southwest Missouri—It is driven South—Concluding Remarks.

Another great battle has been fought between the forces of General Grant and General Bragg, at Lookout Mountain, above the clouds, near Chattanooga, Tennessee, resulting in a grand victory for the Union arms. After the temporary check to the advance of our army under General Rosecrans, on the 19th and 20th of September, the rebel leaders determined to prevent General Grant from reinforcing it, and to use every means in their power to crush it. Jeff. Davis is reported to have stated recently, that Rosecrans' army in Northern Georgia, must be crushed, if it took all the resources of the Confederacy to do it. But the rebel leaders should begin to see by this time, that when General Grant takes command of any grand division of our army in any section, it is sure to win. His presence on the field inspires the troops with confidence of victory. This confidence enables men to brave dangers, endure hardships, and to perform heroic actions, which they could not endure or perform under depressed states of their nervous systems. If a man feels that he is going to get knocked down every time he meets his antagonist in a contest, he is not likely to come to the "scratch" each succeeding round, after the second or third, with much alacrity and buoyancy. So with the enemy. They have been knocked down so many times during the last year, that they are beginning to come to the "scratch" with faltering steps. In the battle at Lookout Mountain or Chattanooga, the other day, according to the despatches, they lost six thousand prisoners and thirty pieces of artillery, and about four thousand men killed and wounded.

The great battles fought in the East and in Tennessee, send a thrill of joy and gladness, or grief and disappointment, according as they have been favorable or unfavorable to our arms, through thousands of loyal hearts even at this great distance from the scenes of operation. Smaller battles affect us in minor degrees, until the smallest do not cause even a ripple upon consciousness.

A large sutler's train arrived on the 2d of December
from Fort Smith, *via* Fort Gibson, loaded principally
with cotton, alleged to have been purchased and captured from the enemy during General McNeil's expedition towards Red River. It is whispered that there
is some crookedness in regard to the manner in which
certain speculators came into possession of this cotton.
Speculators following the army and purchasing cotton
of pretended loyal owners, or disloyal owners, may
find their titles contested by Government agents, who
are commissioned to look after such matters. Sharks
following the army, like sharks following a ship,
should be watched, and not permitted to appropriate
our valuable trophies. And in the present case,
there should perhaps be an investigation to determine
whether or not this cotton has been purchased in a
legal manner. It would be more just that its proceeds
should be distributed to the soldiers, who captured it,
as prize money, than that it should go into the pockets
of sharpers. If rebel planters have left their plantations, and their cotton has fallen into our hands as contraband property, the Government should get the
market price for it, and speculators not allowed to pick
it up for merely nominal sums, as they are reported in
some cases to have been doing. As our armies are
now getting into the cotton-raising regions, the reve-
nues of the Government during the year, from the
sales of contraband cotton, should, if carefully, intelligently and honestly looked after, amount to several
millions of dollars. It would be easy enough for our

supply trains, that come up empty every month, to bring up contraband cotton, for shipment to Leavenworth and Saint Louis, where there would be a market for it. It is possible, however, that the Arkansas River will soon be open to navigation, then it can be shipped by steamboat to Saint Louis, and thence by rail to New York and Eastern manufacturing cities. It can be used to good advantage as breastworks on the boats, to protect the troops and crews from the fire of guerillas at different points along the river.

The peaceful condition of things which has existed for several weeks past along the border has been slightly disturbed by the appearance of guerrilla bands in Southwest Missouri on the 3d instant. But they will probably soon find it an uncomfortable section to operate in, as most of the militia have returned to their stations since Shelby's raid, and are ready to take the field against them. At the different posts in Missouri, the horses of the State troops are generally in good condition, as they are rarely or never short of forage. I mentioned last spring, from my own observations, how the people manage to raise the necessaries of life, even in localities where the men are all absent, in either the Union or rebel army. The people have clung to their homes with wonderful tenacity, and when the army has burned a portion of the rails around their farms, they have generally taken those left to inclose smaller tracts of their lands for cultivation. And while the acreage of nearly every family has thus been contracted, the means of cultivation have also been contracted in about the same ratio. Instead of each family having from one to a dozen fine horses and mules to put into their fields, as in *ante-bellum* times, it is a rare occurrence now to find a family with more than two or three horses or mules, which are generally either old or blind. Families sometimes try to keep their horses concealed in the woods, but this is not very successful as a general thing. The great temptation to keep good, vigorous animals, it has been suggested, has in a number of instances, led to the putting out of the eyes of desirable horses or mules. It is a cruel charge to insinuate were there no extenuating circumstances. But a mother with half a dozen children around her, and her husband away in either the Union or Rebel army, might, rather than take the chances of being reduced to the extremity of seeing them suffer, permit a young son, overflowing with a desire to do something heroic, to destroy the sight of "Charley," the good, reliable family horse. Besides being needed to cultivate and gather the crop, a horse is quite indispensable to take the grain, wheat or corn, to the mill, and to fetch back the flour or meal. In view of what I have seen of the straits to which families in Missouri and Arkansas are reduced to get along, I cannot find it in my heart to condemn an act like the above, which, in peaceful times, would justly be regarded as cruel and barbarous.

It appears by the latest dispatches from Washington, that there is to be a temporary suspension of the

exchanging of prisoners of war between the Federal
and Rebel authorities. At this distance, it is hardly
safe to form a very pronounced opinion as to the wisdom of the Government in adopting such a course,
unless the rebel authorities are unwilling to exchange
on equal terms. It is surely cause for deep regret and
even indignation, to constantly hear of the great sufferings of our soldiers in rebel prisons, while rebel soldiers in our prisons are provided with full rations and
all the comforts that our soldiers in the field have. It
is also announced that the rebel Government refuses
to exchange colored soldiers held as prisoners of war
for rebel prisoners that we hold. It is, perhaps, an un-
looked-for humiliation, that it has come to pass that
the life of a rebel soldier is worth no more than
the life of a plantation negro. But if they regard a
rebel soldier that we hold as worth more to their cause
than the colored prisoner they have captured from us,
they should, to be consistent, be extremely anxious to
exchange. They would not hesitate to exchange an
old and inferior musket for one of our best new patterns. If they can afford to weaken their own cause
by pride, we surely need not regret it. They are too
blind to see that they are fluttering around the lamp
of their own destruction.

A dispatch from Springfield, Missouri, of the 6th
instant, states that General Marmaduke, with a force
of about two thousand men and several pieces of artillery, was, on the 3d instant, encamped on White River
in Arkansas, near the southern line of Missouri. It

is believed that he either intends to make a raid on
Springfield, or to endeavor to capture our supply
trains *en route* between that place and Fort Smith.
There are, probably, nearly three thousand State
troops in southwest Missouri, and should he invade
the State, they will likely soon to be able to check his
movements, and put him to flight. The energy with
which they pressed General Shelby last October, and
their success in capturing his artillery, has given them
great confidence in their ability to meet an invading
force on the field.

General Blunt is still at Fort Smith, but apparently
without a command, much to the regret of his friends.
He is, however, attending to some business in connection with the recruiting and organizing of the Eleventh
U. S. colored regiment. A colored regiment ought to be
raised in that section in a few weeks. It is not likely,
however, that he cares to assume command of the
troops there at present, as there is no organized force
of the enemy in that section that he could hope to
bring to an engagement very soon, though Price's army
occasionally assumes a threatening attitude.

The supply train for Fort Smith moved out on the
morning of December 13th, under command of Colonel W. R. Judson, Sixth Kansas cavalry. He will
have as an escort, including the six companies of the
Twelfth Kansas infantry under Lieut.-Colonel Hays,
about eight hundred men. He will go down through
the border counties of Missouri and Arkansas, instead
of through the Nation *via* Fort Blunt. This will

probably be the last train from this place to Fort Smith, as it is thought that Little Rock will immediately be made a base of supplies for the army in Arkansas. The distance from Little Rock to Fort Smith is not so great as the distance from Fort Smith to this post. And it is probable, too, that in a month or so, light draft steamers can run on the Arkansas River, and thus save overland transportation of supplies to the *Army of the Frontier*. Colonel Phillips' Indian division at Fort Gibson, however, will perhaps continue to be supplied from this place, at any rate until the spring rise in the Arkansas River will enable boats to pass Webber's Falls. As no large force of the enemy can cross to the north side of the Arkansas River without our commanding officers at Forts Smith and Gibson knowing it; and as his trains will pass over a route little infested with guerrillas, they will not require very large escorts and batteries of light artillery, as last spring, to conduct them through safely. This post will henceforward be of less importance in a military point of view. Still, the immense quantities of ordnance, quartermaster and commissary stores kept here, will make it of sufficient importance to keep a force here adequate to its protection.

A dispatch from Kansas City states that General Ewing recently ordered the seizure of the cotton which passed through this place on the 2d instant for Leavenworth. It is also reported that agents of the Government are on the lookout for more contraband cotton. This action of General Ewing is highly com-

29

mendable, and may have a wholesome effect on the army vultures who are always on hand to gorge themselves on the hard-earned prizes of our soldiers.

The morning of the 20th the ground was covered with four or five inches of snow, and the jingling of sleigh-bells reminded us that we were approaching our Kansas mid-winter. From the statements of those who have lived in this vicinity for upwards of twenty years, it seems that we are having a little severer season than usual. The river had scarcely got clear of ice from the cold wave of the tenth of November, when it was frozen over again on the 18th instant. As a general thing the winters are so mild here that the ice does not form on the river two inches in thickness, and ice-dealers are unable to put up enough to satisfy the demands of consumers. Altogether our climate may be regarded as desirable; for during the summer months our southwest breezes are pure and exhilarating, reaching us always after having passed through the cool strata of the atmosphere over the high plateaus of Mexico and the Rocky Mountains. There are here none of those debilitating effects produced by a humid atmosphere in low marshy regions. Though the bracing winds blowing over our vast undulating prairies may have no perceptible effect on the energies of our people in a year or so, I think they will unquestionably in the course of a few generations. They will probably tend to make them wiry and muscular, instead of pulpy and clumsy, like the people of a region where the air is saturated with moisture.

There is a strong probability that the agitation for the removal of General Schofield from the command of this department will be successful in a short time. He has not been popular, and is perhaps not the best officer that could have been placed at the head of this military department, but that he should have been able to give satisfaction to the factions in Missouri and the factions in Kansas, is more than any intelligent person should expect. That President Lincoln should have all along had confidence in him.is surely a good deal in his favor, though it does not necessarily make him a competent commanding general.

A detachment of about fifteen men arrived at this post on the 24th from Fort Gibson, and they report that the enemy are again showing some activity in that vicinity and along the Arkansas line. They also state that Quantrell's force is believed to be *en route* to Jackson county, Missouri, where he will commence his diabolical business again. A force, reported to be his and Standwaitie's, had a lively fight with a portion of Colonel Phillips' command near Fort Gibson about a week ago, and were defeated and scattered in every direction. As the engagement took place on the north side of the Arkansas River, it is thought their broken detachments have moved northward.

A dispatch just received from Fort Smith, Arkansas, states that General Price is collecting his forces together and threatening to attack that place. It does not seem probable, however, that he will be able to organize, out of the Trans-Mississippi rebel forces, an army sufficiently strong to drive our troops from western Arkansas, if General McNeil handles them skillfully.   Including Colonel Phillips' Indian division, we have an army of about eight thousand men in that section, well supplied with artillery.   The army under General Steele, at Little Rock, is also within co-operating distance, should the rebel generals concentrate all their troops in Arkansas, to attack General McNeil at Fort Smith.   Though the enemy may make a bold demonstration, since he is holding no particular place in Arkansas, yet it is not generally thought, from a survey of the field of operations, that he will at present risk a general engagement with our victorious troops.   It is not therefore probable that General Price will be able to fulfill his promise in regard to treating his soldiers with a Christmas dinner from Federal rations at Fort Smith.   His troops, instead of being the victorious legions of a hundred battles, have been so often defeated that it is not easy to conceive with what new hope they can be inspired to undertake a vigorous campaign against our soldiers, flushed with a continuous series of successes.

An attempt was made on the night of the 28th, by an emissary of the enemy to spike one of the Twenty-four pounder seige guns mounted at Lunette "C. W. Blair."   The party was probably disturbed by the guard on his beat walking to and fro, as he left a rat-tail file and hammer on the gun, before completing his work to render it useless.   Nothing has been found which would identify the party engaged in this bold

adventure. Colonel Blair has the four seige guns in
the Forts here carefully inspected every day that they
may be in perfect order in case of an emergency. The
hundreds of tons of hay put up in long ricks, the thousands of bushels of corn in cribs, and the large quantities of ammunition and arms, of quartermaster and
commissary supplies here, are great temptations for
the enemy to attempt a raid on this post for the destruction of this property. And it will require great
vigilance on the part of the post commander to prevent its destruction by secret rebel emmissaries. This
post having been the chief center of our military operations west of Saint Louis since the war, and the
Government having kept a considerable force stationed here, have prevented any serious inroads of the
enemy into southern Kansas. Our people in this and
adjoining counties have therefore pursued their usual
avocations as in times of profound peace. Nor have
guerrilla bands been so troublesome in Vernon county,
Missouri, directly east of us, as in the counties north
and south of it.

It is now known that Quantrell's force, after it
was attacked and dispersed by Colonel Phillips' troops
some ten days ago, continued to move northeast. In
a few days after this, however, he collected together
his scattered detachments, and about the 24th instant
came in contact with a considerable force of the Missouri militia cavalry, near the Arkansas line, and was
again badly beaten and vigorously pursued. But his
force soon broke up into small detachments again, and

it is believed to be their intention to rally at some
point in this vicinity, with the view of attacking this
place. He is after big game. If he could capture
and destroy this place, he knows that it would add to
his notoriety as much as the Lawrence massacre.
Colonel Blair has sent out detachments of cavalry to
the south and southeast of this post, so that we shall
soon know whether he is intending to attack us here,
or is making preparations for a raid into Southern Kansas. It is reported that Quantrell has threatened to
visit this State before he goes south again, and to leave
a track more bloody than Lawrence, and the section he
passes over as desolate as the naked prairies. He seems
to glory in his savage cruelty, and of being a terror to
the loyal people of the border, just like an uncivilized
Indian who is proud of the number of scalps he carries.
That a man born and brought up in the great State of
Maryland, one of our oldest States, as Quantrell was,
with fair advantages, should head a band of fiends,
is quite unaccountable to many. But that he should
get followers in western Missouri is not so strange,
since it is well known to those who have lived in the
West that, for nearly twenty years, the extensive
freighting business from Independence and Kansas
City, to New Mexico and other Western Territories,
has attracted to the two former places adventurers
and desperate characters from all parts of the country.

Three bushwhackers are reported to have been killed
on December 28th, near Humboldt, on the Neosho
River, forty miles west of this post. They belonged

to the party which were in that section about a month ago, committing depredations on the property of loyal people. In different sections of this State there still may be found a few of those who were connected with the pro-slavery movement, and who came here under the Territorial *regime*, to make Kansas a slave State. Nearly all the old pro-slavery element is of course disloyal, and the men belonging to it who have not actually gone South, sympathize with and shield their friends, when they return home or come into this State. A company of cavalry will be stationed at Humboldt during the rest of the winter, and it will keep detachments patrolling the country along the Neosho River below that place, extending to the southern line of the State.

Colonel Blair received information on the night of the 30th, that a force of the enemy, about fifteen hundred strong, under Colonel Coffey, was encamped on Cowskin prairie, in the southwest corner of McDonald County, Missouri, a few days ago. It is not thought, however, that they will be able to march up the border counties of Missouri, as the militia are in considerable force in the counties east and northeast of McDonald County, and have probably moved against them already. The party of rebels that were in the vicinity of Humboldt recently, it is now supposed belonged to Coffey's command. After passing Dry Wood, twelve miles south of this post, we have no other troops stationed in Southern Kansas, and the pressure from Missouri having pushed the enemy into the Cherokee

Nation, several small detachments were able to march up the Neosho River, fifty to sixty miles, without resistance. The main body of Quantrell's men is reported to be with Coffey, though some detachments of them are supposed to have passed near here several days ago, on their way to Cass and Jackson Counties. It is not likely, however, that they will find that section very congenial during a severe winter; besides the headquarters of General Ewing, the commanding officer of the District of the Border, is at Kansas City, adjacent to the region in which Quantrell has been operating since the war. We may therefore hope that they will be speedily driven south again.

The old year is now drawing to a close. The border counties of Missouri and Kansas are comparatively free of guerrillas; and the forces of Coffey and Quantrell are now doubtless sullenly retiring beyond the mountains in Arkansas or the Indian Country. Our armies have been victorious upon almost every important field, and though I have been obliged to note some domestic dissensions, I am fully convinced that the national feeling and love and attachment for the old flag of our fathers has grown stronger. But the Goddess of Liberty may weep, since a sea of blood and tears have been shed in her defense. I have endeavored to faithfully chronicle the most important events connected with the operations of our army along the border during the year. I hope that I have not given, in a single case, an extravagant and sensational account of the number of the enemy killed and wounded in a certain engagement; or of the crimes and cruelties of guerrillas. I was early put on my guard in respect to making exaggerated statements about various matters connected with that division of the army to which I belonged. I am perfectly aware that a work filled with highly-colored statements is more greedily read by a large class of the public, than one containing plain solid facts; yet I do not regret the course that I have followed; for I do not fear to appeal to the common sense and honesty of those with whom I have served in this great struggle, to bear me out in my statements. There are no doubt instances in which I have not done full justice to officers and troops. I regret it even more than the injustice which was done to me.

This attempt to commemorate the actions of our brave, honest and simple-hearted soldiers, in this central part of our great country, geographically speaking, has been to me a source of considerable satisfaction; for I believe that the great contest in which we are engaged will be more worthy the study of future generations than all the wars of the past. And then the thought comes into my mind, will not the millions of people who will inhabit these western prairies, plains, and fertile valleys, during coming generations, wish to know something of the fierce storms that raged along our borders during the great rebellion of the slave-owning section of our country? The history of the world does not furnish another instance of a million of men in arms fighting for a great principle—a principle, too, involving the right of each to "life, liberty and the pursuit of happiness." It is surely a grand thought to contemplate their heroic actions, for, unless the conception of justice changes, future generations can point to their achievements and say "those men fought for a principle, the triumph of which has secured to us the blessings we enjoy." I cannot bid farewell to the expiring year without my thoughts turning with sadness to the thousands of brave and patriotic soldiers who, during this contest, have devoted their lives to their country and to posterity; and to other thousands who lie at this moment upon beds of pain and anguish, with their flesh torn and mangled by shot and shell and small arms; and to still other thousands whose hearts are torn and bleeding on account of the loss of those in the war who were dearest to them on earth.

But firmly believing that we are near the dawn of a brighter day, when the noble sacrifices of our soldiers will be universally acknowledged not to have been in vain, I can simply say, OLD YEAR, I bid you farewell!

INDEX

Adams, Col. 439

Allen County 432

Anderson, Major 382

Anderson, Capt. H. S. 91, 182

Arkansas River 209, 211, 225, 273, 274, 289, 313, 440, 445

Arkansas Troops (US) 1st Cavalry 44, 156, 157, 354

Balltown, MO 374, 394

Barton County, MO 352, 366, 384, 424

Baxter Springs 93, 220, 241, 271, 275, 276, 315, 381, 416, 433

Big Creek 389

Big Spring 112, 137

Benton's Hussars 171

Bentonville, AR 144, 155

Blair's Battery 315, 320

Blair, Col. C. W. 220, 346, 372, 407, 415, 431, 437, 453, 454, 455

Blunt, Gen. James 253, 279, 280, 333, 343, 355, 356, 360, 377, 403, 404, 407, 416, 417, 418, 421, 427, 436, 448

Bourbon County Fair 409

Bowen, Col. Thomas 371, 410

Bowen's Cavalry 171

Bowles, Lt. Col. J.(US) 354, 359, 361

Bragg, General 442

Brooks, Col. (CS) 431

Brother 83, 121, 122, 123

Brown, Col. (CS) 408

Brown, Gen. E. B. 86, 102, 305, 421

Brown, John 400

Brush Creek 344, 417, 418

Buffalo Creek 408

Burch, Capt. Milton 240, 354

Burkhart Prairie 127

Cabell, Gen 220, 221, 225, 228, 258, 290, 298, 309, 326, 344, 357, 393, 402

Cabin Creek 234, 298, 310, 311, 312, 316, 317, 318, 326

Camp Curtis 90

Camp Jim Lane 202

Camp John Ross 207

Camp Moonlight 37, 96, 180

Camp Pomeroy 187

Camp Walker 90

Canadian River 335, 393

Cane Hill 34, 35, 225, 228

Carthage, MO 350, 354, 363, 395, 423

Carroll, Col. (CS) 173, 191

Cass County, MO 373, 456

Cassville, MO 228, 232, 354

Caves 95-98

Charleston, S.C. 189, 382, 413

Chattanooga, TN 408

Cherokee Indians 93

Cherokee Council 141

Chickasaw Nations 440

Choctaw Nations 440

Cholera 366

INDEX

Cincinnati 199, 202, 309

Clarkson, Col. (CS) 233

Cloud, Col. W. F. 61, 140, 240, 354, 411, 427

Cockrall, Gen. F. M. 137

Coffee, Col. 104, 354, 408, 455, 456

Coleman, Capt. 373, 388, 405

Colored Troops 276, 277, 278, 383

Colorado Troops 2nd Infantry 315, 316, 317, 341

Conkey, Capt. Theo. 128

Conscripts 48

Coon Creek 139

Cooper, Col. (CS) 220, 223, 225, 226, 252, 357, 403

Copperheads 425

Corn Coffee 194

Corwin, Col. David B. 206

Cove Creek 58, 59

Cowskin (Elk) River 125, 145, 235, 237

Cowskin Prairie 236, 455

Crafts, Capt. Fred. 164, 182

Craven, Col. (CS) 363

Crawford, Capt. S. 34

Creek Indians 93, 440

Creek Agency 255

Crittenden, Col. T. T. 239, 354

Cross Hollows 102

Crump, Col. (CS) 62

Curtis, Gen. S. R. 165

Curits, Major H. Z. 377, 409, 414, 419

Davis, Lt. Jefferson 207, 208

Davis, Gen. Jeff C. 166

Davidson, Gen. 402

Deserters 296

District of SW MO 140

District of the Border 422

Dodd, Lt. Col. Theo R. 302, 316, 319

Doubleday, Col. 104

Dripping Springs (Battle) 62, 63, 64, 70, 71

Drywood 128, 438, 455

Drywood Creek 371

Dutch Mills 191, 199, 202

Eighth & Ninth District of MO 104

Elk Creek 303, 309, 343, 355, 357

Elm Springs 75

Emancipation Proclamation 151

Ewing, Gen. 384, 390, 401, 422, 423, 424, 426, 449

Fayetteville, AR 38, 156, 158, 161, 221

Flat Rock 310

Flat Rock Creek 342

Flint Creek 179

Forage 163

Forman, Maj. John A. 86

Fort Davis 72

Fort Gibson 72, 205, 206, 207, 208, 209, 421, 422, 438

Fort Scott 346, 374, 377, 439

Fort Smith 3, 402, 413, 427, 430, 438, 439, 440

Foster, Maj. Emory S. 137

INDEX

Gad Fly 244
Gallaher, Capt. Wm. 140,
    231, 232, 333
Gambling 272, 273
Gettysburg, PA 247
Gilmore, Gen. 382, 404
Gilpatrick, Dr. 226
Gordon, Cy 420, 423
Grand River 100, 208, 209,
    211, 224, 225, 235, 274,
    275, 288, 299, 312, 317
Grand Falls 113
Grand Saline 232, 235, 299,
    309, 312, 313, 326, 338
Grandby 120
Grant, U. S. 304, 305, 442,
    443
Green, Capt. H. S. 139, 357
Greenleaf 276
Greenleaf Prairie 257, 293
Guerillas 126, 127, 128, 133,
    134, 340, 350, 383
Hall, Lt. Joseph 199
Haskell, Capt. J. G. 377
Harris, Lt. John G. 35
Harrison, Col. M. LaRue 157,
    191, 221, 227, 228, 232,
    238, 239, 408
Harrisonville 389
Hart, Martin 441
Harvey, Capt. 373
Hay Mowing Machines 337
Hayes, Lt. Col. 440, 448
Herron, Gen. F. J. 38, 80,
    244, 355
Hilterbrand's Mills 191, 278

Honey Springs (Battle)
    355-360
Hopkins, Capt. Henry 358
Hopkin's Battery 104, 176,
    218, 227
Horse Creek 343
Hoyt, Col. 399, 400,
Hudson, Capt. J. K. 35
Hudson's Ford 310, 315
Humbolt, KS 432, 454, 455
Hunt County, TX 441
Hunter, Gen. 188
Hunter, (CS) 420
Illinois River 184, 187, 199,
    207
Illinois Troops
    3rd Cavalry 171
    10th Cavalry 44
    25th Infantry 171
    35th Infantry 171
    36th Infantry 171
    37th Infantry 44, 46, 169,
    171
    39th Infantry 171
    44th Infantry 171
    59th Infantry 171
    94th Infantry 44, 46
    Peoria Battery Lt. Artillery
    44
Indian Delegation 160
"Indian Expedition" 54, 234,
342
Indians 127, 339, 340
Indian Troops 200, 201, 225,
    280, 281, 421, 452, 449
    1st Brigade 292

INDEX

2nd Regiment 201, 219, 227
3rd Regiment 80, 90, 154, 175, 182, 206, 312
4th Regiment 184, 187
5th Regiment 184, 187
Cavalry 321
Indiana Troops
  1st Infantry 44
  2nd Infantry 44
  3rd Infantry 44
  8th Infantry 169, 171
  18th Infantry 171
  22nd Infantry 169, 171
  26th Infantry 44, 46
  1st Cavalry 44
  2nd Lt. Artillery 44, 183, 240
  3rd Battery Artillery 136, 137
Insley, Capt. M. H. 377, 384
Iowa Troops
  4th Infantry 171
  9th Infantry 169, 171
  19th Infantry 44, 46
  20th Infantry 44, 46
  3rd Cavalry 171
  Light Artillery 171
Ivansville 227
Jackson, Claiborn 111
Jackson County, MO 136, 373, 451, 456
Jasper County, MO 128, 352, 353, 363, 423
Jayhawker 110
Jennison, Col. C. R. 394, 399, 400, 437, 438

Jewell, Lt. Col. Lewis 35, 36
Johnson, Lt. John 35
Josling, Lt. B. F. 433
Judson, Col. W. R. 39, 40, 61, 154, 342, 358, 407, 448
Kansas City, MO 383, 388, 439
Kansas Troops
  1st Cavalry 408
  2nd Cavalry 34, 44, 54, 61, 140, 354
  6th Cavalry 34, 44, 54, 61, 63, 64, 139, 156, 174, 180, 215, 218, 294, 317, 321, 361, 373, 422, 425, 448
  9th Cavalry 44, 315, 321, 373, 405,
  11th Cavalry 389
  14th Cavalry 372, 413, 414, 431, 433, 434, 438
  15th Cavalry 437
  10th Infantry 44, 46, 80
  11th Infantry 44, 46, 180
  12th Infantry 427, 448, 439
  13th Infantry 44, 46, 371
  14th Infantry 391, 394
  15th Infantry 391, 394
  1st Colored Infantry 241, 276, 310, 315, 317, 319, 321, 327, 359, 360
  2nd Colored Infantry 427
  1st Light Artillery 44
  2nd Light Artillery 44
  3rd Light Artillery 44
Lamar, MO 395, 431

Lane, Gen. James H. 81, 180, 387, 394, 400, 424, 425
Lane, Lt. John 81
Lawrence, KS (destruction of) 385-388, 439
Lead Mines 120
Leavenworth City 398, 445
Lee's Creek 62
Lewis, Lt. R. J. 422
Little Rock, AR 402
Livingston, Maj. Thomas (CS) 128, 172, 173, 180, 243, 271, 340, 352, 432
Lone Jack (Battle) 136, 342, 383

Locust Grove (Battle) 89, 233, 235
Lookout Mountain 442, 443
Lucas, Capt. N. B. 191, 405
Lunette "C. W. Blair" 452
Lynch's Mills 236
Marmaduke, Gen. John 86, 102, 103, 305, 411, 447, 448
Marmaton River 434
Marshall, MO 421, 422
Masterton, Lt. 183
Maysville, C. N. 34, 281
McDonald County, MO 125, 144, 455
McFarland, Lt. Col. Samuel 50
McIntosh's Indian Regiment 326
McNeil, Gen. John 393, 424, 427, 440, 444, 452

Mefford, Capt. David 180
Meteors 158
Mississippi River 347
Missouri River 333
Missouri Troops
    1st Cavalry 44, 46, 171
    4th Cavalry 171
    5th Cavalry 171
    7th Cavalry 38, 44, 46, 112, 136, 137, 239
    8th Cavalry 44, 46
    9th Cavalry 171
    1st Lt. Artillery
        Battery E 44, 46
        Battery F 44, 46
        Battery L 44, 46
    2nd Lt. Artillery 171
    1st. Infantry 116
    2nd Infantry 169, 171
    3rd Infantry 112, 171
    12th Infantry 169, 171
    15th Infantry 171
    17th Infantry 171
    24th Infantry 169, 171
    25th Infantry 171
    Phelp's Regiment 171
Missouri State Militia 221, 244, 352
    2nd Battalion Infantry 136
    6th Infantry MSM 136
    7th Infantry MSM 136, 140
    8th Infantry MSM 136, 354
    1st Cavalry MSM 389
    8th Cavalry MSM 240
Moody, Capt. Joel 140
Moonlight, Col. Thomas 180, 433

Moonlight's Battery 180
Morgan (CS) 392
Mount Vernon, MO 154, 240
"Mountain Federals" 441
Neosho, MO 86, 112, 425,
   426
Neosho River 210, 220, 275,
   298, 315, 316, 344, 372,
   432, 454, 455, 456
Nevada, MO 409
Newton County, MO 118,
   240, 354
Newtonia, MO 118, 240, 354
New York Draft Riots 369
New York Tribune 375
North Fork Town 226
Ohio Troops
   2nd Cavalry 57, 104
   2nd Lt. Artillery 171
Old Fort Wayne (Battle of)
   90
Old Military Road 221
Orahood, Capt. John W. 80
Osage Mission, 423, 431, 437
Osterhaus, Col. P. J. 171
Ovens 214, 215
Paola 388, 393
Park Hill, C. N. 198, 202,
   280
Pea Ridge (Battle of) 164-168
Pea Ridge (Battlefield of)
   168-170
Perryville, C. N. 402
Phillips, Col. 435, 449, 451,
   452
Phillips, Lt. Maxwell 154

Pickets 275, 281, 282, 283,
   295, 296
Pineville, MO 144, 155, 238
Pin Indians 198
Plumb, Major 389
Pomeroy, Senator (KS) 187
Pond, Lt. 417, 420
Port Hudson 347
Pothloholo 440
Potoe River 402
Prairie Grove (Battle of)
   39-44, 52
Pratt, J. R. 195
Price, Gen. Sterling 451
Punishment of Soldiers 149
Quantrell 373, 384, 385, 416,
   417, 418, 420, 421, 439,
   451, 453, 454, 456
Ransom, Maj. W. C. 425
Rapid Ford 255, 259, 270,
   (Skirmish at) 262-264
Red River 341
Reduction of Transportation
   84
Rhea's Mills 37, 54
Richie, Col. Harvey 115
Rogers, Capt. John 174
Ross, Chief John 93
Ross, Lewis 232
Rump Legislature 111
Saint Louis, MO 445
Salt Works 234, 338
Saysear, Col. 389
Schaurte, Lt. Col. F. W. 227,
   295, 361
Schofield, Gen. John 79, 140,
   141, 390, 404, 451

INDEX

Scott's Mills 125, 145, 235, 237

Seminole Indians 93

Shelby, Gen. Jo 137, 411, 416, 419, 420, 421, 422, 448

Sherwood, MO 344

Shoal Creek 113

Sigel, Gen Franz 119

Skullyville 421

Smalley, Lt. W. M. 191

Smallpox 176, 367

Smith, Capt. A. E. 342, 358

Solomons, Gen. 9th WI 55

Spavinaw Creek 236

Spillman, Capt. A. C. 139

Springfield, MO (Raid on) 86, 102, 103, 447

Spring River 128, 352, 353, 354

Standwatie, Col. 205, 236, 292, 326, 451

Standwatie's Indian Regiment 326

Standwatie's Mills 236

State Militia 118, 119

Steamboats 64, 65

"Steamer Rose Douglas" 68

Steele, Gen (CS) 371, 404

Steele, Gen (US) 452

Stewart, Capt. 321

Stockton, MO 352, 364

Sugar Creek 155, 165

Supplies 53

Supply Train 438

Tahlequah 205, 260, 276

Taylor, Capt. (CS) 365

Tennessee 347

Texas Troops
  20th Texas Regiment 361
  27th Mounted Regiment 326
  29th Mounted Regiment 326

Thatcher, Major 389

Tough, Capt. W. S.

Union League of Fort Scott 406

Van Buren, AR 164, 228

Van Dorn, Gen. 165

Vernon County, MO 365, 366, 374, 384, 409, 412, 453

Verdigris River 209, 260, 289, 423

Vicksburg, MS 304, 347

Water's Mills 155

Wattles, Col. 292, 293, 294, 370

Webber's Falls 211, 216, 217, 225, 229, 258, 281, 411, 421, 449, (Skirmish at) 225, 226

Weir, Col. Wm. 36, 80, 233, 237

White River 155, 447

Whitesides (Indian Scout) 374

Wild Cat Creek 77

Wild Turkeys 155

Willets, Capt. 431

Williams, Col. James M. 241, 276, 278, 310, 311, 315, 319, 321, 352

INDEX

Wisconsin Troops
  2nd Cavalry 44
  3rd Cavalry 44, 63, 128,
  315, 381, 413
  9th Infantry 44, 137, 217
  12th Infantry 137
  20th Infantry 44, 46
Wooden Cannon Balls 259
Yellow Pine Lumber 146, 147
Young soldiers 285, 286

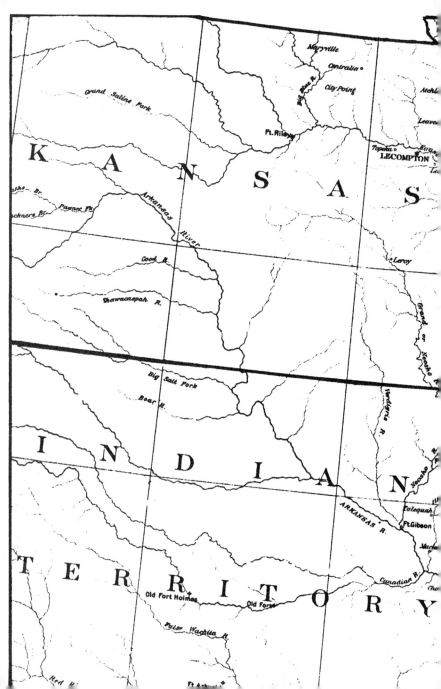